'Unhappiness in Culture', a critical, annotated translation of Freud's *Das Unbehagen in der Kultur.*[1]

Dr. David Burke Griffiths

---

[1]*Das Ungluck in der Kultur* ('Unhappiness in Culture') is the title which Freud (hereafter often SF) liked the most, although he deferred to Joan Riviere's translation title *Civilization and its Discontents* (1930). We prefer 'Unhappiness in Culture' because 'unhappiness' is a stronger term than 'discontents' and degrees of unhappiness are inevitable within mass capitalist or state socialist societies with high degrees of repression. The term 'civilization' should also be questioned. Nowhere in *Das Unbehagen in der Kultur* (hereafter DUK; vol. 2 *Anwendungen der Psychoanalyse* of *Werkausgabe* (1978) does SF use the term *Zivilization,* although there are several cases where *Kultur* should be translated by 'civilization,' e.g. Bk 3,385-6, 390; Bk 4,388.

On the two terms, Thomas Mann wrote on November 1914: "Civilisation and culture are not only not one and the same: they are opposites (*Gegensätze*)." This comment is relevant to the exclusive translation of *Kultur* with English 'civilization', e.g. throughout the *Standard Edition* (24 volumes, hereafter S. E). However, the two terms had a complex interactional history: often diverged but sometimes merged or one was the shadow of the other, but by the early 20th century and the rise of militant nationalism both had become politicized. The translation by Joan Riviere and by James Strachey, general editor of the S. E., used 'civilization' for *Kultur* regardless of context and turned Freud's '*Ich,*' '*Es,*' '*ÜÜber-Ich*' into the neo-Latin 'ego,' 'id,' 'super-ego.' [Some of the material in some of our notes, often so long they smother the text, appeared in a 2012 publication of ours by the same press. We thank Sayoko Koga and Rory Britto for technical assistance, N. W. Warren and M. Edlich for textual help].

ud

'Unhappiness in Culture', a critical, annotated translation of Freud's *Das Unbehagen in der Kultur.*

For: Amalia Griffiths Astin

I

One cannot resist the impression that human beings commonly use false standards of measurement in what they seek for themselves and admire in others: Power, Success and Wealth (*Macht, Erfolg und Reichtum*), and that they undervalue (*unterschätzen*) what is of true value in life (*wahren Werte des Lebens*). And yet, in making general judgments like this, we risk forgetting the variety and diversity (*Buntheit*) of the human world and its mental life.

There are some individuals admired by their contemporaries, although their greatness depends upon qualities and achievements (*Eigenschaften und Leistungen*) foreign to the goals and ideals of the multitude.[2] It would be easy to suppose that only a minority appreciates

---

[2] a)   The contrast of great ones and the multitude (*der Menge*) reminds us of Nietzsche's (1844-1900) Exceptional One or the *Übermensch* in *Also Sprach Zarathustra* (1883-85). SF's admiration of 'great men,' legendary or historic, included Moses (Abraham was ignored) and in his rumination

ud

on Moses versus the mob in the *Collected Papers*, 4, 259-60, he portrayed Moses as a paradigmatic hero. The historical figure of Hannibal , revenger against Rome, was important to SF, although his 'great men' were the 18th century 'poets and thinkers', especially Goethe and Schiller. SF used *der Menge* (masses) in descriptive and pejorative ways. Etymologically speaking, he was not a 'democrat', e.g. in *Future of an Illusion* (1927) he called the masses lazy and unintelligent and hence needed to be governed by a minority. His preference for leaders over *der Menge,* in the context of the 'present state of America,' was expressed in Bk. 5, 403. (This bias for 'leaders' had more nuance than the term 'elitist' conveys, and speaking loosely it resembled a Germanic romantic tradition from Hegel to Herder to Weber). M. Heidegger (hereafter often MH) was also deeply influenced by Nietzsche; and Heidegger's contrast between the masses, as *das Man*, and the authentic individual fore-running his death was elaborated in *Sein und Zeit* (1927). b) MH, who ignored Freud, shared an anti-American bias with him, although SF's bias was far more rational and unlike MH he loved England and read and wrote in English, in fact he told E. Jones that for ten years he had only read books in English. His half-brothers had immigrated to England in the 1850's and SF made his first visit in 1872. He named his second son Oliver after Oliver Cromwell, perhaps because of his role in the readmission to Jews to England. In respect to America, SF complained about American 'prudery' but was fond of Mark Twain and in 1909 had a walk and talks with William James, then very ill. (Freud, *An Autobiographical Study* (1935), p. 89). SF was eager for American disciples yet when E. Jones asked him for a 'source book ' of his writings, Freud replied "…the whole idea is very repellent to me, typically American. One can be sure that when such a 'source books' exists no American will ever touch the original writings." (E. Jones, *Life and Work*, Vol. 3, p. 143).

c) In contrast, SF was very fond of French 'civilization' and liked the joke about the couple: "If one of us should die, I shall move to Paris." Freud was fond of jokes. In *Jokes and their Relation to the Unconscious* (1905c, *Der Witz und seine Beziehung zum Unbewussten*) he classified them as hostile, cynical, skeptical. With the possible exception of Plato's story about the servant girl who laughs when Thales falls in a ditch while searching the Heavens and Bergson's essay on humor, philosophers have avoided the dimension of jokes. In some cases, this might correlate with a narrow view of ethics, e.g. did Kant ever tell, let alone write a joke? d) SF was an Austrian Jewish political liberal and unlike Heidegger, who joined the

ud

these great men, while the majority wants to know nothing about them ("*nichts von ihnen wissen will*"). But it cannot be that simple thanks to the discrepancies (*Unstimmigkeiten*) between people's thoughts and actions, and the diversity of their wishful impulses (*Vielstimmigkeit ihrer Wunschregungen*).

In his letters, one of these exceptional men calls himself my friend. I had sent him my small book that treats religion as an illusion,[3] and he

---

NSDP on May 1, 1933, he was terrified by the rise of political anti-Semitisms. SF, unlike Heidegger, was nuanced on technology, noting benefits and dangers. MH, however, viewed technology as uprooting Dasein from the earth and yet he supported the German war machine, and after the war was silent or relativized the Catastrophe or Shoah. Contrast SF and his anxiety in 1930 over the possibility of 'exterminating one another to the last man' ("*einander bis auf den letzten Mann auszurotten*"). *DUK*, Bk. 8, 424).

[3] **Bk. 1, 367. a) The first use of the keyword 'religion' is set within the experience of a gift to a friend and his response. This gives a human concreteness to the discourses in *DUK*. According to his *Autobiography* (pp. 12-13) Freud's publicly expressed interest in 'religion' and the psychology of religion went back to his *Obsessive Actions and Religious Practices* of 1907 (*S.E.*, IX, 117-204) in which he developed an analogy between obsessive neurosis and religious ritual. According to Freud in *Totem und Tabu* (1912-1913, III, 4, 84-5), the neuroses had a significant correspondence (*Überinstimmungen*) to the great social productions of art, religion, and philosophy (*der Kunst, der Religion und der Philosophie*). However, they were also a distortion and caricature of them, e.g. religion was a caricature (*Zerrbild*) of a compulsion neurosis. Obsessive behavior and religious ritual share renunciation of instinctual drives, and individuals in both cases may not be aware of that. b) Freud's aversion to religious ritual may have had an obsessive quality, e.g. according to Peter Gay, *Freud* (1988) Freud did not allow his wife Martha Bernays (1861-1951) to light the Shabbat candles. He seemed not to recognize any positive role of emotion in religious practice. He wrote Ludwig Binswanger on 10 September 1911 that the frequency of crucifixes (*Herrgötter*) in the Tyrol had persuaded him to make a study of the psychology of religion. (*The Sigmund Freud---Ludwig Binswanger Corresondence 1908-1938*, p. 74). [This probably refers to his work at the time on *Totem and Taboo*]. c) Freud's comments on 'religion' were not always consistent. By linking it with art and science he accorded it value in life because art, science, religion can all replace or represent each other (Bk. 2, 374). But this is not very clear, and contradicted by statements in *Das Ich und das Es* [*S.A.* vol.3, 1923b, *The Ego and the Id*], and the type of 'religion' in question is that of the 'common man' ("*gemeine Mann*"), a comment which expressed his belief that the masses lacked a full understanding of reality. However, he also appreciated that 'religion' had recognized the role that a sense of guilt played in culture/civilization: "*Die Religionen wenigstens haben die Rolle des Schuldgefühls in der Kultur nie verkannt*" (Bk 8, 417). Secondly, he stated in *The Future of an Illusion* that: "by accepting the universal neurosis he is spared the task of forming a personal neurosis" (*Die Zukunft einer Illusion*, Bk. 8, 358). c) Freud's view of the adaptive usefulness of ' religion', derived from evolutionary**

ud

answered that he fully agreed with my judgment of religion, but regretted (*bedauerte aber*) that I had not appreciated the essential (*eigentliche*) source of religiosity (*Religiosität*).[4] This was a special feeling, that had never left him,[5] which he found confirmed by many others, and which he supposes is present in millions of people. A feeling which he would like to call a sensation of 'eternity', a feeling as of something Unlimited, Unbounded, so to speak, 'Oceanic.' This feeling is a pure subjective fact, not a proposition of faith (*kein Glaubenssatz*); it brings with it no assurance of personal continuance (*keine zusicherung persönlicher Dauer*), but is the source of religious energy that is seized by various churches and religious systems, directed by them into definite channels and doubtless also exhausted by them. Only on the ground of this oceanic feeling can one call oneself religious, even if one rejects every belief and every dream (*Illusion*).
[6]   These views of my revered friend, who himself at once praised the

---

theory, was not incompatible with his belief that religious propositions were forms of wish-fulfillment, and that the truth they contained was so distorted (*entstellt*) and systematically disguised (*systematisch verkleidet*) that most people could not recognize it. Idem, Bk. 8, 358. Obviously, Freud did not include himself within 'most people' (*die Masse*). He also did not recognize that the elitist and soteriological dimension of the psychoanalytic movement functioned like a 'religion', i.e. with polemics, 'converts', excommunications. Freud's attack on 'religion' is a valuable counter to dogmatic God-talk that silences discourse, but his reductive psychological approach led to distortion and omission. To understand ancient near-eastern and modern 'Western' religions, and he ignored the rich North East, South East, and Far East noetic traditions, one must study their central cultural productions and symbolic dimensions: the sacred texts and liturgies, calligraphy and cathedrals. One should also have noted and appreciated that the development of notions of moral law within the monotheistic traditions and Dharma/Dhamma within other traditions checked or challenged the monopoly of power by the varied sovereigns. d) Freud's 'atheism' applies only to classical images of a Deity whose existence can be proved by reason. He avoids the formal arguments for the existence of Deity (Aristotle on the 'unmoved mover', Anselm's the ontological argument, and the 'Five Ways' of Aquinas). He was disdainful of Deism (Bk. 2, 374) and not tempted by agnosticism, which was attributed to Darwin. However, SF's search for a ground of ethics independent of religious authority is valuable and that ethics can be independent of religion is more important than the question of theism vs. atheism (debates between them are a current fashion). Nevertheless, SF's view of 'religion' is too thin: it is not enough to say that the gods are wish-fulfilling projections and 'religion' is opposed to scientific understanding. *See also*, Appendix 1.

[4] *DUK*, idem. James Strachey (hereafter JS), p. 36 has "true source of religious sentiments."

[5] Bk. 1, 367. The phrase is "*das ihn selbst nie zu verlassen pflege.*"

[6] Bk. 1, 368. Freud is describing the thought of his friend here and hence the concluding word '*Illusion*', if translated as 'illusion', is rather odd; and in the previous sentence, the same might be said of "*auch aufgezehrt werde*" ('also exhausted by them'). A negative use

ud

magic of illusion in a poem,[7] caused me no small difficulty.[8] I cannot discover in myself (*nicht in mir entdecken*) this 'oceanic feeling.' It is not easy to treat feelings scientifically. One can try to describe their physiological signs. Where that is not feasible (*nicht angeht*), and I also fear that the oceanic feeling will elude[9] this kind of characterization, nothing remains except to keep to the representational-thinking content (*Vorstellungsinhalt*)[10] most easily associated with the feeling. If I have

---

of *Illusion* fits Freud's critique more than that of his friend, R. Romain. The German '*Illusion*' is not always negative, e.g. deception in art and magic is not negative. In *The Future of an Illusion* (1927) the meaning of the term is negative (hence *Täuschung* would have been more precise); but if one reads Freud from the late work *Moses and Monotheism* (*Der Mann Moses und die monotheistische Religion: Drei Abhandlungen* (1939a, S.A. vol. 9) to the early works (sometimes an intuitive insight is gained from moving backwards), one sees not only a deep interest in 'religion' but a qualification of any simple negative verdict on it.

[7] Idem. "*poetisch gewürdigt hat.*" "*Poesie*" is poem; the adj. '*poetisch*' is 'poetic', however no other rendering makes sense.

[8] Idem. a) The phrase 'brought me no small difficulty' ("*brachte mir nicht geringe Schwierigkeiten*") proved to be sadly true. In the first month of 1920, Freud was deeply hurt by the death of Sophie Freud Halberstadt, his 26 year old daughter, from influenza. He wrote his close friend Sándor Ferenczi (1873-1933, founder of the Hungarian Psychoanalytic Society), that: "Since I am profoundly irreligious there is no one I can accuse, and I know there is nowhere to which any complaint could be addressed…Quite deep down I can trace the feeling of a deep narcissistic hurt that is not to be healed." (cited in E. Jones, vol. 3, p. 20). b) This page in *DUK* has a fn. by Freud [added 1931] # 1. "Since the appearance of both books *La vie de Ramakrishna* (1929) and *La vie de Vivekananda* (1930) I no longer need to hide that the friend in the text is Roman Rolland."

[9] Idem. '*entziehen*', JS (p. 37) has 'defy' which is perhaps too strong. The term has a sense of 'withdrawal', 'remove', 'evade.'

[10] Bk. 1, 368. a) On '*Vorstellungsinhalt*': the more standard translation of '*Vorstellung*' is 'representation' as in Kant and Schopenhauer (*Die Welt als Wille und Vorstellung*, 1818). The important compound *Vorstellungsrepräsentanz* does not appear in *DUK*. The term '*Vorstellung*' was first used in a philosophical sense by Christian Wolff, a disciple of Leibniz who influenced Kant and while now largely forgotten was a powerful presence in 18th century Germanic philosophical circles. *Vorstellung* as a verbal noun translates as intellectual processes in consciousness that is somehow inseparable from contents. It contains the notion of 'idea', but the core of the meaning is psychical, mental representation or interpretation of meaning through meaning. The translator of *The Unconscious* (*S.E.*, 14, p. 166) has "the idea which represents an instinct" (so P. Ricouer, *Freud and Philosophy*, p. 116, fn. 2). JS (p. 37) has 'ideational content.' b) After Hegel, speaking very generally, 'representation' loses out to 'conceiving' or '*begreifen.*' However, Heidegger used '*begreifen*' as a form of "*vorstellendes Denken.*" There is also thinking representationally, as in Schiller's *darstellend denken*. While tracing lines of influence are difficult, I am confident of Schiller's importance to Freud but not aware that he was influenced by Hegel except in a general sense of mental climate, or by Heidegger in any respect, although he probably knew about Heidegger through Binswanger. [Jacques Lacan, who rethought Freud on some levels, was influenced by Heidegger.] Heidegger and Freud

ud

understood my friend correctly, he means the same thing by it as the consolation offered by an original and somewhat eccentric poet-dramatist (*Dichter*) to his hero before his self-chosen death (*freigewahlten Tod*): "We cannot fall out of this world."[11] Thus a feeling of an indissolvable bond, of belonging together (*Zusammengehörigkeit*) with the external world as a whole. I want to say that to me this has the character of an intellectual insight (*Einsicht*), which is certainly not without an accompanying feeling-tone but only like any other act of thought of similar range. In respect to myself, I could not become convinced of the primary nature of such a feeling. But therefore I cannot deny that it occurs (*Vorkommen*) as a fact for others. The only question is whether it is correctly interpreted and if it should be regarded as the "*fons et origio*" of all religious needs (*aller religiösen Bedürfnisse*).

I have nothing to suggest which could have a decisive influence on the solution of this problem. The idea that human beings receive notice (*Kunde*) [12] of their connection with the environment through an immediate feeling, directed from the outset to that purpose, sounds so strange (*fremdartig*) and fits so badly with the fabric of our psychology that one

---

were both concerned with origins but from conceptually opposite poles, i.e. the future as radical temporality compared to the primacy of the past. In his *An Autobiographical Study* (*Selbstdarstellung*, 1925), Freud acknowledged the large area of agreement between psychoanalysis and Schopenhauer, but stated that he had read Schopenhauer 'very late' in his life; and that he 'avoided' Nietzsche 'for a long time' because his 'guesses and intuitions' were often close to psychoanalysis. In a letter of May 11, 1934 to Arnold Zweig, the 79 year old Freud wrote: "In my youth he [Nietzsche] signified a nobility which I could not attain." (E. Jones, vol. 3, 460). c) Freud also had high regard for Thomas Mann and wrote in *An Autobiographical Study* that Mann "had found a place for me in his history of modern thought" (p. 124). And see his letter of praise to "Thomas Mann, on his sixtieth birthday" (1935, in *S. E.*, vol. 22, 225). Freud was deeply influenced by the first volumes of Mann's tetralogy *Die Geschichten Jakobs* (1933-1944, American title: *Joseph and His Brothers*). The respect was mutual, but Mann's evaluation of Freud's theories as Schopenhauer's 'metaphysics translated into psychology' was exaggerated and probably reflected Mann's own deep immersion in Schopenhauer. Freud's meaning-use of 'belonging together with the external world' is not framed by an idea of Will but by his idea of mentalities and their formation in relation to cultural memory and genetic processes.

[11] Idem. Freud's footnote 2: "D. Chr. Grabbe, *Hannibal*: "*Ja, aus der Welt werden wir nicht fallen. Wir sind einmal darin.*" From his early teens Hannibal was one of Freud's heroes. This connection related to his early reading and his bond with his father who had suffered discrimination and humiliation.

[12] Bk. 1, 368. JS (p. 37) has 'intimation' but the word is too weak; the noun '*Kunde*' has the primary meaning of 'known, public.'

ud

will be justified in seeking a psychoanalytical, i.e. a genetic derivation (*Ableitung*)[13] of such a feeling. Then the following line of thought is in order: normally there is nothing more certain than the feeling of our self, our own 'I.'[14] This 'I' appears to us as autonomous and unitary, well-marked off from everything else. That this appearance is a deception, that the 'I' itself is on the contrary continued inwards, without sharp boundaries in an unconscious mental essence (*Wesen*),[15] that we describe as 'It' (*Es*), for which it forms a façade (*Fassade*);[16] this was first learned

---

[13] Idem. JS (pp. 37-38) has 'explanation' for '*Ableitung*.' This is questionable.

[14] Idem. Bk. 1, 368. Descartes' image of mind "*je pense, donc je suis*" is hinted at here; but instead of a dualism of *res extensa* and *res cogitans,* Freud had a more fascinating concept of the 'I' and the "three strict superiors": the *Es*, or Id, and the *Über-ich* or superego (*New Introductory Lectures on Psycho-Analysis, Neue Folge der Vorlesungen zur Einführung in die Psychoanalyse,* S. A., vol. 1, 1933a). However, if taken literally, as Freud intended, the struggle between Eros and the Death drive is an ontic-type dualism. JS breaks the sentence into two, glosses the first part, and, as always, renders *Ich* as 'ego.'

[15] a) Arthur Schopenhauer and John S. Mill, and Laycock and Carpenter, the psychologists who explored hypnosis, knew about the Unconscious long before Freud. There were, however, deep differences in the conceptualizations (see James Miller, "Revelations of Hypnosis" *The New York Review of Books* (April 20, 1995). Hypnosis, an outgrowth of mesmerism, contributed to the emergence of psychoanalysis but was soon almost forgotten. 'The Unconscious' became dominant. While without boundaries, it also functions like a system of restraints on language and behavior. Jung broadened Freud's concept of the unconscious to include all psychic material beneath the threshold of consciousness. Sartre, however, rejected the concept of the unconscious. There is a fissure within consciousness but the unconscious is simply self-consciousness as intentional positing of objects. In Sartre's existential psychoanalysis, the human Dasein is what s/he is not, and Dasein must constantly make itself. He often cited Freud in his *Being and Nothingness* and used Freud in his later biographical studies, and Freud's presence on problems of motivation and existential teleological categories lurks behind the novels and Nausea and the plays *Dirty Hands* and *No Exit*. b) The neo-rationalism of a linguistic unconscious may be a modern alternative to a Freudian unconscious. However, Freud's 'the Unconscious' was not a place or organ of the brain but a psychic and biological function that managed mechanisms of rationalization and displacement. I suspect Freud would have welcomed neuroscience and the new MRI imaging. His 1895 "Project for a Scientific Psychology", which he abandoned, was a neurological account of the brain in light of current information. It might anticipate recent work in cognitive psychology and computational models. Freud had no idea of a digital computer or of the specific algorithms, of the last four decades or so, but he and his contemporaries had an idea of the brain as a computational structure that executed algorithms. See Clyde Glymour, our bibliography.

[16] Bk. 1, 369. a) The tripartite structure of *das Ich, Es, Über-Ich* was developed in *Das Ich and Das Es* (Vienna, 1923, translated as *The Ego and the Id* (New York, 1961, *S.E.*, vol.19, 3-66). Freud was influenced by Nietzsche's use of '*Es*', but said that he borrowed the term '*Es*' from Georg Groddeck, author of *Das Buch vom Es. Psychoanalytische Briefe an eine Freundin* (Zurich, 1926). Groddeck's image of the *Es* as the great unknown differed from Freud's later image of an unmeasurable chaos and 'death-wish.' c) In his later thought the

Page 8

ud

through psychoanalytical research, which still has much more information (*Auskünfte*) for us about the relation of the 'I' to the It.[17] But to the outside, at any rate, the 'I' appears to maintain clear and distinct boundary lines. There is only one state, an extraordinary one to be sure but not one that can be judged as sick, in which this does not happen (*wird es anders*). At the peak of being in love the boundaries of 'I' and Other threaten to become blurred (*verschwimmen*).[18] Against all the evidence of the senses, the one in love maintains the oneness of the I and You,[19] and is prepared to act as if it were a fact (*als ob es so wäre*). What can temporarily be overcome through a physiological function must naturally also be open to disturbances by morbid processes (*krankhafte Vorgänge*). Pathology has taught us about a great number of conditions in which the boundary lines of the 'I' and the external world are uncertain or in which the boundaries are incorrectly drawn; cases in which a part of his own body, yes, even portions of his own mental life (*seelenlebens*), his perceptions, thoughts, feelings appear alien and not belonging to his 'I', there are other cases in which he ascribes to the external world things that obviously originate in the 'I' and that ought to be acknowledged by it.[20] Thus even the 'I'-feeling is subject to disturbances and the 'I'-boundaries unstable (*nicht beständig*).

On further reflection: this 'I'- feeling of adults cannot have been the

---

Es or It is much more than the desire/instinctual substrate of consciousness. As the repository of self-destructive patterns, it is more than the repressed. The *Es* is the realm of the wild Nay-saving of Mephistopheles in Goethe's *Faust* (*Ich bin der Geist, der stets verneint!*) but it is also subject to 'sublimation'. The expressions of the *Es* in art and wit confront and challenge rather than conform. c) In part, the topology of *Ich, Es, Über-Ich* replaced the earlier division of conscious, preconsious, unconscious. The structural theory of *Ich, Es, Über-Ich* (ego, id, and super-ego) seeks to explain the aims and functions of the mind. However, it appears to confuse mechanics with phenotype; and it is unclear how it translates into modes of functioning within environment, self-autonomy, and sociality (*Umwelt, Eigenwelt, Mitwelt*).

[17] Idem. JS (p. 38) inserts 'a discovery' in the sentence. Freud's first of two footnotes on this page refers to his "*Die Struktur der psychischen Persönlichkeit*" in Bd. I of the *Werkausgabe*.

[18] JS' (p. 38) 'melt away' is too strong.

[19] *DUK*, idem. JS (idem) puts single quotation marks, not in the text, on 'I' and 'you' (*Ich* and *Du*). This is the only place where *Ich* is translated as 'I.' The *Ich und Du* of this sentence immediately invokes Buber's famous treatise of 1923, but Freud's point is entirely different.

[20] *DUK*, idem. a) Freud's reflection on boundary lines relates to the 'I' and the external world and the 'I' (ego) and the raw materials of the *Es* (Id), and these boundaries are learned through experience. How the *Ich* confronts the *Es* is analogous to how the agent or person (an identity qua identity which cannot be duplicated) confronts the external world.

ud

same from the beginning. It must have gone through a process of development (*Entwicklung*), which naturally cannot be demonstrated (*nicht nachweisen*), but can be reconstructed with a fair degree of probability. [21] The infant at the breast does not yet distinguish his 'I' from the external world as the source of the influx of sensations. He gradually learns it from various stimulations (*verschiedene Anregungen*). He must be strongly impressed that some of the sources of excitation, which he will later recognize as his bodily organs, can send on (*zusenden*) [22] sensations at any time, whereas others evade him from time to time-among them his mother's breast which he desires the most-and only reappear as a result of his demanding screams for help. In this way, the 'I' is first set over against an 'Object', as something which exists 'outside' (*außerhalb*)[23] and is forced to appear only through a special action. [24] A further incentive (*Antrieb*) to the disassociation (*Loslösung*) of the 'I' from the mass of sensations, hence to the recognition of an 'Outside', an external world, is given by the frequent, manifold, unavoidable sensations of pain and unpleasant sensations (*Unlustempfindungen*), the overcoming (*aufheben*) and avoidance of which is demanded by (*heißt*) the pleasure principle (*Lustprinzip*) in its unrestricted domination. A tendency arises to separate from the 'I' everything that can become a source of such unpleasure (*Unlust*),[25] to throw it outside, and to build a pure Pleasure-'I', which is confronted by a foreign, threatening Outside (*Draußen*). The boundaries of this primitive Pleasure-'I' (*primitiven Lust-Ichs*) cannot escape correction through experience. Some of the things that give one pleasure that one is unwilling to surrender are not the 'I', yet some of the things one seeks to expel prove to be inseparable from the 'I' because of their inner origin. One comes to learn a technique which through a deliberate direction of one's

---

[21] *DUK*, Bk. 1, 369. Freud's footnote to this sentence reads: "Cf. the many works on the I-development and I-feeling, from Ferenczi's *Development Stages of the Sense of Reality* (1913) to Federn's contributions of 1926, 1927 and later."

[22] Idem. '*zusenden*' [ir. v. a.] < *zuschicken*, 'send on.' JS (p. 39) has "provide."

[23] Idem. '*Außerhalb*' and '*Objekt*' have double quotation marks in the German.

[24] The inconstancy of sensation is the key to the emergence of the I-Other structure.

[25] a) Freud's 'pleasure principle' suggests the influence of J. Bentham (1748-1832) and a utilitarian ethics of pleasure/pain. For Freud, however, humans seek the reduction of suffering more than they seek happiness. Second, Freud's 'pleasure principle' is countered by the 'reality principle' and the innate tendency toward destructiveness. b) Our 'unpleasure' is a neologism, but 'displeasure' is not precise or strong enough.

ud

sensory activities and suitable muscular action one can differentiate between the inner---what belongs to the 'I' and what is external---what originates (*Entstammendes*) from the external world; and in this way one takes the first step toward the introduction of the Reality-principle which should dominate future development. Of course, this differentiation serves the practical purpose of defending against sensations of unpleasure which one feels, or is threatened by. That the 'I' in order to fend off certain unpleasant sensations arising from within, can use no other methods than those used against unpleasure from the outside, is the starting-point of important pathological disorders.

In this way, the 'I' detaches itself from the external world. Expressed more accurately: originally the 'I' contained everything, later it separates an external world from itself. Our present I-feeling is therefore only a shrunken residue of a more inclusive, yes, an all- embracing feeling which corresponded to a more intimate bond between the 'I' and surrounding world. If we assume that this primary 'I'-feeling has persisted in the mental life of many people to a greater or lesser degree, it would be side by side with the narrower and more sharply bounded (*umgrenzten*) maturity like a kind of counterpoint placed by it, and its appropriate representational-thinking content (*Vorstellungsinhalts*) would be precisely those of unboundedness and unity with the All, the same 'oceanic feeling' which my friend elucidated. But have we a right to the assumption of the survival of something originally there, next to what was later derived from it? Undoubtedly, there is nothing strange in such an event (*Vorkommnis*) in either the mental field or elsewhere. [26] In the animal order we hold strong to the assumption that the most highly developed species have developed from the lowest, yet among the living today we find all the simple life forms. These species (*Geschlecht*) of the great saurians are extinct today and the mammals have taken their place, but a true representative of this species, the crocodile, still lives among us. The analogy may be too remote, also weakened by the circumstance that the lower species surviving today are generally not the true ancestors of the present-day higher developed

---

[26] **JS (idem) has 'phenomenon' for '*Vorkommnis*' and turns '*Unzweifelhaft*' into a single sentence!**

species. [27] As a rule, the intermediate links have died out and are known only through reconstruction. Whereas in the field of the mind, the primitive (*des Primitiven*) is so frequently preserved alongside the transformed version that evidence through examples is unnecessary. Generally when this happens a bifurcation (*Entwicklungsspaltung*) follows. A quantitative part of an attitude, instinctual impulse (*Triebregung*), remains unchanged, while another part experiences further development. [28]

We move with this to the more general problem of preservation in the sphere of the mind (*Erhaltung im Psychischen*),[29] as yet the subject has hardly been studied, but it is so interesting and important that we can turn our attention to it for a while, even though our motive (*Anlaß*)[30] is insufficient. Since we overcame the error of supposing that our common forgetting signified a destruction of the trace of memory (*eine Zerstörung der Gedächtnisspur*), that is, its annihilation, we have been inclined to the opposite assumption that in mental life nothing that has been formed can perish, that everything is somehow preserved and that in suitable circumstances, for example when regression goes back far enough, can once more be brought to light.[31] Let us try to make clear what this assumption involves through a comparison (*Vergleich*) from another field. We choose as an example the development of the Eternal City. [32]

---

[27] It is characteristic of Freud's style in *DUK* to state a proposition and then interrogate it.

[28] Our translation of '*Triebregung*' (Bk. 1, 370) as 'instinctual impulse' is justified because the context is biological evolution. Jacques Lacan in *The Four Fundamental Concepts of Psycho-Analysis* (1977, French, 1973) noted that '*Trieb*' relates to the 'psychical *pulsion*' whereas '*Instink*' has a biological context. This is not always the case in *Das Unbehagen in der Kultur,* but it is sometimes implied by context, and JS fails to make the distinction when needed. Freud does not use the term '*Instink*' in *DUK,* but J.Rivere and JS always translated '*Trieb*' as 'instinct.'

[29] The "sphere of the mind" is a gloss. Freud is using the German form of the Greek word for 'soul, breath.'

[30] Bk. 1, 371. JS's 'excuse' does not work. The phrase is an example of Freud's occasional fake modesty and tendency to exaggerate his originality. The subject had been studied, e.g. by Johann Friedrich Herbart (1776-1841). See Frank J. Sulloway, *Freud: Biologist of the Mind* (1979, Harvard, 1992), p. 67 *passim*.

[31] Freud used commas in this sentence. JS used dashes and one set of parentheses.

[32] Bk. 1, 371. [The sentence in the text and the three ones following ones, except for one change and some German insertions, are identical to J. Rivere and JS's translation.

Freud cites "Nach *The Cambridge Ancient History*, T. VII, 1928. "The founding of Rome" by Hugh Last."

a) It has been said that Freud had a "Rome neurosis" in the sense of a deep fascination for Rome combined with an

emotional block on visiting the city. There is evidence that from his youth his mind had

ud

Historians tell us that the oldest Rome was the Roma Quadrata, a fenced settlement on the Palatine. Then followed the phase of the septimontium, a federation of the settlements on the different hills, after that the city bounded by the servian wall, and still later, after all the transformations of the republican periods and the early Caesars, the city which the Emperor

---

been filled with classical lore, but he was blocked from visiting Rome until he done four years of self-analysis. These began in 1897 shortly after the death of his father. He and his brother Alexander visited Rome in the late summer of 1901.

Freud called this event "the high-point of my life." He made seven visits in all. He disliked medieval and baroque Christian Rome but he loved classical Rome. His adoration of Athena and her embodiment in the Roman Minerva was fundamental to this affection. See Carl Schorske, *Fin-de-siècle Vienna* (Knopf, 1979), E. Jones, *The Life and Works of Sigmund Freud,* one vol. edition, pp. 245-248.

b) A few years later the fascination with classical Greece and Rome was eclipsed by reflections on Jewish origins and Egypt. James Breasted's *The History of Egypt*, 1905 was his principal source. In seeking those origins in Egypt, Freud sought to go deeper than the standard Jewish and Christian traditions. In that process he made Moses an Egyptian and Ikhnaton (Akhenaten) a proto-Jew (this is somewhat simplified). SF's deep interest in Moses began, according to Jacob Taubes, around 1913. It was apparent in his writing on Michelangelo's Moses in the Church of San Pietro in Rome and in his last work *Der Mann Moses und die monotheistische Religion* (1937-1939; G.W., 16, 103; translation *Moses and Monotheism:Three Essays* (London and New York, 1939); *S.E.*, 23, 7-137). Philip Rieff claimed that Freud identified with Moses, but Jacob Taubes pointed to a deeper identification with Paul through suspension of the Law and a deep concern with redemption from guilt. While Freud's ruminations on Moses displeased many Jews, it was a major influence on Charles Olson, the American poet (1910-1970). In his *Call Me Ishmael* (City Lights, 1967), an original and early monograph on Herman Melville, he identified Captain Ahab as "*the Father*", the White Whale as the Mother, and the crew as the exiled sons. Many English speaking poets and critics were influenced by Freudian terminology but without knowing its clinical genesis.

Or they knew but rejected much of the terminology and conceptual structure, as with D. H.Lawrence and V. Woolf (late in her life she found his works on *Kultur* of great value, and noted in her *Diary*, that she began reading Freud in 1939: "to enlarge the circumference, to give my brain wider scope, to make it objective; to get outside"). Leonard Woolf, her husband, in 1914 after reading the first translation of Freud's major work *Interpretation of Dreams*, wrote the first review for non-specialist readers of Freud (in *The New Weekly*). This was enclosed within his review of *The Psychopathology of Everyday Life*. Until the mid-1930's, Virginia had little interest in SF and is quoted as regarding his ideas as 'silly,' however, the Woolfs hosted lectures by Melanie Klein in 1925 and on January 28, 1939 Virginia and Leonard visited the very ill Freud in London (he died Sept. 23, 1939). Virginia said of Freud that he was an "old fire now flickering."

Olson knew and accepted both the terminology and content but Pound who did not like Freud still used some of the Freudian vocabulary.

ud

Aurelian enclosed with his walls. We will not follow the changes which the city went through any further; and ask ourselves what a visitor, whom we imagine equipped with (*ausgestattet denken*) the fullest historical and topographical knowledge, can still find left of these earliest stages of the Rome of today. He will see the wall of Aurelian almost unchanged except for a few gaps. In some places he will find stretches of the servian wall which have been excavated and brought to light (*zutage gefördert finden*). If he knows enough—more than current archaeology ---, he may perhaps be able to trace out in the plan of the city the whole course of that wall and the outline of the general character (*Stadtbild*) of the Roma Quadrata. Of the buildings, which once occupied this ancient space, he will find nothing or scanty remains because they exist no more. At the most (*Das Äußerste*) the best information about Rome in the republican era would only enable one to point out the sites where the temples and public buildings of that time stood. Ruins now take their place, but not ruins of themselves but of restorations of later times after fires and destructions.

It is hardly necessary to mention that all these remains of ancient Rome are stratified (*Einsprengungen*) in the jumble of a great metropolis which has developed in the last few centuries since the Renaissance. Much that is old is certainly still in the soil of the city or buried beneath its modern buildings. This is the way the past is preserved, that is encountered (*entgegentritt*), in historical sites like Rome.[33]

Now we make a fantastic assumption, suppose that Rome is not a human dwelling-place (*Wohnstätte*) but a psychical entity with a similiarly long and abundant past,[34] in which nothing that once happened (*zustande gekommen war*) has perished, also at the side of all the earliest developmental phases the latest phase continues to exist (*noch fortbestehen*). [35] [The six following sentences are identical to JR and JS's translation.] This would mean that in Rome the palaces of the Caesars and the septizonium of septimius severus would still be rising to their old

---

[33] *DUK*, idem. JS (p. 43): "This is the manner in which the past is preserved in historical sites like Rome."
[34] It is curious why the Freud who loved (but not without some ambivalence) Vienna's richly stratified memory traces and presences preferred Rome as a model for a psychoanalytical theory of memory.
[35] Bk. 1, 371. JS (p. 44) has "...in which nothing that has once come into existence will have passed away and all the earlier phases of development continue to exist alongside the latest one."

ud

height on the Palatine and the castle of S. Angelo would still be carrying on its battlements the beautiful statues which graced it until the siege by the Goths, and so on. But more than this. In the place occupied by the Palazzo Caffarelli would once more stand-without the Palazzo having to be removed-the Temple of Jupiter Capitolinus; and this not only in its latest shape, as the Romans of the Empire saw it, but also in its earliest one, when it still showed Etruscan forms and was ornamented with terra-cotta antefixes. Where the Coliseum now stands we could at the same time admire Nero's vanished Golden House. On the Piazza of the Pantheon we should find not only the Pantheon of today, as it was bequeathed to us by Hadrian, but, on the same site, the original edifice erected by Arippa; indeed, the same piece of ground would be supporting the church of Santa Maria sopra Minerva and the ancient temple over which it was built. And the observer would perhaps only have to change the direction of his glance or his position in order to call up the one view or the other. [36]

There is obviously no sense in spinning out this fantasy further; it leads to the unimaginable, even to the absurd. If we want to represent historical sequence in spatial terms we can only do it through juxtaposition in space; the same space cannot tolerate (*verträgt*) two different contents. Our attempt seems to be an idle game; it has only one justification: it shows us how far we are from mastering the characteristics of mental life through pictorial representation (*anschauliche Darstellung*). There is one more objection (*Einwand*) which must be considered. The question may be posed of why we chose to compare the past of a city to the past of the mind. The assumptions that everything past is preserved are valid [even] for mental life and only holds good if the organ of the *Psychē* [37] has remained intact, its tissues (*Gewebe*) not damaged by trauma or inflammation (*Entzündung*). Destructive influences, which one can compare to causes of illness like these, are never lacking in the history of a city, even if it had a less agitated

---

[36] **These inessential details manifest Freud's fascination with Roman history and antiquities. The emotional distress of the present can be traced back in time and situation. Digging down and back is a simile that Freud used of his own psychanalytical work. But the analogy between the analyst and the archaeologist is limited, i.e. the mind does not have spatial layers. In the sentences immediately following, he calls the analogy a "Phantasie", a term which points out the limitations of pictorial or graphic representation. It is characteristic of his thought in DUK to propose perspectives and analogies and then critically assess them.**

ud

(*eine minder bewegte*) past [38] than Rome, and even if like London if has hardly ever suffered from the visitations of an enemy (*Feind heimgesucht wurde*). The most peaceful development of a city include (*einschließt*) [39] demolitions and replacement of buildings and therefore a city from the start (*vornherein*)[40] is unsuited for a comparison of this kind with a mental organism.

We give way (*weichen*) to this objection; renounce our effort toward an impressive contrast (*eindrucksvolle Kontrastwirkung*) and turn to what is after all a more closely related object of comparison (*Vergleichsobjekt*), the body of an animal or human being (*menschliche Leib*). But also here we find the same thing. The earlier phases of development are in no sense still preserved, they have been taken into (*aufgegangen*) the later phases for which they have supplied the material (*Stoff*). The embryo cannot be discovered in the adult, the thymus gland of the child is replaced after puberty by connective tissue, but no longer exists itself; in the marrow-bones of the adult I can (*kann ich*), it is true, trace the outline of the child's bones, but it itself has gone (*aber dieser selbst ist vergangen*),[41] having lengthened and thickened (*streckte und verdickte*)[42] until it has attained its final (*endgültige*) form. The fact remains (*Es bleibt*) that it is possible only in the mind to preserve the earlier stages alongside their final form (*Endgestaltung*), and we are not in a position to represent this event (*Vorkommen*) in pictorial terms. [43]

---

[37] Idem. Freud uses the Greek word for 'breath, soul'. JS (idem) has 'mind.'

[38] JS has "even if it had a less chequered past" but 'chequered' [from chess] does not match well with '*bewegen.*'

[39] *DUK*, idem. JS (p. 45) has 'occur.'

[40] JS (idem) has the odd word choice of '*a priori.*'

[41] The reference here could be the embryo, the thymus gland, or the child.

[42] Bk. 1, 373. The complementary parallelism of "*streckte und verdickte*" illustrates a feature of Freud's style which used forms of "parallelismus membrororum" (synonymous, antithetical, synthetic) identified long ago in ancient Hebrew by Bishop Robert Lowith. The sentence also reveals Freud's training in research science which he pursued until taking up studies in medical science. It also shows how he often brought his own 'I' into the narrative and analysis.

[43] Freud's rejection of a fixed type of pictorial method contrasts significantly with his method of understanding through the symbolic which repudiated the bigoted nonsense of the visual type of "essence" method used by the British eugenist Francis Galton in the 1890's. See Sander L. Gilman, *The Case of Sigmund Freud* (1994), pp. 42-64, Gilman, *The*

ud

Perhaps (*vielleicht*) we are going too far in this assumption. We perhaps (*vielleicht*) ought to make do (*begnügen*) with asserting that the past in mental life *can* be preserved and is not *necessarily* destroyed.[44] It is always possible that even in the *Psychischen* some of what is old is effaced or destroyed (*verwischt oder aufgezehrt*) - in the normal or exceptional state of things - to an extent that it cannot be restored or revivified (*wiederhergestellt und wiederbelebt*) [45] by any means, or that preservation in general is dependent on certain favorable conditions. It is possible but we know nothing about it. We can only hold fast to the fact that the preservation of the past in mental life is more likely the rule than the displeasing (*befremdliche*) exception. [46] Thus we are perfectly ready (*bereit*) [47] to acknowledge that the 'oceanic' feeling exists in many people and inclined to lead it back to an early phase of the 'I' feeling,[48] so the further question then arises as to what claim this feeling has to be regarded (*angesehen*) as the source of religious needs.

The claim does not seem compelling to me. After all, a feeling can only be a source of energy if it is itself the expression of a strong need. To me the derivation of religious needs from the infant's helplessness and the lively (*geweckten*)[49] longing for the father is inevitable (*unabweisbar*), [50]

Jew's Body (1991), p. 204.

[44] Bk. 1, 373. '*vielleicht*' ('perhaps', 'maybe'), one of his frequent words, has a touch of modesty and hints at an interactive style. Both '*kann*' and '*notwendigerweise*' are in italics in the text.

[45] Note the two cases of synonymous conceptual parallelism.

[46] a) This rejects a fixed biological model of successive epochs and/or generations. JS has "We can only hold fast to the fact that it is rather the rule than the exception for the past to be preserved in mental life." b) On a surface level, Freud's concern here with the preservation of the past reminds one of Proust's *À la recherche du temps perdu*. However, that complex work, 1913-1927, confronts the way retrospection can become reinterpretation. It is possible that Freud read it (I owe this suggestion to N. W. Warren). The two minds are linked through their focus on the primal role of highly mobile desire, obsession, and aggression. Proust and Freud were both moralists with a focus on sexuality and its representations. "Proust echoes Freud's account of the child's wish to know abut sex as the prototypical form of all later intellectual endeavour" (M. Bowie, 1998, 44). There is no mention of Proust reading Freud in Jean-Yves Tadié's definitive biography, *Marcel Proust: A Life*, translated by Euan Cameron (Viking, 2000; Edition Gallimard, 1996). We know that he was not psychoanalyzed, but should also note his comment that everything great has come to us from neurotics.

[47] JS has 'prepared', but that would be '*bereitwillig.*'

[48] JS has 'ego-feeling'and instead of using a conjunction breaks up the sentence.

[49] JS ignores the word.

[50] JS's 'incontrovertible' confuses evidence with process.

ud

especially since the feeling is not simply prolonged from childhood days, but is permanently sustained through the *Angst* before the superior power of Fate (*Übermacht des Schicksals*). [51] I don't know any need in childhood as strong as the need for the protection of the father. Hence the role played by the oceanic feeling, which might seek something like the restoration of unrestricted narcissism, is pushed out from the foreground (*Vordergrund abgedrängt*). The origin of the religious attitude can be traced back in clear outline to the feeling of childhood helplessness (*der kindlichen Hilflosigkeit*) There may be something still behind this, but it is covered in obscurity.

I can conceive (*vorstellen*) that the oceanic feeling later became connected with religion.[52] The Oneness with the All (*Eins-sein mit dem All*), that constitutes its conceptual content (*Gedankeninhalt*), sounds

indeed like a first attempt at a religious consolation (*Tröstung*),[53] as though it were another way of denying the danger which the 'I' recognizes as threatening it from the external world. I admit once more that it is very difficult for me to work with these barely tangible quantities (*kaum faßbaren Größen*). Another friend of mine, whose insatiable drive for knowledge has led him to make unusual experiments and ended by giving him extensive knowledge (*Allwisser*),[54] has assured me that through the practice of Yoga, by withdrawing from the world, by concentration of the attention on bodily functions and by peculiar methods of breathing one can

---

[51] **Bk. 1, 373. a) This discourse on yearning for the father as the origin of religious feeling requires a clearer distinction between 'religion' and 'religious feeling.' The yearning is a basic theme in this treatise and in *The Future of an Illusion*. b) JS has 'fear' for "*Angst*", a mistake that he and Joan Rivere constantly made; although in fairness, the word according to the OED was not a naturalized English term until ca. 1944 (I owe this comment on the *OED* to N. W. Warren). b) The 'superior power of Fate', perhaps a borrowing from Nietzsche, is a religious proposition in tension with Freud's reductive critique of 'religion.' But we may be over-interpreting this because Freud often used the German term for 'fate' and one of his favorite expressions was "*man darf nicht mit dem Schicksal hadern*" ('it is no use quarreling with fate'). Cited in E. Jones, *Life and Work*, vol. 3, p. 145.**

[52] **Idem. Freud, often cautious about the limits of knowledge, was vague and careless in his use of 'religion'. [Hence our use of scare quote marks]. While SF sometimes mentions 'Jews' and 'Christians', he flattens out the rich diversity of traditions and Christian Science is the only specific cult or denomination named in the text.**

[53] **This conceptually important word is used at the very end of Bk. 8.**

[54] **JS has 'encyclopaedic' but the German has an implication of 'superficial' which 'encyclopaedic' lacks.**

ud

actually evoke new sensations (*Emfindungen*) and general feelings (*Allgemeingefühle*)[55] which he understands as regressions to primordial, long overlaid states of mind. He sees in them a physiological ground, as it were, of much of the wisdom of the mystics.[56] There are close connections here to several obscure modifications of mental life, like trance and ecstasy (*Trance und Ekstase*).[57] But I am only pressed to declaim in the words of Schiller's diver:

"…Es freue sich, wer da atmet im rosigten Licht." 'Let him rejoice who breathes in the illuminating light!' [58]

II

In my *Future of an Illusion* [59] I dealt (*handelte*) much less with the

---

[55] Bk. 2, 374. a) J.Rivere has 'new sensations and diffused feeling.' This is better than the horrific 'coenaesthesias' of JS (p. 48). That coinage, based on a Greek compound, 'common' plus 'perception', was first used by Sr. W. Hamilton as "The Vital sense" (1877). OED has "The general sense or feeling of existence arising from the sum of bodily impressions, as distinct from the definite sensations of the special senses". b) Note the complementary parallelism of 'sensations and general feelings' (*Emfindung und Allgemeingefühle*).

[56] I suspect that Jung, who had the interests indicated, is the 'another friend' mentioned here. Freud had once called him his "son and heir", but in April 1912 wrote Ludwig Binswanger (1881-1966) that Jung was "playing out his father complex against me, for which I certainly provide no cause…" (*Freud – Binwanger Correspondence*, p. 83). In a letter (10,1909) to O. Pfister, SF mentioned his 'father complex' in relation to the need to correct his father. The father-son struggle (the topic itself was over-theorized) worked both ways, and shortly after the defections of Adler and Stekel, Jung reproached SF, his friend and mentor, with "playing the father." However, substantial differences of ideas were involved here, e.g. the development of the theory of libido, and SF's animus (like Kant's) to anything that resembled the 'mystical.' They had begun a vigorous correspondence in April 1906 and it lasted almost seven years. The severance hurt Freud emotionally, as it also did Anna Freud years later. However, Freud respectfully mentions Jung in Bk. 6 of *DUK*. In his letters to Binswanger he was not exactly kind about Jung, who developed a messianic type savior complex, and one suspects that his friendship with Binswanger, a Swiss psychiatrist and philosopher and founder of *Daseinanalysis*, helped him cope with Jung's defection. (Ernest Jones, *Life and Works*, cited above, pp. 252-3; and see Elisabeth Young-Bruehl, *Anna Freud. A Biography*, second edition, (Yale University Press, 2008), pp. 425-6.

[57] Bk. 2. 374. Notice the synonymous parallelism. JS (p. 48) has 'trances and ecstasies.'

[58] Schiller, "*Der Taucher.*" This use of Schiller's lyric appears to be poetical sarcasm. It is a exhortational statement and appeal to the clarity of reason over against trance and ecstasy and religious constructs like 'oceanic feeling.' One could translate '*rosigten*' as 'rosy,' 'shining' 'roseate,' 'brightest.'

[59] Bk. 2, 374. Freud's footnote: "[1927c, oben, S. 329ff.]"

ud

deepest sources of the religious feelings than with what the common man (*gemeine Mann*) understands by his religion, with the system of doctrines and promises (*Lehren und Verheißung*),[60] which on the one hand explains to him the mysteries (*Rätsel*) of this world with enviable fullness, and on the other hand assures him that an attentive Providence will watch over his life and will make amends (*gutmachen wird*) in a future existence for whatever denials (*etwaige Versagungen*) [he suffers here]. [61] The common man cannot imagine this Providence otherwise than in the person of a hugely exalted father. Only such a being can understand the needs of the children of men and be moved (*erwecht*) by their prayers and calmed (*beschwichtigt*) by the signs of their remorse.[62] The whole thing is so patently childish, so foreign to reality that anyone with a friendly attitude toward humanity finds it painful to think that the great majority of mortals will never be able to rise above this view of life.[63] In addition, it is more humiliating to learn how large a number of people alive today, that must

---

[60] **Idem. Note the non-synonymous parallelism.**

[61] **Idem. JS (idem) has 'any frustrations.'**

[62] **Idem. JS (idem) has 'softened' for "*erwecht*" and 'placated' for "*beschwichtigt*."**

[63] **Bk. 2, 374. a) In this passage Freud seems to equate 'common man' with 'the great majority of mortals'. The puzzling statement that 'the religion of the common man is the only one which ought to bear the name' might suggest a double truth doctrine, found in some forms of Buddhist thought and late medieval Scholasticism. It posits one level of truth for the masses and another for the enlightened and/or the elites. For instance, there is a God of the philosophers (as in Spinoza), but only superstition for the masses. There is a hint of this in his citation of Goethe on the page following and in his later reflections on Ikhnaton (Amenhotep IV) as the source of 'monotheism.' b) Freud's treatment of 'religion' is complex to the point of inconsistency. It is a 'mass-delusion' and a palliative measure, but it also addresses the question of the purpose of life. That aside, his atheism failed to distinguish symbols of ineffable experience and the numinious, from an eternal, single, self-existent Being, as posited in St. Thomas and Moses Maimonides (1135-1204). His atheism, based to some extent on Feuerbach's image of a projected trans-human Being, is an alternative to classical theism. It does not rationally rebut the mystical traditions of knowing Deity through unknowing, it reduces them to an infancy stage of development. c) The deconstructive method he applied to 'religion' was not applied to psychoanalysis, which depended upon substitutional relationships, for instance, eyes and blindness and the male organ in the castration complex. Nor was a deconstructive method applied to his belief that "scientific work is our only way to the knowledge of external reality" (*Die Zukunft einer Illusion*, Bk. 6, 349). The classical Marxists likewise exempted their concept of consciousness from their critique of 'false consciousness', i.e. consciousness is derivative of social relations from which ideas arise. However, that relationship—crudely put as 'base and superstructure'— was loosened up by Engels in his later years and is not attested in Marx's manuscripts of 1844.**

ud

see that this religion is not sound (*nicht zu halten ist*),[64] yet try to defend it piece by piece in pitiful rearguard battles (*Rückzugsgefechten*). One would like to mix among the row of believers in order to meet these philosophers who believe they can save the God of religion by replacing him with an impersonal, shadowy abstract principle, and to address (*vorzuhaltung*) them with the warning (*Mahnung*) words: "Thou shalt not take the name of the Lord in vain!" If some of the great minds (*Geister*) [65] of the past acted in the same way, it is no precedent for us. One knows why they did so. [66]

We return to the common man and to his religion, the only one, which ought to bear this name.[67] The first thing that comes to us is the famous saying of one of our great poets and sages (*Dichter und Weisen*) [68] concerning the relation of religion to art and science. It runs:

> "He who possesses science and art also has religion; but he who posesses neither, let him have religion!" [69]

---

[64] Bk. 2, 374. JS has 'tenable.' As stated before, Freud does not break down the term 'religion', or even give an etymology; presumably he is referring to Judaism and Christianity. I found no reference to Islam in *DUK* or in *The Future of an Illusion*. This might appear puzzling because of Freud's affection for Goethe who found in Islam, the drinking issue aside, a counter to the moralising sentimentality of Christianity. See Goethe's *West-Östlicher Divan*, inspired by Háfiz and medieval Persian poetry, and especially the poem "*In tausend Formen magst du dich verstecken*" ('You may conceal yourself in a thousand forms', 1815). But there is the fascinating comment in *Der Mann Moses* (1939): "the founding of the Mohammedan religion seems to me to be an abbreviated repetition of the Jewish one...Allah proved himself to be much more grateful to his chosen people than Jahve had in his time." (translation by Katherine Jones, p. 118).

[65] Idem. JS (idem) has 'men.'

[66] Bk. 2, 374. Note the biting sarcasm of the 'impersonal, shadowy abstract principle', a barb thrown at what was called Deism in the 18th -19th century. The view was widespread among the 'Founders' of the USA but also attested in Newton, one of Freud's heroes. This fascinating atheistic attack uses an ancient Hebrew prohibition of idolatry with a coded reference to religious conformity as evidence of lack of 'science' and 'art.'

[67] Idem. This is in tension with the earlier "*tiefsten Quellen des religiösen Gefühls*" ('deepest sources of the religious feelings'). The meaning of 'the religion of the common man' needs more clarity.

[68] Idem. Note the near-synonymous parallelism. 'Poets and thinkers' (so JS) is acceptable for *Dichter und Weisen,* a famous phrase often used by Germanic cultural nationalists. Heidegger used it in his Parmenides lectures of 1942-3: "*Das Volk der Dichter und Denker*" (people of thinkers and poets). However, '*Weisen*' has a wider meaning-range than '*Denker.*' Freud's attraction to poets and sages was often perspicacious and intuitive, but it was also in tension with the topological schemata of "*Ich*", "*Es*", and "*Über-Ich*".

[69] Bk. 2, 375. Freud's note: "Goethe in the *Zahmen Xenien* IX (*Gedichte aus dem Nachlaß*)". The first stich is easy to translate but the "*der habe*" of the second implies that 'religion' is like a second best consolation. We thank Marion Edlich for discussion of this

ud

This saying on the one hand brings religion into contrast with both of the highest achievements of humankind and on the other asserts that in respect to their value in life, they [achievements and religion] can represent or replace (*vertreten oder ersetzen*)[70] each other. If we seek to deprive the common man of his religion, we clearly don't have the poet's authority on our side.[71] We will try (*versuchen*)[72] a special way to bring us closer to an appreciation of his words. Life, as we find it, is too difficult for us, it brings us too much pain, disappointments, impossible demands.[73] In order to endure it, we cannot do without (*entbehren*) means of relief (*Linderungsmittel*). (Theodor Fontane told us that we can do nothing without structures of relief (*Hilfskonstruktionen.*)[74] There are perhaps three: powerful diversions (*Ablenkungen*),[75] which cause us to make light of our misery, substitute gratifications (*Ersatzbefriedigungen*), which lessen it, and intoxicating substances, which make us insensitive to it

point.

[70] Idem. Observe the parallelism of contrast. The relationship between art and religion is not explored in *DUK*. His essays on Leonardo (1910c) and Michelangelo (1914b) show more respect for religion expressed in art than do his comments on religion as an institution and as a palliative for suffering. However fleeting, and there is more than a touch of Schopenhauer here, the suspension of suffering in great art is a victory of the '*Ich*' over the *Über-Ich*.

[71] Bk. 2, 375. JS (p. 51) adds the explanatory phrase ['who has neither science nor art'] after 'the common man.' The phrase is not necessary, and JR does not have it. JS takes '*Dichters*' to refer to Goethe, and this is supported by the "*seines Satzes*" in the following sentence and by the preceding citation of Goethe. Freud, a committed atheist, is not denying the value of 'religion' for the 'common man'. Hence, I doubt he favored favored militant regimes that sought to outlaw organized religion. Freud called himself 'a godless Jew' but he was something of a religious (*un religieux*) in his many   years of devotion to reducing human suffering, and his own deep concerns with religious questions. In *Der Mann Moses*, his last book (1939), he wrote: "To all matters concerning the creation of a religion—and certainly to that of the Jewish one—pertains something majestic, which has not so far been covered by our explanations. Some other element should have part in it: one that has few analogies and nothing quite like it, something unique and commensurate with that which has grown out of it, something like religion itself" (transl. by K. Jones, Vintage Books, 1967, p. 164). Cited in Appendix II.

[72] Bk. 2, 375. JS (p. 51) has 'choose' but that would be *wählen*.

[73] Idem. This is one of the most moving sentences in *DUK*.

[74] JS (idem) has 'auxiliary constructions' which sounds like architecture. The Theodore Fontane quote refers to chemical and organic substances that lessen pain. That quotation is not within quotation marks in the text and is enclosed in brackets; JS removed the brackets, put the statement in single quotation marks, and in a footnote says: "It has not been possible to trace this quotation."

[75] JS (idem) has 'deflections.'

ud

(*unempfindlich machen*). Something of the kind is indispensable.[76] Voltaire has diversions in mind when he ends *Candide* with the advice to cultivate one's garden; [77] and scientific (*wissenschaftliche*) activity is also such a diversion.[78] The substitute gratifications which art offers are illusions in contrast to reality, but they are none the less psychically effective thanks to the role which fantasy (*Phantasie*) has assumed in mental life. The intoxicating substances influence our body and alter our chemisty. It is not simple to locate the position of religion within this succession (*innerthalb dieser Reihe*). We must expand our field.[79]

---

[76] Idem. Freud's footnote: "*Auf erniedrigtem Niveau sagt Wilhelm Busch in der <u>Frommen Helene</u> dasselbe: 'Wer Sorgen hat, hat auch Likör.'*" 'On a lower plane, Wilhelm Busch in *Die Fromme Helene* said the same thing: 'He who has cares also has brandy.'" But 'brandy' is too narrow a definition of *Likör* = 'liqueur.'

[77] Idem. A parody of the theodicy of Leibniz: this world is the best possible one, on the ground of God's omnipotence and moral perfection, and according to the principle of sufficient reason. However, it is doubtful that Voltaire (1604-1778) had understood that 'the best of all possible worlds' was a comparative judgment that did not imply that this world was a pleasant one. Freud shared Voltaire's hostility to revealed religion, judicial torture, and the stulification of institutions.

[78] Bk. 2, 375. This seems overstated and at odds with Freud's love of research science, and his attempts at a bio-psychological science of the mind. The German '*Wissenschaft/lich*' has a wider meaning range, e.g. 'learned,' 'scholarly,' than English 'science' and 'scientific.'

[79] On the role which fantasy has in mental life, see Freud's "Formulations on the Two Principles of Mental Functioning" (1911b) in *Collected Papers*, IV, 16-17 and S.E. vol. 12; and also see the chapter "Phantasy and Utopia" in H. Marcuse's *Eros and Civilisation* (1966). Phantasy or imagination links the sexual drives and the deeper levels of the unconscious with art and the higher products of consciousness. On this level there is some affinity between Freud and Surrealism. But there is no affinity with the utopian elements within early Marxist texts because the transition of the pleasure principle into the reality principle leaves phantasy behind. b) On locating 'religion' within this succession, i.e. structures of relief, we should note that Freud in 1927 and in *DUK* viewed 'religion' as a type of mass delusion, without much cultural specificity or symbolic value. However, he did not deny that 'religion' had pragmatic value. As we mentioned, objective neurosis is more comforting than an individual neurosis, which as an infancy-based projection of the unconscious must be decoded. But as he stated in *Die Zukunft einer Illusion* an 'illusion' is not the same as an error. While the illusion-versus-reality model is simplistic, given the positive role accorded to sublimation, e.g. in the form of art, it is possible to construe 'illusion' in a way that is much less threatening to a religious praxis. For instance, if 'religion' is viewed not as a fixation but as a 'transitional object' (the phrase is D. Winnicott's). c) But this perspective on 'religion' is text specific. In the late work *Der Mann Moses,* Freud claimed that hidden behind the normative Jewish tradition was the 'historical truth' that Moses was an upper-class Egyptian, 'monotheism' was developed from an Egyptian cult, and Moses was murdered by his own people. He expressed this also in a letter of 6. 1. 1935 to Lou Salomé. The question that drove him was "what has really created the particular character of the Jew, and came to the conclusion that the Jew is the

ud

The question concerning the purpose of human life has been raised countless times; it has not yet found a satisfactory answer and perhaps it does not allow one. Some of the questioners (*Fragesteller*) have added that if it turns out that it has no purpose it would lose all value for them. But this threat changes nothing. It looks, on the contrary, as if one had a right to dismiss the question. [80] It's pre-assumption (*Ihre Voraussetzung*) [81] appears to be that of human arrogance, many other expressions (*Äußerungen*) [82] of which are already known. No one talks about the purpose of the life of animals, if their regulation (*Bestimmung*) does not consist of serving humans.[83] However, that also does not hold because with many animals, humans can do nothing - except to describe, classify, study - and countless animal species have avoided (*entzogen*) this use by living and becoming extinct (*lebten und ausstarben*) before humans had seen them. Once again, only religion can answer the question of the goal of life. One can hardly err in concluding that the idea of a purpose to life stands and falls (*steht und fällt*)[84] with the religious system. [85]

Therefore we will turn to the less ambitious question of what humans show by their behaviour to be the purpose and intention (*Zweck und Absicht*)[86] of their lives, what they demand of life, wish to obtain. [87]

---

creation of the man Moses." But the Jews were not "able to tolerate the exacting faith of religion of Aten..." Freud then cited the work of E. Sellin on the rebellion against Moses and his slaying. Over the course of six to eight centuries, 'Jahve' the god of Moses, triumphed. This illustrates the "return of the repressed" and that the strength of religion "lies not in its *material*, but in its *historical* truth." (italics in the original, letter in *Sigmund Freud and Lou Andreas-Salomé LETTERS*, pp. 204-205).

[80] Bk, 2, 375. JS (p. 52) uses a comma and a linking 'for' to connect separate but thought-continuous elements. (Our 'thought-continuous' is rather ungainly).

[81] JS (idem) has 'for it seems to derive.'

[82] JS (idem) has 'manifestations.'

[83] Bk. 2, 375: "*Von einem Zweck des Lebens der Tiere wird nicht gesprochen, wenn deren Bestimmung nicht etwa darin besteht, dem Menschen zu dienen.*" JS (idem) has "Nobody talks about the purpose of the life of animals, unless, perhaps, it may be supposed to lie in being of service to man." The remedy of this condition, rooted in the Bible, Augustine, Descartes, began with J. Bentham and is present today in works by Peter Singer, Franz de Waal, and others.

[84] Idem. Note the two cases of antithetical parallelism.

[85] Bk. 2, 375-6. Read literally, this contradicts the thesis that 'religion' is an illusion. However, he quickly moves to a 'less ambitious question' which engenders the contention that the pleasure principle decides the purpose of life, although it is blocked by discontent imposed by the body, the outside world, and by relations with others. This assertion leads to the great line that happiness is not included in the 'plan' of creation.

[86] Notice the synonymous parallelism.

ud

The answer to this can hardly be in doubt; they strive after happiness, they want to become happy and to remain so.[88] This striving has two sides, one positive and one negative goal, absence of pain and unpleasure (*Schmerz und Unlust*),[89] and on the other side the experiencing of stronger feelings of pleasure (*stärker Lustgefühle*).[90] The word 'happiness' ("*Glück*") in its narrow senseonly relates to the last. In conformity with this dichotomy in their goals (*Zweiteilung der Ziele*) human activity develops in two directions, as it seeks to realize one or the other of these goals—mainly or even exclusively.[91]

It is, as we see, simply the programme of the pleasure principle that decides the purpose of life. This principle dominates the operation of the mental apparatus from the beginning; and there can be no doubt about its efficacy, yet its programme is in discord (*Hader*)[92] with the whole world, with the macrocosm as much as with the microcosm.[93] There is no possibility of its being carried through, as all the arrangements of the universe (*Einrichtungen des Alls*)[94] oppose it; one wants to say that the intention that humans should be "happy" is not included in the plan of

---

[87] Bk. 2, 376. JS turns this into two sentences and inserts a question mark which is not in the German.

[88] The theme of happiness (*eudaimonia*) was fundamental in Aristotle's ethics. He did not equate *eudaimonia* with pleasure, noting "…[the] many things we should be keen about even if they brought no pleasure…" *Nicomachean Ethics,* 10. 3. Consciously or not, Freud followed Aristotle on this point. Pleasure alone cannot account for the value attributed to many objects of both choice and desire.

[89] Idem. Again: synonymous parallelism. At first sight, 'unpleasure" may appear anamalous but it is in the *Oxford Dictionary of English* (2003): "[mass noun] "Psychoanalysis" the sense of inner pain, discomfort, or anxiety which results from the blocking of an instinctual impulse by the ego". We thank N. W. Warren for this reference and for discussion of *Unlust* as 'unpleasure' or 'displeasure.'

[90]   In current terminology, '*Lustgefühle'* would likely be described in terms of dopamine.

[91] This dichotomy of goals would not have been needed if Freud had followed Aristotle on happiness as '*eudaimonia'*: flourishing activity, with pleasure as a by-product, and according to Bk. 10, 1178b of *NE*, contemplation as the highest level of human activity. Aristotle's view of *eudaimonia* influenced Greek Stoics, and later Roman Stoics, e.g. Marcus Aurelius Antonius (121-80 CE.) noted in his *aureus libellus* ('little golden book' entitled "Meditations") that: "Happiness, by derivation, means 'a good god within'; that is, a good master-reason" (translation by Maxwell Staniforth).

[92] Bk. 2, 376. JS has 'loggerheads.'

[93] JS divides the sentence into two.

[94] JS, who breaks the sentence into two, has 'all the regulations of the universe.' The knowledge claim of '*Alls'*, a philosophical term, contradicts the image of the dynamic historicity of the *psychē*.

ud

"Creation."[95] What one calls happiness in the strictest sense comes from the preferably sudden satisfaction (*Befriedigung*) of needs that have been dammed up to a high degree, and it is from its nature only possible as a transitory phenomenon (*episodisches Phänomen*).[96] When any situation greatly desired by the pleasure principle is prolonged,[97] it produces only a feeling of mild comfort; we are so constituted that we can derive intense pleasure only from contrast and very little from a state of things (*Zustand*).[98] Consequently our possibilities of happiness are already restricted through our constitution. Unhappiness is much less difficult to experience. Suffering threatens us from three sides, from our own body, which is destined (*bestimmt*)[99] to decay and dissolution (*Verfall und Auflösung*),[100] and cannot even do without pain and anxiety (*Schmerz und Angst*)[101] as warning signals from the outside world, which rage against us with overpowering, pitiless, destructive force, and finally from our relations with other human beings. The suffering which comes from this source is perhaps more painful than any other; we are inclined to look on it, to a certain extent (*gewissermaßen*), as a superfluous extra; it can hardly be any less fatefully inevitable than suffering from another origin (*Herkunft*).[102] No wonder if under the pressure of these possibilities of suffering,

---

[95] Bk. 2, 376. JS (p. 53). **The comment has great significance: if creation has no plan then humans must make their own, and there is no ontological foundation for ethical standards. (One of Sartre's basic motifs is expressed here. While critical of Freud, Sartre was indebted to him, see *L'être et le néant*, pp. 84-89, passim).**

[96] Idem, '*Befriedigung*' is a keyword in this treatise. According to P. Ricouer in *Freud and Philosophy,* p. 322, it was used since the "Project" of 1895 to indicate "that quality of pleasure that requires the help of others." JS (p. 53) puts brackets, not in the text, around 'preferably sudden,' and has 'episodic phenomenon.'

[97] The syntax of the first clause is difficult to follow. JS breaks the sentence into two.

[98] Bk. 2, 376. This reminds one of a line by Epictetus on 'happy' as 'not being miserable'. b) However, happiness as *eudaimonia* or 'doing well' or 'flourishing,' as in Aristotle, is not far from Freud's image. But in this passage the image of 'happiness' is overladen with images of mechanical energy, charge and discharge. Also, Freud in *DUK*, compared to Aristotle in *Nicomachean Ethics*, is more interested in unhappiness than enjoyment, more impressed by suffering and how people are attached to it, and more troubled by aggression. c) Freud adds a footnote: "Goethe, indeed, warns that 'nothing is harder to bear than a succession of fair days.'" Freud then commented: "*Das mag immerhin eine Übertrebung sein*" ('But this may be an exaggeration').

[99] JS (p. 53) has 'doomed.' The matrix of the term [past part. of *bestimmen* 'to decide,'] is the musical sphere of notation.

[100] Bk. 2, 376. Note the synonymous parallelism.

[101] Idem. Observe the synonymous parallelism.

[102] Idem. JS breaks the sentence into two, and translates "*das Leiden anderer Herkunft*" as

ud

human beings reduce their demands for happiness (*unter dem Druck dieser Leidensmöglichkeiten die Menschen ihren Glücksanspruch zu ermäßigen pflegen*), just like the pleasure principle which under the influence of the outside world changed into the more modest reality principle (*bescheideneren Realitätsprizip*), if one takes oneself to be already happy having avoided being unhappy or to have survived suffering, and if in general the task of avoiding pain pushes gaining pleasure into the background. Reflection teaches that the solution of this task can be attempted along very different paths; and all these ways are recommended (*empfolen*) by individual schools of wisdom and practiced by human beings. An unrestricted satisfaction of all needs presents itself as the most enticing method of conducting one's life, but that means putting enjoyment before caution (*Genuß vor die Vorsicht*) and soon brings its own punishment. The other methods, in which avoidance of unpleasure (*Unlust*) is the predominant purpose, are differentiated according to the source of unpleasure to which their attention is mainly turned. Some of these methods are extreme and some moderate, some are one-sided and some attack the problem at the same time from several positions. The best safeguard against suffering that derives from connection with others is willed isolation (*gewollte Vereinsamung*). One understands that the happiness which can be achieved along this path is that of peace (*Ruhe*).[103] One can only defend oneself against the fearful external world by some form of turning away, if one intends to solve the task by oneself. Of course, there is another and better (*anderen und besseren*) [104] way in which one, as a member (*Mitglied*) of a human community, with the help of a technique guided by science, goes on the attack against nature and subjects her to the human will.[105] Then one is working with all for the good of

---

'the suffering which comes from elsewhere.'

[103] Bk. 2, 377. a) Freud does not give any specific information on 'individual schools of wisdom' which advocate 'very different paths.' It is possible that he knew the Latin translation (1823) of the *Gītā* and its enumeration of the path of knowledge, path of devotion, selfless action, and meditation. b) Our 'peace' for '*Ruhe*,' is stronger than JS's 'quietness.'

[104] Complementary parallelism.

[105] This attitude conflicts with those ecological psychologists who view harmony with Nature as in dialectical tension with civilization. But Freud is thinking of nature in terms of natural disasters beyond human control.

ud

all.[106] However, the most interesting method of avoiding suffering is through influence on our own organism. All suffering, finally, is only our own experience; it exists only in so far as we experience it, and we experience it according to the characteristics (*Einrichtungen*) of our organism. [107]

The crudest, but also among the most effective of these methods of influence, is the chemical one, intoxication. I don't believe that anyone fully understands (*durchschaut*) [108] its effect; however, it is a fact that there are foreign materials present in blood and tissue that directly produce sensations of pleasure (*Lustempfindungen*) but also change the conditons of our sensory life (*Empfindungslebens*) [109] so that we become incapable of receiving unpleasureable impulses (*Unlustregungen*). The two effects not only occur at the same time but seem to be intimately bound up with each other. But there must be substances in the chemistry of our own body which have similar effects, because we know at least one pathological condition, that of mania, in which a condition similar to intoxication arises without the administration (*eingeführt*) [110] of an intoxicating drug. Moreover, our normal mental life shows variation between a comparatively easy or difficult (*erleichterter oder erschwerter*)[111] connection to pleasure (*Lustenbindung*), parallel with which is a diminished or increased (*verringerte oder vergrößerte*)[112] sensitivity to displeasure. It is very regrettable that this toxic side of mental processes has up to now eluded scientific examination (*wissenschaftlichen Erforschung bisher entzogen hat*). [113] The effect (*Leistung*)[114] rendered by means (*Rauschmittel*) of

---

[106] Invoking J. Stuart Mill, and reminding one of the Marx of the 1844 manuscripts.

[107] Philosophically, this is weak. If we only can know X through our own experience there is no way we can contrast it with any Y beyond our experience and hence we could not know how X related to any non-X. Second, our mind-body organism has shared characteristics with other human and sentient beings.

[108] Bk. 2, 377. JS (p. 55) has 'mechanism.'

[109] Idem. JS (idem) has 'sensibility.'

[110] Idem. Following JS (p. 56). Initially I had 'introduction' but as a noun this does not fit the past participle *eingeführt*. (We thank N. W. Warren on this point).

[111] Notice the antithetical parallelism.

[112] Again, antithetical parallelism.

[113] Bk. 2, 377. The assertion is exaggerated. Freud probably means that they have not yet been examined by the method he prefers: *wissenchaftlichen Erforschung* (scientific research). Freud thought psychoanalysis was a scientific world view; a rational perspective based on closely observed data from a variety of sources, e.g. one-to-one interactions, dreams, sculptures, paintings, literary works. The term 'modernist' is vague, but Freud's

ud

intoxication[115] in the struggle for happiness and to keep misery away is so very prized as a benefit that individuals and peoples (*Völker*)[116] have given them a firm place within their libido-economies (*Libidoökonomie*).[117] We owe to them [118] not only the direct yield of pleasure, but also a highly desired degree of independence from the outside world. One knows that with the help of these 'breakers of cares' ("*Sorgenbrechers*")[119] one can at any time withdraw from reality and find refuge with better conditions of sensibility in one's own world. It is well known that exactly this property of

fascination with the archaic and the primitive and the unconscious in fact is modernist. He was also a 'modernist' in his affirmation of the significance of immediate perception. In terms of the even more vague 'postmodernist' construct, one could say that his respect for research was hostile to epistemic relativism and any fundamental deconstruction, e.g. that scientific knowledge is a social construction.

[114] Bk. 2, 377. JS (p. 56) has 'service.'

[115] Idem. JS (idem) has 'media' for 'means of intoxication.'

[116] '*Völker*' has a chilling effect because of its widespread use during this period as a racialistic and nationalistic term. Unlike W. Benjamin and G. Scholem, Freud was a nationalist at the time of the First World War. His sons Ernst and Martin served in the army and SF supported it. I don't know why. (Thomas Mann, but not his brother Heinrich, supported the German effort, thinking the war might teach Europe something, even purify it.) The slaughter, hysteria, and falsehoods of the war soon alienated Freud from not only war but nationalism and the aggression inherent in power. We see that in *Thoughts for the Times on War and Death* (*Zeitgemässes über Krieg und Tod*, S.A.vol. 9; S. E. vol.14). b). In his letter of Sept. 1932 to Einstein, an ardent pacifist, he wrote that "we pacifists have a constitutional intolerance (*konstitutionelle Intoleranz*) of war, an idiosyncrasy magnified, as it were to the highest degree (*eine Idiosynkrasie gleichsam in äußerster Vergrößerung*)." In closing he asked: "*Wie lange mussen wir nun warten, bis auch die andern Pazifisten werden?*" (And how long shall we have to wait before the rest of mankind become pacifists too?). He went on: 'There is no telling, but it may not be an utopian hope (*utopische Hoffnung*) that these two factors, the cultural attitude and the justified anxiety of the consequences of a future war, may result in a measurable time in the end of war (*ein Ende setzen wird*).' (*Warum Krieg?* in *Freud ZB*, vol. 2, 483-493, quotation on p. 493; *S.E.*, 22, pp. 203-215). This was written a few months before the Nazis assumed power in Germany. We do not know if the evils to come would have altered Freud's correlation between the growth of *Kultur* and opposition to war. Although in great physical pain from cancer of the palette, he followed the grim news and the last entry in his daily logbook was "*Kriegspanik*", 'war panic' (Young-Bruehl, *Anna Freud*, p. 238). The small degree of hope about the development of culture in *DUK* is qualified by the sentence added in 1931. However, the letter to Einstein was written several months later when the dominant 'cultural attitude' was: "War always finds a way" (B. Brecht).

[117] Bk. 2, 377. The pleasure and unpleasure principle rests upon this mechanistic and materialist image of energy and its need for constancy. However, 'libido' and the drives have an intersubjective context. Without that context, there would be no need for repression, sublimation, wish-fulfillment, and so forth.

[118] That is, the means of intoxication. JS again inserts 'media'.

[119] Initially we had 'downers of cares', but N. W. Warren suggested that the metaphor is 'break' rather than 'bring down.'

ud

intoxication also determines their danger and their injuriousness (*Gefahr und Schädlichkeit*). [120] The complicated structure of our mental apparatus also admits, however, of a whole series of other influences. Just as the satisfaction of a desire is a joy, so severe suffering is caused if the outside world lets us starve: it refuses satisfaction (*Sättigung*)[121] of our needs. One can also hope through influence on these impulses of desire (*Triebregungen*) [122] to be free of a portion of suffering. This type of defense against suffering no longer assails the sensory apparatus (*Empfindungsapparat*): it seeks to master the internal sources of our needs. In the extreme form of this, one kills the drives (*die Triebe ertötet*)[123] as the life wisdom of the East (*die orientalische Lebensweisheit lehrt*) and yoga practice (*Yogapraxis*) teaches.[124] If it succeeds, then the subject has of course given up all other activities (his life sacrificed)[125] and by another path has once more only achieved the happiness of peace. We follow the same path when our aims are reduced, if one only attempts to control our life desires. The governing elements are the higher psychic authorities (*Instanzen*)[126] which have submitted themselves to the reality principle (*Realitätsprinzip unterworfen haben*). Here the aim of satisfaction is in no way overcome, but a certain amount of protection against suffering is secured, in that non-satisfaction is not so painfully felt in the case of desires kept in dependence as in the case of uninihibited (*ungehemmten*) ones. But

---

[120] **Antithetical parallelism.**

[121] **Bk. 2, 378. JS (p. 56) has 'to sate', but *Sättigung* is a noun.**

[122] **Idem. JS (idem) has 'instinctual impulses.'**

[123] **Idem. JS (p. 57) has 'killing off the instincts,' but that requires *Instinkte*.**

[124] **Idem. JS (idem) has 'worldly wisdom' and 'prescribed'. Freud's point is overgeneralized. 'Yogapraktiken' is also used in *DUK*, Bk. I, p. 373. The term is a Sanskrit [m.] noun (literally) "the act of yoking, joining..." and has many referents and different forms, e.g. the school of Patanjali and the Buddhist *Yogācāra* ("mind only") school. Freud's observations on this may have come from Jung and Rolland Romain but they are superficial compared to the deep interest he had in ancient Egypt. Also Eastern tradition yoga does not teach 'killing off the instincts.' and in Jain praxis only the highest meditative level can reach that. But the Jain recognition that 'renunciation of desire is not enough because the wish still exists' would have pleased Freud (Bk. 7, 411).**

[125] **Bk. 2, 378. JS (p. 57) deletes Freud's parenthetical brackets.**

[126] **Idem. Here, and later, we use 'psychic' instead of 'psychical' because 'psychic' in current English has a greater frequency of use. However, the term has the danger of suggesting occult and medium practices which Freud rejected. One should note, however, that several of the early analysts in the UK were active in 'psychic research.' JS (idem) has 'psychical', and renders '*Instanzen*' as 'agencies.' However, '*Instanzen*' (*Instanz*, singular dictionary form) has a juridical context: 'courts', 'authorities.'**

ud

set against this is an undeniable reduction of the possibilities of enjoyment. The feeling of happiness derived from the satisfaction of a wild, untamed by the 'I', desire impulse (*vom Ich ungebändigten Triebregung*) is incomparably more intense than the satiety of a tamed desire (*Sättigung eines gezähmten Triebes*).[127] The irreversibility of unnatural (*perverser*) impulse and perhaps the general stimulus (*Anreiz*)[128] of the forbidden may find here an economic explanation. [129]

Another technique to avoid suffering is the use of libido displacements (*Libidoverschiebungen*) which our mental apparatus permits and thorough which its function [mental apparatus] gains so much flexibility (*Geschmeidigkeit*). The task to be solved here is to move the aims of desire (*Triebziele*)[130] in such a way that they cannot come up

against frustration from the external world. The sublimation (*Sublimierung*) of the desires lends its help to this.[131] One gains the most if one can

---

[127] Bk. 2, 378. JS (idem) has "…a wild instinctual impulse untamed by the ego is incomparably more intense than that derived from sating an instinct that has been tamed."

[128] Idem. JS (idem) has 'perverse instincts', and translates '*Anreiz*' as 'attraction.'

[129] Freud's 'economic explanation' (*ökonomische Erklärung*) posits something like a general tendency of mental life to save energy and hence hold on to pleasure. The notion underlies the theory of 'sublimation,' that is, the creation of new aims requires that energy shift from object-focussed libido to *das Ich* and narcissistic libido. While on a different dimension, this process has some resemblance to Hegel's concept of self-consciousness.

[130] Bk. 2, 378. JS (p. 57) has 'instinctual aims' for '*Triebziele*.' *Trieb* and *Instinkte* are not the same.

[131] Idem. a) On 'sublimation': chemistry was likely the context at the origin of this frequently used keyword. The psychoanalyic sense entered English by 1900 (so Pfeffer and Cannon, p. 321). However, the noun had been in use in English for centuries, and Freud's psychoanalytic sense is attested in 1910, see *OED* 2. The verb 'sublimate' is attested in 1896, perhaps earlier than the German '*sublimieren*'. The German noun, from late Latin, is used in a letter to W. Fliess in 1897. We thank N. W. Warren on this point. b) Freud's '*Sublimierung*' differed, but not always that much, from earlier English uses of the term. In somewhat of a paraphrase of *OED*, Pfeffer and Cannon have: "The refining and discharging of instinctual energy, esp. sexual, in socially acceptable ways…" Freud used the term in the footnote on page 369, the page that follows this one. The word is widely and uncritically used in English. c) One can often redirect energies but this common practice leaves the phenomena subject to sublimation unanalyzed by the process. They are left as they were, and there is no rational marker for why some things yield to sublimation but not others. Consider two examples: Freud's addiction to cigars (many a day) and Dostoyevsky's addiction to gambling were not sublimated by the respective scholarly and literary creative activity of the individuals. But suppose they had been. It would not follow that either person's creative activity was a sublimate of cravings for cigars or the adrenlin of gambling. The effectiveness of sublimation is relative to situation and intentionality.

ud

sufficiently heighten the yield of pleasure (*Lustgewinn*) from the sources of psychical and intellectual work (*psychischer und intellektueller Arbeit*). [132] Fate then can barely touch one. A satisfaction of this type, like the joy of an artist in creation, in giving body to his/her visions (*Verkörperung seiner Phantasiegebilde*),[133] or a researcher's (*Forschers*) in solving problems and in discerning the truth (*Erkennen der Wahrheit*),[134] has a special quality that we certainly one day will be able to characterize as metapsychological (*metapsychologisch*). At present we can only say figuratively that such satisfactions seem 'finer and higher' ("*feiner und höher*")[135] but their intensity is subdued (*gedämpft*) compared to the crude, primary (*primärer*) satiety (*Sättigung*) of desire impulses (*Triebregungen*) [136]; it does not convulse our physical being. But the weak point of this method is that it is not applicable generally, it is accessible only to a few

---

Sublimation does not work well if people do not like or seek the imputed results or if a strong religious sense of guilt is at play. In the Dostoyevsky case (a gifted paradoxalist), the possibility of sublimation decreased because of his strong religious views which reinforced his guilt. See Freud's *Dostoyevsky and Parricide* (*S.E.*, 21, p. 187). In *DUK*, Freud indirectly concedes the limitation of sublimation in the recognition that given the natural aversion to work sublimation does not work well (Bk. 2, fn. 1). The limitations of sublimation reflect the topography of the *Ich, Es, Über-Ich* model. This model should be recast as the dialectical dimensions of knowing and willing and judging. d) One is reminded of how the base-superstructure function in standardized Marxist thought was modified by Engels in his later years. On guilt, see Herman Westerink, *A Dark Trace: Sigmund Freud on the Sense of Guilt*, translated from the Dutch (Leuven University Press, 2009), p. 165 and footnotes 120, 121. Hereafter cited as *A Dark Trace*. The author of this valuable study sadly used the *S.E.* terminology and translations.

[132] Observe the near-synonymous parallelism. "*Arbeit*", especially in compounds, is a key Freudian term, e.g. *Traumarbeit* (dream work), *Trauerarbeit* (work of mourning). *Durcharbeit* (working through) is what we are attempting in this translation.

[133] JS (p. 58) has 'giving his phantasies body', but one suspects that the Greek '*phantasia*', 'a making visible,' underlies '*Phantasiegebilde*.'

[134] Bk. 2, 378. Freud's "*Erkennen der Wahrheit*" questions a view of him as an epistemic relativist. JS (idem) has 'discovering truths.'

[135] Idem. On '*metapsychlogisch*' see our note to Introduction. His hope for a metapschological dimension of psychology, i.e. to ground the understanding of neurosis in psychical regulative concepts or principles began in 1894; but he soon turned away from the project. However, in *DUK* (1929-31) he is again expressing hope that 'one day' we can characterize a 'special quality' in metapsychological terms. The term was not used often in later works and/or works dealing with the practical application of psychoanalysis. It occurs only once in *DUK*, once in *Jenzeits des Lustprincips* (1920) and twice in *Massenpsychologie und Ich-Analyse* (1921). Note the synonymous parallelism placed within double quotation marks.

[136] Bk. 2, 378. '*primärer*' (adj.) is Austrian dialect. JS (p. 58) has 'sating' for '*Sättigung*,' 'mild' for '*gedämpft*,' 'instinctual impulses' for '*Triebregungen*,' and he divides the sentence in two.

ud

people. It presupposes the possession, infrequent to any practical degree, of special talents and gifts (*Anlagen und Begabungen*). [137] And even to the few, this cannot guarantee (*gewähren*) complete protection from suffering, it creates no impenetrable armour against the arrows of fate (*Schicksals*) [138] and it habitually fails [139] when the source of suffering is a person's own body. [140]

While this procedure already clearly shows an intention of making oneself independent of the external world, in that one seeks satisfaction in inner psychical processes, the next [procedure] brings out those features

---

[137] **Bk. 2, 379. Notice the near-synonymous parallelism. JS (idem) has 'dispositions' for 'Anlagen.' The contrast here between the 'few' and the 'many' has a note of distaste for 'people', although different terms and unclarity of reference may be involved. Cf. Bk. 2, 385: 'diese Personen' of 'primordial dullness' ("ursprüngliche Stumpfheit".) In a gloomy letter (March, 1922, as cited in Jones, vol. 3, 83-84) to S. Ferenczi, whom he trusted, he complained about "earning money which is never enough, and to continue with the same psychological devices that for thirty years have kept me upright in the face of my contempt of people and the detestable world."**

[138] **Idem. 'Schicksals' is a keyword, used for example on pp. 421, 424. JS (idem) has 'fortune.'**

[139] **Idem. JS's (p. 59) 'it habitually fails' for "sei pflegt zu versagen" is puzzling. Pflege and pflegen ('care', 'care for') do not have an implication of temporality. JS splits up the sentence.**

[140] **This sentence on suffering and fate has a deep and moving basis in his life experience. Freud's footnote (idem, note 1: "When there is no special disposition (Veranlagung) in a person which prescribes what direction his/her interest in life should take, the ordinary professional work open to everyone can play the part advised by Voltaire. It is not possible within a short survey to discuss the benefits of work for the economics of the libido. No other technique for the conduct of life (Lebensführung) attaches the individual so firmly to reality as the emphasise on work, for his/her work gives at least a portion of reality, a secure place in the human community (in die menschliche Gemeinschaft sicher einfügt). The possibility it offers of displacing a large amount of libidinal components, narcissistic, aggressive and even erotic, onto professional work (Berufsarbeit) and onto the human relations connected with it, gives it a value not second to the indispensabe preservation and justication (Behauptung und Rechtfertigung) of existence in society. Professional activity (Berufstätigkeit) is a means of special satisfaction if it is freely chosen, and also if it makes possible by means of sublimation the use of existing inclinations of persisting or constitutionally (Fortgeführte oder konstitutionell) reinforced instinctual impulses (Triebregungen). And yet work as a way to happiness is not highly prized by men/women. One does not run after (drängt) it like other possibilities of satisfaction. The great majority of human beings only work under necessity and this natural aversion to work raises most difficult social problems."**
This comment should be in the text, although it needs temporal and cultural specificity, i.e. is he talking about Austrian working people of the 1920s? The sentence would be strengthened by a distinction between work for survival and work as creative expression, although that distinction is hinted at in "freely chosen" work.

ud

even more strongly.[141]   In it, the connection with reality becomes further loosened and satisfaction is gained from illusions, which are recognized as such, without the deviation (*Abweichung*) from reality being allowed to disturb enjoyment. The field from which these illusions arise is the life of fantasy (*Phantasielebens*), it comes into being at the same time as the development of the sense of reality took place, this region was expressly exempted from the demands (*Anspruchen*) of reality-testing (*Realitätsprüfung*) and was set apart for the purpose of fulfilling wishes (*Wünsche*) which were difficult to carry out. At the top of these fantasy satisfactions (*Phantasiebefriedigungen*) stands the enjoyment of the works of art, an enjoyment made accessible through the mediation (*Vermittlung*) [142] of the artist to those who are not themselves creative.[143]   Those who are receptive to the influence of art cannot praise it enough as a source of pleasure and consolation. Nevertheless the mild narcosis (*Narkose*) given us by art cannot be more than a fleeting distancing (*flüchtige Entrückung*) [144] from the misery (*Nöten*) of life, and is not strong enough to make us forget real suffering. [145]

Another method operates more energetically and thoroughly, it views reality as the only enemy, as the source of all suffering, with which it is impossible to live, so that if one is to be in any way happy one must break all relations with it [reality].[146]   The hermit turns his back on this world and

---

[141] **Idem. The second German clause seems clumsy.**

[142] **Bk. 2, 379. JS (idem) has 'agency.'**

[143] **Freud's footnote, number 2. "Cf. 'Formulations on the Two Principles of Mental Functioning' (1919b), and Lecture XXIII of *Introductory Lectures on Psycho-analysis* (1916-17)." Compare this common-use of 'fantasy satisfactions' insight on 'phantasy' as imagination with André Breton's "*La seule imagination me rend compte de ce qui peut être.*"**

[144] **Idem. JS (p. 60) has 'transient withdrawal.'**

[145] **Idem. The sentence has a touch of Schopenhauer's ontic gloom. Freud was less hesitant in acknowledging the influence of Schopenhauer than he was with Nietzsche (easier to do given Nietzsche's talent for self-contradiction); but Freud, like M. Heidegger, was touchy about acknowledging sources. Schopenhauer was probably the stronger influence, at least in respect to art and sublimation and the dimension of feeling. In the *Collected Papers* 4, 355 he states that Schopenhauer's unconscious 'Will' is equivalent to the view of the drives/instincts in psychoanalysis. [But this is a large exaggeration]. And see Herman Westerink, *A Dark Trace*, pp. 118-121, esp., p. 118-19, fn. 147, 151. In his *An Autobiographical Study* (1925), Freud acknowledged three main areas of agreement with Schopenhauer: dominance of emotions, sexuality, and repression. Freud may also have been influenced by Jung's interest in Schopenhauer.**

[146] **Idem. This slightly clumsy sentence reads better if broken in two.**

ud

will have nothing to do with it.[147] But one can do more than that, one can try to transform it, to build up in its place another world in which its most unbearable (*unerträglichten*) features are erased (*ausgetilgt*) and replaced by others in conformity with one's own wishes. Whoever in desperate rebellion (*verzweifelter Empörung*) takes this way to happiness will as a rule attain nothing; reality is too strong for him (*die Wirklichkeit ist zu stark für ihn.*) He becomes a mad man who in carrying through his madness will for the most part find no one to help him. But it is asserted that every one of us behaves in some respect like a paranoiac; corrects some aspect of the world unbearable to him/her by the construction of a wish, and introduces this delusion into reality (*diesen Wahn in die Realität einträgt*). A special importance attaches to the case in which this attempt to obtain a certainty of happiness and a protection against suffering (*Glückversicherung und Leidenschutz*)[148] through a delusional remoulding of reality is made by a considerable number of people in common. We must also classify the religions of mankind among such mass delusions (*Massenwahn*).[149] A delusion is of course never recognized for what it is by those who share it (*Den Wahn erkennt natürlich niemals, wer ihn selbst noch teilt*).[150]

I don't believe I have made a full enumeration of the methods (*Aufzählung der Methoden*) by which human beings strive to gain happiness and keep suffering away, and I also know that the subject matter might have been differently arranged. There is one prodecure I have not brought up (*angeführt*), not that I had forgotten it but because it will concern us later in another connection. And how is it possible to just forget this technique in the art of living? It distinguishes itself through a remarkable combination of characteristics. It naturally strives for independence from fate (*Schicksal*), as it is best to call it,[151] and in this

---

[147] **Idem. JS (idem) has 'on the world and will have no truck with it.'**
[148] **Bk. 2, 380. Note the near-synonymous parallelism.**
[149] **Idem. JS (p. 60) uses 'among' for "*solchen*"? Freud's "religions of mankind", as mass-delusions, is the type of loose generalization that damaged *The Future of an Illusion* and *Moses and Monotheism*.**
[150] **This is an example of Freud's sharp irony. The sentence is difficult to translate. It could mean no one who shares (*teilt*) the madness recognises themselves as doing so, or no one who shares it recognizes it as a delusion, or no one who shares a delusion recognizes it as such. JS (idem) has "No one, needless to say, who shares a delusion ever recognizes it as such." We thank N. W. Warren for his insight on this sentence.**
[151] **Bk. 2, 380. The use of 'fate' with qualifier indicates Freud's distance from normative Rabbinic Judaism and Christianity. In those traditions 'fate' is a 'pagan' and pre-theistic**

ud

goal locates satisfaction in inner mental processes, in so doing making use of the displaceablity of the libido (*Verschiebbarkeit der Libido*), as we mentioned a while ago, but it does not turn away from the external world, on the contrary clings to objects belonging to that world and obtains happiness from an emotional relationship (*Gefühlsbeziehung*) with them.[152] Nor is it content with the avoidance of unpleasure; a goal, so to speak (*gleichsam*),[153] of weary resignation, it heedlessly goes past this and holds fast to the original passionate striving (*leidenschaftlichen Streben*) for a postive fulfillment of happiness. Perhaps it does really come closer to this goal than any other method. Naturally I am speaking of the way of life (*Richtung des Lebens*) which takes love as its central point (*Mittelpunkt*), and expects all satisfaction from love and being loved. Such a psychical attitude comes naturally enough to all of us (*liegt uns allen nahe genug*)[154]; one of its manifest forms (*Erscheinungsformen*), sexual love, has given us the strongest experience of an overwhelming sensation of pleasure and hence given us a model for our striving for happiness (*Glücksstreben*). [155] In seeking happiness, what is more natural than that we persist on the same path on which we first encountered it.[156] The weak side of this technique of living is easy to bring to light (*klar zutage*), otherwise it would not have occurred (*eingefallen*)[157] to anyone to abandon this path to happiness for any other (*für einen anderen zu verlassen*). We are never so defenseless against suffering as when we love, never so helplessly unhappy as when we

---

concept, although the late Hebrew text *Kohelet* contained a Stoic-like image of 'fate' with the Heb. term at times interchangeable with '*Elohim*' (Deity). Freud distinguished between 'fate' as the force of parental agency and the explicit 'religious' use of the notion.

[152] Idem. JS (p. 61) divides this complex sentence into two.

[153] Idem. '*gleichsam*' = adv. 'as it were,' 'as if,' 'as though,' 'almost.'

[154] Idem. To posit 'love' as the 'central point' must also recognize that there were different forms along a continuum: friendship, parental, erotic, and selfless.

[155] Bk. 2, 380. JS (pp. 61-62) has 'pattern' for "*Vorbild*" and 'search for happiness' for "*Glücksstreben*."

[156] Idem. This is a stretch. The first encounter with 'love' is the non-instrumental agape-type nurturing love. The assumption of the priority of sexual love reflects a biological evolutionary context. In terms of a social-psychological perspective, that assignment of priority is an overreaction to repressional models which depend upon a quantitative standard of excitation rather than depth as quality, as in *philia*, friendship love, and agape as selfless and non-calculative love. An investigation of 'love' should recognize emotions as complex mixtures of feeling, cognition, and variable social contexts.

[157] Idem. '*eingefallen*', [v.] 'Fall in, collapse inward, occur, come to mind, suggest itself...' JS (idem) has 'thought of.'

ud

have lost our love object or its love.[158] But this does not dispose of the way of living (*Lebenstechnik*) [159] grounded in love, for there is much more to say about it.

One can go on from here to consider the interesting case in which happiness in life is predominantly sought in the enjoyment of beauty, wherever beauty presents itself to our senses and our judgment, the beauty of human forms and gestures (*Formen und Gesten*), of natural objects and landscapes (*Naturobjekten und Landschaften*), of artistic and even scientific creations. [160] This aesthetic attitude to the goal of life offers little protection against the threat of suffering, but it can compensate for much. The pleasure of beauty has a special mildly intoxicating characteristic of feeling. The use of beauty is not obvious (*liegt nich klar zutage*), its cultural advantages are not apparent, and yet civilization (*Kultur*) could not do without it (*vermissen*).[161] The science of aesthetics (*Wissenschaft der Ästhetik*)[162] investigates the conditions under which the beautiful may be sensed (*das Schöne empfunden wird*),[163] but has been unable to give any

---

[158] Bk. 2, 380. Freud's father Jacob was the son of Reb Schlomo (Freud's Jewish name was Schlomo) and was raised in a *shtelt* in Tysmenitz in the East European area of Galicia. He died when Freud was 43. Freud's mourning lessened with time but in his letter of consolation to Ernest Jones upon the death of his father early in 1920, Freud told his friend, disciple and biographer, that the death of his own father had "revolutionized my soul." He was also deeply wounded in late January 1920 by the sudden death of his 'beloved' daughter Sophie from influenza. See Peter Gay, *Freud* (1988), pp. 390-393.

[159] Idem. '*Lebenstechnik*' is also used in Bk. 2, 380. JS (p. 62) has 'technique of living.' In this compound, Freud is using *Technik* in the Greek sense of 'art,' 'craft'. Within his context of science and culture, he is elaborating upon ways to reduce suffering. These ways parallel the more explicitly noetic idiom of Buddhist, Jaina, and 'Hindu' paths to the cessation of suffering (*moksha*, emancipation from the cycle of birth and death). JS divides the sentence.

[160] Bk. 2, 380-381. Note the parallelism in this beautiful sentence. Schopenhauer's aesthetics, minus his odd image of the Will, is probably the basis of this reflection on beauty and suffering.

[161] Bk. 2, 381. JS weakens the powerful sentence by dividing it into two; but his and JR's use of 'civilization' here for '*Kultur*' is correct, as is also the case in Bk.6, 407. The phrase 'aesthetic attitude to the goal of life' sounds like Kierkegaard as poetic experimentator but his aesthetic dimension, hedonist in essence, was followed by the ethical stage of value and fulfillment, and then followed by two dimensions of the religious attitude. Freud would have rejected those stages along with Kierkegaard's (1813-1855) 'crucifixion' of reason in the interest of faith.

[162] Idem. We don't know Freud's source for this "science of aesthetics." As a self-conscious discipline, aesthetics was an 18th century phenomenon, and the term was coined, on the basis of the Gr. '*aisthesis*' by A. G. Baumgarten in his *Aesthetica* (1750-1758).

[163] Idem. *Empfunden*(s) = 'feeling, sensation, perception, sentiment', *emfinden* [ir. v. a.] =

ud

explanation of the nature and origin of beauty; and, as usual, lack of success is concealed under a flood of resounding, empty words. [164] Unfortunately, psychoanalysis also has little to say about beauty. The only thing that appears certain is its derivation from the field of sexual sensation (*sexualempfindens*), it seems a (*es wäre ein*) [165] perfect example of an aim or goal-inhibited impulse (*zielgehemmten Regung*). "Beauty" and "attraction" (*Reiz*) are original characteristics of the sexual object. [166] It is remarkable that the genitals themselves, the sight of which is always exciting, are still seldom judged to be beautiful; instead, the quality of beauty is attached to certain secondary sexual characteristics (*sekundaren Geschlechtsmerkmalen*). [167]

In spite of this incompleteness, I will venture a few remarks as a conclusion to our inquiry (*Untersuchung*).[168] The programme of becoming happy, impelled by the pleasure principle, cannot be fulfilled, yet we must not and cannot give up (*nicht aufgeben*) our efforts to bring it nearer to fulfillment.[169] One can follow (*einschlagen*) [170] very different paths in that direction, and we may give priority to either the positive content of the goal (*den positiven Inhalt des Ziels*), gaining pleasure, or the negative content, avoiding unpleasure. By none of these paths can we obtain all that we desire (*begrehen*). Happiness, in the reduced sense in

---

'feel, perceive, sense'. JS (p. 62) has 'things are felt as beautiful.'

[164] It is not clear whom Freud is attacking here. It is a mistake to merge aesthetics with the question of the beautiful, especially in relation to Kant (*Critique of Judgement*, 1790) and Hegel's lectures on aesthetics in the 1820's.

[165] Bk. 2, 381. The referent of 'it' could be either beauty or the love of beauty. JS (p. 63) divides the sentence into two, beginning the second with "The love of beauty...".   On the topic of beauty, what Freud does claim for psychoanalysis is as speculative as any of the major aesthetic theories.

[166] Idem. The quotation marks are in the original. '*Reiz*' has a range of meanings and 'stimulus' might be slightly better than 'attraction.' Freud's footnote, not given in the JS translation, refers to his *Three Essays on Sexual Theory* (1905d).

[167] This judgment on 'sight' and 'exciting' and 'beautiful' is overgeneralized. That 'the quality of beauty is attached to certain secondary sexual characteristics' is teasingly unspecific because it sounds banal to say that humans are attracted to lovely breasts and shapely bums.

[168] Idem. This important keyword '*Untersuchung*' has the range of: 'examination, inquiry, investigation, inspection, probing, research.' (*Cassell's German-English Dictionary*, p. 504). It is also used in Bk. 5, 418 and at the beginning of Bk. 8, 418.

[169] Idem. JS (p. 63) adds: 'by some means or other'– an elaboration of the adj. '*irgendwie*.'

[170] Idem. JS (idem) has 'be taken.' In this context, '*einschlagen*' seems a curious word choice by SF because its dominant image is 'driving,' 'beating,' 'striking.'

ud

which it is recognized as possible, is a problem of the economics of the individual libido. There is here no advice (*Rat*) that suits all (*der für alle taugt*);[171] each one must find out for himself in what particular fashion he can become happy (*auf welche besondere Fasson er selig werden kann*).[172] Manifold (*mannigfachsten*) factors will operate to direct his choice of way (*die Wege*).[173] It comes to a question of how much real satisfaction he (*er*) can expect from the real world and how far he is led to make himself independent of it (*ihr*); and finally how much power he feels he has for changing the world to fit his wishes (*Wünschen abzuändern*). Already in this, his psychic constitution, regardless of external consideration, plays a decisive part. The predominantly erotic person (*erotische Mensch*) will give preference to his emotional relationships (*Gefühlsbeziehungen*) to other people; the narcissistic (*Narzißtische*) person, who inclines more (*eher*) to self-sufficiency, will seek essential satisfaction in inner mental processes (*inneren seelischen Vorgängen suchen*); the person of action (*Tatenmensch*) will not give up (*nicht ablassen*) the external world on which he (*er*) can test his power (*er seine Kraft erproben kann*). As regards the type in the middle, the nature of his talents (*Begabung*), and the extent

---

[171] **Bk. 2, 381. JS (idem) inserts the gloss: "There is no golden rule which applies to everyone…" a) Freud recognized the need for balance (see p. 382) and that there was no single rule for all. Like Kant but with a different premise and intention, he rejected a Golden Rule; but not if formulated in a certain way, see our fn. 442. The thought in this and the two following sentences reflects a libertarian theme of self-ownership and choice, but within the context of diverse environmental factors. b) If we understand happiness as flourishing activity it should not be restricted to 'the economics of the individual libido.' However, Freud states (p. 382) that the transformation and reordering of libido components is 'indispensable for later achievements.'**

[172] **Idem. a) JS (p. 62) renders 'selig' as 'saved.' This appears to be a mistake, although 'selig werden' may be used here as a secular idiom (so N. W. Warren). 'Selig' with 'werden' can mean 'attain salvation'. The Christian terms 'saved' and 'salvation' were not pleasing to Freud, hence he was probably using the phrase in a figurative and satirical way. The "*Auch die Religion kann ihr Versprechen nicht halten*", a few lines later, establishes that the pericope is anti-religious. JS's translation misses Freud's aversion to Christianity and how it reflects and inflects varied contexts. b) The footnote by JS reads: ["The allusion is to a saying attributed to Frederick the Great: 'in my State every man can be saved after his own fashion.' Freud had quoted this a short time before in *The Question of Lay Analysis* (1926[e]), *S.E.*, 20, 236."] *Die Frage der Laienanalyse* is in *Zwei Bänden*, vol. 1, 17-69. There are no quotation marks in the German text which attribute this saying to Frederick the Great. The collocation with *Fasson* (style/fashion) indicates that it was a quotation which was probably familiar to a well-read audience.**

[173] **Idem. JS (idem) leaves out "*die Wege*."**

ud

of desire sublimation (*Triebsublimierung*) [174] possible for him, will determine where he locates his interest (*er seine Interessen verlegen soll*). Any choice pushed to an extreme will be punished by exposing the individual to the dangers which arise when any technique of living chosen as exclusive (*ausschließen gewälten Lebenstechnik*) should prove inadequate (*Unzulanglichkeit*). Like a cautious businessman who avoids tying up all his capital in one place, so, perhaps, worldly wisdom (*Lebensweisheit*) advises not to expect all satisfaction from a single aspiration (*einzigen Strebung zu erwarten*). [175] Success is never certain; it depends on the convergence of many factors, perhaps none more important than the capability (*Fähigkeit*) of the psychical constitution to adapt itself to the environment and to exploit that to gain pleasure (*der Umwelt anzupassen und diese für Lustgewinnen ausunützen*). [176] Someone born with a particularly unfavorable instinctual constitution (*Triebkonstitution*) and who has not properly undergone [177] the transformation (*Umbildung*) and reordering (*Neuordnung*) of his libido components (*Libidokomponenten*) indispensable for later achievements,[178] will find it hard to obtain happiness from an external source, especially if faced with difficult tasks. As a last technique of living, which will bring at least some substitutive satisfactions, he is offered the flight (*Flucht*) into neurotic illness –which he usually performs (*vollzieht*) when still young. One who sees his pursuit of happiness as vain (*vereitelt sieht*) in later years can find consolation in gaining pleasure from chronic intoxication or undertaking the desperate search for rebellion of the psychoses (*Auflehnungsversuch der Psychose*). [179]

---

[174] **Bk. 2, 381. JS (p. 64) has a misleading 'instinctual sublimation.' The use of "*Mensch*" permits 'person' rather than 'man', but the personal pronouns establish that Freud is addressing 'men'.**

[175] **'Striving' and 'endeavour' are also acceptable.**

[176] **Notice the verbal parallelism and euphony.**

[177] **Bk. 2, 382. That is, according to the correct rule ("*nicht regelrecht durchgemacht*"). A 'rite de passage' structure is implied here.**

[178] **Note the near-synonymous parallelism of "*Umbildung*" and "*Neuordnung*."**

[179] **Idem. '[C]hronic intoxication' and 'the psychoses' are rather grim choices. b) The 'young' motif is a sub-theme in DUK, e.g. in the brillant analogy on the preparation of the young for life being like equipping people for a polar expedition with summer clothes and maps of the Italian lakes (Bk. 8, 416). Freud's focus on the significance of early and middle childhood development, more fully developed by his youngest daughter Anna, is widely accepted. However, the flight, often a comforting one, into neurosis is not a monopoly of the "*jungen Jahren.*" Freud adds a foonote (1931) to this passage in which he points out**

ud

Religion restricts this play of choice and adaptation (*Auswahl und Anpassung*),[180] since it imposes equally on everyone its own path to the acquisition of happiness and protection from suffering (*ihrem Weg zum Glückserwerb und Leidensschutz allen in gleicher Weise aufdrängt*).[181] Its method (*Technik*) consists in decrying the value of life (*Wert des Lebens herabzudrücken*) and [hence] distorting the picture of the real world in a delusional matter, which presupposes an intimidation of the intelligence (*was die Einschüchterung der Intelligenz zur Voraussetzung hat*).[182] At this price, through a powerful fixation in [a state of] psychical infantilism (*psychischen Infantilismus*) and drawing them (*Einbeziehung*) into a mass delusion (*Masswahn*), religion succeeds in sparing many people from an individual neurosis.[183] But more: there are, as we have said, many paths which may lead to happiness, as attainable by human beings, but none which does so for certain (*keinen, der sicher dahin leitet*).[184] Religion cannot even keep its promise (*Versprechen*). If the believer finally finds

---

gaps left in the discussion, and that a grasp of the connection between narcissism and object libido is required.

[180] Note the lexical parallelism in this lovely sentence. It is troubling that Freud, trained in the specificity of scientific research, constantly used 'religion' as a generic noun.

[181] Observe the exquisite parallelism: attainment of happiness and protection from suffering.

[182] The sentence is not fully clear to me but the last clause probably relates to '*Technik.*' This keyword, often used in compounds, combines the Eng. for 'technology' and 'technique'; *technē* is a keyword for Aristotle with the meaning of skill, craft, art. b) The phrase about distorting the picture 'of the real world' shows that Freud would not have agreed with a constructivist view of science and religion—a debate that raged since Darwin's work of 1859 and currently spins around 'intelligent design' and 'creationism.' Some argued then and do so now that science and religion are not in conflict because they are different types of activity within different intellectual and language communities that answer to different needs. But Freud thought science and religion were antagonists; and religious dogmas, the products of repression, should be replaced by the results of rigorous, rational mental efforts ("*rationellen Geistesarbeit zu ersetzen*", in *Die Zukunft einer Illusion*, Bk. 8, 358). c) The motif of 'decrying the value of life' is from F. Nietzsche. Freud bought his collected works in 1900. However, according to Peter Gay, Freud "treated Nietzsche's writings as texts to be resisted far more than to be studied." (Gay, *Freud* (1988) p. 45). The term 'resisted' probably relates to an affinity to Nietzsche, something which troubled Freud's desire for originality. He also feared distraction, a fact that may have motivated his avoidance of classical music, given its erotic dimension. However, he liked Wagner's *Die Meistersinger von Nürnberg,* and in 1883 wrote his fiancée Martha Bernay about the G. Bizet's *Carmen*, Mozart's *The Magic Flute, Don Giovanni,* and *The Marriage of Figaro.*

[183] Freud footnoted *Die Zukunft einer Illusion* (1927c) with page reference (vol. 2 of *Freud ZB*, p. 375 f. and p. 358, Anm. 2.) JS omitted this footnote.

[184] Bk. 2, 382. JS (p. 65) divides the sentence and puts 'may' in italics.

ud

himself obliged (*genötigt*) [185] to speak of God's 'inscrutable decrees' ("*unerforschlichem Ratschluß*"), he is admitting that all that is left as a possible consolation and source of pleasure (*Trostmöglichkeit und Lustquelle*) is unconditional submission (*bedingungslose Unterwerfung*). [186] And if he is ready for that, he could probably have spared himself the detour (*Umweg*). [187]

III

So far, our investigation of happiness (*Untersuchung über das Glück*) has not taught us much that is not already common knowledge (*allgemein bekannt ist*). [188] And even if we proceed with the question of why it is so difficult for human beings to be happy, there appears to be no great prospect of learning anything new (*Neues zu erfahren*). We have already given the answer by indicating the three sources from which our suffering comes (*aus denen unser Leiden kommt*): superior power of nature, the feebleness of our own bodies, and the inadequacy of the institutions which govern the mutual relationships of human beings in the family, the state, and society (*Unzulänglichkeit der Einrichtungen welche die Beziehungen der Menschen zueinander in Familie, Staat und Gesellschaft regeln*). [189] In regard to the first two, our judgment cannot hesitate long (*unser Urteil nicht lange schwanken*), it forces us to recognize those sources of suffering and to submit to the inevitable (*und zur Ergeben ins Unvermeidliche*). We can never fully control (*beherrschen*) nature, our organism itself a part of that nature will always be a transitory formation, restricted in adaptation and achievement (*vergängliches, in Anpassung und Leistung beschränktes Gebilde bleiben*). [190] This recognition does not have a paralysing effect; on the contrary it points to the direction of our activity (*Tätigkeit die Richtung*). If we cannot remove (*aufgeben*) [191] all suffering,

---

[185] 'inclined' would work here but the 'obliged' of JS is better. That 'religion' cannot even keep its promises is a basic premise of Christopher Hitchens' *god is not Great: How Religion Poisons Everything* (2007), although that work is more polemic than scholarship.

[186] This is a central theme in Islamic and Calvinistic theology.

[187] Freud's ironic wit often worked like a surprise punchline at the end of a narrative.

[188] Bk. 3, 383. '*allgemein*' also means 'general' and was often used by Hegel and Heidegger in the sense of 'universal.'

[189] Idem. Our 'institutions' for *Einrichtungen* is preferable to JS's (p. 67) 'regulations.'

[190] Again, the powerful use of parallelism.

[191] Idem. The basic meaning of "*aufgeben*" is 'give up.' It is a keyword in Freud, and in a different context in Hegel's dialectic. It has a range of meanings: sublate (< L. *subāt-us;* first use 1694, OED), cancel, elevate, and preserve (*tollere, elevare, conservare*).

ud

we can remove some, and mitigate some (*und anderes lindern*); many thousands of years of experience (*Erfahrung*) has convinced us of that. We [have] a different relation to the third souce, [i.e.] the social source of suffering. We will have nothing to do with this one: we cannot see why the institutions made by ourselves should not on the contrary be a protection and benefit (*Schutz und Wohltat*) for all of us. [192] And yet, when we consider how bad we have been in precisely this affair (*Stück*) of preventing suffering (*Leidverhütung gelungen ist*), a suspicion awakens that here too a piece of unconquerable nature lies behind, this time our own psychic constitution (*psychischen Beschaffenheit*).

In the process of considering this possibility we come upon a contention which is so astonishing that we must linger with it (*bei ihr verweilen wollen*).[193] It holds that what we call our civilization (*Kultur*) is largely responsible for the guilt at our misery (*der Schuld an unserem Elend*),[194] and we would be much happier if we gave it up (*aufgeben*) and returned to primitive conditions (*primitive Verhältnisse zurückfinden werden*).[195] I call it astonishing because—however we may define the concept of civilization—it is a fact that all the things we use to protect against the menace (*Bedrohung*) deriving from the sources of suffering are part of that very same civilization.

How was it possible that so many people have come to this point of view of strange hostility to civilization (*Auf welchem Weg sind wohl*[196] *so viel Menschen zu diesem Standpunkt*[197] *befremdlicher Kulturfeindlichkeit gekommen*)?[198] I believe the basis of it was a deep and long-standing

---

[192] **This is lovely near-synonymous parallelism.**
[193] **Idem. JS (p. 68) has 'dwell upon it.'**
[194] **The keyword "*Schuld*" is used about ninety times in *DUK*. It is also a keyword in *Totem and Taboo* (1911-1913). b) Guilt is a decisive experience in culture and in the relationship between the individual and culture or civilization. See Herman Westerink, *A Dark Trace*, cited above.**
[195] **Bk. 3, 383. JS (p. 68). The last phrase is perhaps directed at J. J. Rousseau (1712-78). It could also target the *völkisch* return-to-nature, proto-fascist movements of the 1920's. Later in *DUK*, Freud gave specific historical contextualization to his generalization. b) In this context 'civilization' is the best translation of *Kultur*. c) On the phrase 'guilt at our misery,' JS omits "*der Schuld*" and has only 'our misery.'**
[196] **Idem. "*Auf welchem Weg sind wohl*" = lit., 'on which way probably are.' JS (p. 68) has 'how has it happened.'**
[197] **Idem. "*Standpunkt.*" JS (idem) has 'attitude.'**
[198] **Bk. 3, 383. JS (p. 68). This 'hostility' arises because the renunciation demanded for security does not secure enough of it. The demands subject to renunciation are the**

ud

dissatisfaction with the respective state of civilization and on that basis, occasioned (*Anlässen*) by certain historical events, a condemnation was built up. I believe I know what the last and next to last of these occasions were, but I am not learned enough to trace the chain of them far back enough in the history of the human species. A factor of cultural hostility must have already been involved (*beteiligt gewesen sein*) in the victory of Christendom over the heathen religions. For it [hostility to civilisation] stood very near to the low evaluation (*vollzogenen Entwertung*) of earthly life by Christian doctrine (*christliche Lehre*). [199]

The next to last of these occasions was when the progress of voyages of discovery led to contact with primitive peoples and races (*primitiven Völkern und Stämmen*).[200] As a result of insufficient observation and a mistaken view of their manners and customs (*Sitten und Gebräuche*),[201] they appeared to Europeans to be leading a simple, happy life, low in needs (*bedürfnisarmes*); a life unattainable to their visitors with their superior civilization. Later experience has corrected many of those judgments; in many cases one had wrongly attributed a degree of ease of life (*Lebenserleichterung*), [which was] provided by the abundance of nature and the easy satisfaction of substantial needs, to the absence of complex cultural demands. The last occasion is especially familiar to us; it arose when people came to know the mechanism of neuroses which threatened to undermine the small degree of happiness of civilized human beings (*Kulturmenschen*). One discovered that a person becomes neurotic because he cannot withstand the amount of denial (*Versagung*) society imposes on

---

satisfaction of needs, not only sexual but also aggressive impulses. He gave three examples of this hostility: the victory of Christianity over the 'pagan' religions, the hostility of colonials toward 'primitive' people (there is a hint here of an anti-colonial attitude), and the modern neurotic patterns of civilization. These neurotic patterns are protests against dominant cultures which promise happiness but don't fulfill the promise.

[199] Bk. 3, 383. Nietzsche's thought informs this sentence and paragraph.

[200] Bk. 3, 384. Note the near-synonymous parallelism of "*Völkern und Stämmen*". b) The keyword "*Fortschritt*" (progress) is used in several ways, most importantly in relation to *Kultur*. The notion of 'primitive' as applied to peoples in terms of temporal stage and normative evaluation is less the point than how early ethnologists got things wrong. Through his sources, and especially Robertson Smith, Freud also got it wrong, especially in *Totem und Tabu*. However, humility is shown in the endnote citing Andrew Lang "Nowhere do we see absolutely primitive man, and a totemic system in the making." *Secret of the Totem*, p. 29". Cited on page 151 of *Totem and Taboo*, translation by A. A. Brill (1913, new edition, Barnes & Noble 2005). Lang is cited 17 times in the German text.

[201] Synonymous parallelism.

ud

him in service of its cultural ideals (*im Dienste ihrer kulturellen Ideale auferlegt*) and it was concluded from this that the abolition or great reduction of those demands signified a return to the possibilities of happiness (*daß es eine Rückkehr zu Glücksmöglichkeiten bedeute, wenn diese Anforderungen aufgehoben oder sehr herabgesetzt werden*). [202]

There is also an added factor of disappointment. In the last generations humankind has made an extraordinary progress in natural science and in their technical application, and domination over nature has been established in a way unimaginable before (*in einer früher unvorstellbaren Weise befestigt*).[203] The details (*Einzelheiten*)[204] of this progress are general knowledge and it is unnecessary to enumerate them. Human beings are proud of their exploits and have a right to be. But they seem to have observed (*glauben bemerkt*) that this new-won power over space and time (*Raum und Zeit*),[205] this subjugation of the power of nature, this fulfillment of a thousand year old longing (*Sehnsucht*) has not increased the amount of pleasure-satisfaction (*Lebensbefriedigung*) expected from life, and it has not made them feel happier (*nicht glücklicher gemacht hat*). From the realization of this finding one should be content to conclude that power over nature is not the only preconditon of human happiness. Just as it is also not the only goal of cultural striving, we should not infer from it that technical progress is valueless for the economics of our happiness (*Wertlosigkeit der technischen Fortschritte für unsere Glücksökonomie daraus ableiten*).[206] One would like to object, is it then

---

[202] Cf. the "back to the garden" counter-cultural trends in the 1960's and early 1970's in North America. There was also the less innocent embrace of nature in the *völkisch* attitudes of the German Youth movements of the 1920s.

[203] Bk. 3, 384. *DUK* is an inquiry into progress, repression, aggression and the struggle of the *Ich* with the *Es*. Freud noted in this treatise and in *The Future of an Illusion* (1927) that advances have been made in the control of nature, but risks arose with advances: for instance from new weapons, and from the gap between the social dimension (*mitsein*) and the growth of science and technology. b) This view of the loss of connection to 'roots' (*Bodenständigkeit*) was developed in ethically disturbing ways by Heidegger and other reactionary modernists in the 1930's.

[204] Idem. JS (p.70) has 'single steps.'

[205] Idem. A famous lexical pair: cf. Heidegger's *Sein und Zeit* (1927). I am not implying that Freud coined "*Raum und Zeit*", a long established pair.

[206] Idem. a) Anxiety is rooted in the helplessness of being thrown (*Geworfenheit*) into different worlds. Antidotes to helplessness through attempts to subjugate the natural world are not the solution; although some control is needed, e.g. over fire and flood, and some controls are possible. b) The Freud of *DUK* avoids extremes on technology and

ud

not a positive gain of pleasure, no unambiguous (*unzweideutiger*) increase of my feeling of happiness, if I can hear the voice of my child living hundreds of kilometers (*Kilometern*) [207] away, if I can hear in the shortest possible time that my friend has safely landed after a long and difficult voyage? Does it mean nothing, that medicine has succeeded in enormously reducing infant mortality and the danger of infection for women in childbirth, and indeed, in lengthening considerably the average lifespan of a civilized person (*Kulturmenschen*)? And we could cite (*anführen*) a long list of benefits of this kind which we owe to the much-despised era of scientific and technical progress; but here the voice of pessimistic criticism allows itself to be heard, and warns that most of these satisfactions follow the model of 'cheap enjoyment' ("*billigen Vergnügens*") extolled (*angepreisen*) in the anecdote. The enjoyment obtained by (*Man verschauf sich diesen Genuß*) putting a bare leg out in the cold winter night and then drawing it in again.[208] If there had been no railroad to overcome distances, then my child would not have left his hometown and I would not need a telephone to hear his voice. If no ocean liners (*Schiffahr über den Ozean*) my friend would not have gone on his voyage, and I would not need a telegraph to relieve my concern (*Sorge*) about him.[209] What is the use of reducing infantile mortality when that extreme prevention (*Zurückhaltung*) forces a reduction in procreation so that we rear no more children than in the days before the reign of hygiene, while at the same time we have

---

happiness. The denunciation found in the post-*Sein und Zeit* Heidegger is absent, and Freud avoided the full endorsement of technology found in T. Veblen and B. Fuller. If we interpret 'happiness' in a more inclusive and integral way than satisfaction of a pleasure principle, we can find in *DUK* a critique of the search for power over nature and the non-human lifeworld. Although the textual problems must be specified, interpreting the pleasure principle along the lines of Aristotle's *eudaemonia* as 'flourishing activity' gives the concept a wider reach, and makes it compatible with current neo-Jungian eco-psychologists, although perhaps not with its animistic forms; but radical environmentalism includes a myriad of categories, e.g. eco-feminism, eco-socialism, eco-humanist 'Marxism.' We thank Dr. Paul Astin for discussion of, and literature on, this and related points. c) JS (p. 70) makes two sentences out of this one and twice puts 'only' in italics.
[207] **JS (idem) has 'miles.' One may get the impression that in this pericope, Freud is playing 'devil's advocate for technophobia' (N. W. Warren, personal communication).**
[208] **JS links this sentence with the preceding one and thus makes it a clause.**
[209] **Bk. 3, 385. These negative past conditionals on the gains and loses of technology have a light rhetorical feel, and address a different issue than the disturbing counter-negative in the sentence that follows. JS (p.71) has 'anxiety' for *Sorge*, and makes one sentence out of two.**

ud

created difficult conditions for our sexual life in marriage and probably worked against the benefits of natural selection (*natürlichen Auslese*)? And finally what good to us is a long life if it is difficult, poor in joy and so rich in misery that we welcome death as a solution (*Erlöser bewillkommnen*). [210]   It seems certain that we do not feel well in our present-day civilization (*unserer heurigen Kultur nicht wohl fühlen*),[211] but it is very difficult to form an opinion (*Urteil*) whether and in what degree persons of an earlier time felt happier and what part their cultural conditions played in that. We always tend to view the misery of others objectively; that is, to put ourselves with our own demands and susceptiblities (*Anspruchen und Emfänglicheiten*) [212] in their conditions and then to examine (*prüfen*) which occasions we find in them for experiencing happiness and unhappiness. This form of observation which appears objective because it ignores (*absieht*) subjective variations of sensibility is naturally the most subjective because it puts one's own mental attitudes (*Verfassungen*) in the place of all unknown others.[213]   But happiness is itself essentially

subjective (*Das Glück ist aber etwas durchaus Subjektives*).[214]   We

---

[210]   Idem. The sentence on the 'benefits of natural selection' confuses the is/ought or fact-value distinction. If infanticide was sometimes required by natural selection that reveals a morally dark side of the process, i.e. reducing infant mortality is a human good, regardless of context. On the other hand, the sentence questioning the value of a long life if one is not happy assumes the fact-value distinction. An assumption based on evolutionary biology that a longer life is better than a shorter one does not provide a standard of value for that life. Freud's model wavered between life-philosophy and scientific status as a fact-based methodology. This claim ran ahead of the evidence, could not clarify the is/ought distinction; and it made major category mistakes, e.g. driving affections from infantile sexuality rather than from the value of the primary mother-child relationship.

[211]   Idem. JS (p. 71) has 'comfortable' for "*wohl*". The term is a synonym of "*gut*", "*gesund*". In English usage, 'feel well' often refers more to a state of health, whereas "*wohl*", as here, refers to mental and attitudinal condition.

[212]   Idem. Note the lovely correlative parallelism. JS has 'wants and sensibilities,' but the basic meaning of "*Empfang*" is 'reception.'

[213]   Bk. 3, 385. This is an odd inversion of the meaning of empathy (*Einfühlung*) as a feeling of 'one-with'.

[214]   Idem. This assertion on the subjectivity of 'happiness' may mean that it cannot yield a standard of justice and social welfare. Otherwise, the sentence is a tautology like the Japanese proverb 'ten people, ten colors.' How it connects with the sentence following is problematic, i.e. if happiness is subjective why do 'we shrink back in horror from some situations…'? It is also unclear to me how happiness as essentially subjective relates to the topography and mechanics of *Ich, Es, Über-Ich*. Lastly, the assertion ignores how drive and desire (*Trieb*) connect us with others, shapes 'happiness' and forms of the good like active agency as embodied intersubjectivity.

ud

shrink back in horror from some situations) — the ancient galley-slave, the peasant in the 30 years war, the victims of the Holy Inquisition, Jews waiting for a pogrom — but it is still impossible for us to feel our way into those people, to guess (*erraten*) the transformations of primordial dullness, a gradual stupefication (*allmähliche Abstumpfung*), cessation of expectation, that crude or more refined methods of narcotization (*Weisen der Narkotisierung*) have produced upon their susceptibility to sensations of pleasure and unpleasure.[215] Morever, in the situation of the most extreme possibilities of suffering, special mental protection devices come into operation. It seems to me unfruitful to pursue this side of the problem any further.

It is time that we concern (*kümmern*) ourselves with the nature of culture on whose value [as a means] for happiness doubts have been raised (*Zweifel gezogen wird*).[216] We will not look for a formula that expresses this essence in a few words until we have learned something about it through research. It is enough for us to repeat that the word 'civilisation' ("*Kultur*") describes the whole sum of achievements and institutions (*Leistungen und Einrichtungen*) which distinguishes our lives from our animal ancestors and serves two purposes: to protect human beings from nature, and the regulation of their mutual relationships.[217] To understand more, we will bring together the features of culture individually, as they are exhibited in human communities. We allow ourselves to do so without hesitation [because we are] guided by linguistic usage, or as it is also called linguistic feeling (*Sprachgefühl*), in the trust (*Vertrauen*)[218] that

---

[215] Idem. a) The examples are vivid and powerful. However, the whole passage is obscure and it seems to blame the victims. However, 'Jews waiting for a pogrom' has a bitter sarcastic edge. Freud rejected Jewish passivity and the *Kiddush ha-shem* (Santification of the Name). b) It is not clear if the 'gradual stupefaction' and 'cessation of expectation' are the products of the 'methods of narcotization', and if not what connects this glimpse of human suffering with "*Das Glück ist aber etwas durchaus Subjektives.*"? The passage contradicts that statement, and it contradicts Freud's odd objection to a concept of empathy. Happiness and discontent are logical and existential correlates and hence the project of an analytic of culture and its discontents presupposes that they are not 'subjective.'

[216] Idem. Literally, 'called in.' JS (p. 72) has 'as a means to happiness doubts have been thrown.'

[217] Note the parallelism in this sentence which gives the most concise definition of *Kultur* in *DUK*. In this context, the term is best translated as 'civilisation.' Italics in the original. '*Einrichtungen*' is literally: 'fittings, furnishings', but JS (p. 73) has 'regulations.'

[218] Bk. 3, 386. In contrast to the Stracheyese neologisms in *DUK* and the *S.E.*, the passage

ud

we shall be doing justice to inner insights (*inneren Einsichten*)[219] which resist expression in abstract terms.

The beginning is easy: we recognize as cultural all activities and values (*Tätigkeiten und Werte*)[220] useful for making the earth servicable for human beings, protecting them against the violence of the forces of nature, and so forth. About this side of cultural life there can hardly be any doubt. If we go back far enough, the first cultural acts (*die ersten kulturellen Taten*)[221] were the use of tools, control over fire, and the construction of dwellings. Among these, the taming of fire stands out as an extraordinary, unexampled achievement,[222] while the others opened up paths followed ever since, the stimulus to which is easily guessed. With all his tools man is perfecting his own organs—whether motor or sensory—or removing the limits on their functioning. Motor power places gigantic forces at his

---

shows nominalistic caution toward abstract expressions.

[219] 'inner insights' appears tautological. JS (p. 73) has 'inner discernments.'

[220] Idem. Note the near-synonymous parallelism. JS (p. 73) has 'activities and resources.' However, 'resource' would be '*Mittel.*'

[221] Bk. 3, 386. This a case where '*kulturellen Taten*'could be rendered: 'acts of civilization.'

[222] On Freud's footnote: he seems to have forgotten his initial caution about the speculative and the peril of using 'legends' and 'fables' as evidence; and we observe simplistic equations: flame with penis, hearths and dwellings with the womb. b) Freud's footnote: "Psychoanalytic material, incomplete and not open to clear interpretation, still admits of a speculation (*Vermutung*), a fantastical sounding one, about the origin of this human feat. It is as if primal man had the habit, when he came in contact with fire, of satisfying an infantile desire (*eine infantile Lust an ihm zu befriedigen*) by putting it out with a stream of urine. The legends that we have leave no doubt about the original phallic interpretation of tongues of fire shooting upward. Putting out fire by urination, a theme to which the modern giant child Gulliver in Lilliput and Rabelais' Gargantua refer back to, was therefore a kind of sexual act with a male and enjoyment of male potency in homosexual competition (*homosexuellen Wettkampf*). The first to renounce this desire and spare the fire was able to carry it off and subdue it and use it for himself. Through damping down the fire of his own sexual excitation he had tamed the natural force of fire. This great cultural conquest was also the reward for his renunciation of instinct (*Triebverzicht*). Further, it was as if woman had been made guardian of the fire, held captive on the domestic hearth, because her anatomical structure (*anatomischer Bau*) made it impossible for her to yield to the temptation of this desire (*Lustversuchung nachzugeben*). It is remarkable, too, how regularly analytical experience attests (*bezeugen*) to the connection between ambition, fire and urethral erotism." Freud now referenced a later study (1932a) "The Acquisition of Fire" (*Zur Gewinnung des Feuer*s (Imago, 1932) in *Zwei Bänden*, vol. 2, 512-16; in *S.E.* 22, 183-193). This essay focussed on Prometheus, the culture hero who stole fire from the gods and hence was punished, and on the antithetical functions of the penis (*Glied*) of urination and erection. Many find anti-women motifs in SF, but in this passage women as 'guardian of the fire' are the essential source of *civilization.*

ud

disposal, which, like his muscles, he can use in any direction, and [thanks to] ships and airplanes, his motion over water or air cannot be hindered. With glasses he corrects defects of the lens in his eye, with the telescope he sees into the far distance, and through the microscope he overcomes the limits of visibility set by the structure of the retina. In the photographic camera he has created an instrument which retains fleeting visual impressions (*flüchtigen Seheindrücke festhält*), just as a gramophone disc retains the equally fleeting auditory impressions (*Schalleindrücke*);[223] fundamentally both are materializations of his power of remembrance (*Erinnerung*), his memory (*Gedächtnisses*). With the aid of the telephone he can hear at a distance which even in a fairy tale would be considered unattainable. Writing in its origin was the voice of an absent person, and the dwelling-house (*Wohnhaus*) was a substitute for the womb, the first lodging (*Behausung*), which probably man still longs for, and in which he felt safe and at ease. [224]

These things not only sound like a fairy tale, they are a direct fulfillment of almost every fairy-tale wish, these things that human beings through their science and technology (*Wissenschaft und Technik*)[225] have brought about on this earth, on which he first appeared (*auftrat*) as a weak animal organism and on which each individual of his species (*jedes Individuum seiner Art*) must make its entry-'*oh inch of nature*'-[226] again as a helpless suckling. He can claim all these possessions (*Besitz*) as his cultural acquisition (*Kulturerwerb*). A long time ago he formed an ideal

---

[223] *'Schall' is Austrian dialect: 'wound, ring, peal, resonance, noise.' Note the assonance seheindrücke/ Schalleindrücke.*

[224] *Bk. 3, 386-7. This section has three major points: tools extend human capacities, the roots of technology need human communication, and communication depends upon memory. b) The term 'Erinnerung' ('remembrance', 'recollection') was a keyword in Hegel. In the sentence following 'Wohnhaus' and 'Behausung' invoke Heidegger's 1951 lecture Bauen Wohnen Denken ("Building Dwelling Thinking"). Both thinkers sought 'origins' but on different dimensions and in different ways.*

[225] *Important parallelism.*

[226] *In English. According to Freud's footnote, James Strachey established that the phrase is not from Shakespeare but from George Wilkins' 1608 novel The Painfull Adventures of Pericles Prince of Tyre. Pericles says the words to his infant daughter. Freud adds that the phrase is in the Danish critic Georg Brandes' William Shakespeare (1896). The footnote to the 2005 edition of Civilization and its Discontents notes that Freud "greatly admired the Danish critic..." Brandes, a devotee of Enlightenment ideals, also wrote the two volume study of Wolfgang Goethe (authorized translation by Allen W. Porterfield, Vol. I (Frank-Maurice, 1924).*

ud

conception of omnipotence and omniscience (*Allmacht und Allwissenheit*) which he embodied (*Verkörperte*) in his gods. [227] He attributed to these gods everything, which seemed unattainable to his wishes or forbidden to him. Therefore, one can say that these gods were cultural ideals (*Kulturideale*). Now he has come very close to the attainment of this ideal, he is almost a god himself.[228] Of course, only as ideals are attained through the general judgment of humanity (*Freichlich nur so, wie man nach allgemein menschlichem Urteil Ideale zu erreichen pflegt*).[229] Not fully, in some cases not at all, in others only half way. Man has become, so to speak, a kind of prosthetic god, quite magnificent when he puts on his auxillary organs, but they have not grown on to him and occasionally cause him too much (*noch viel*) trouble.[230] He has; by the way, the right to console

---

[227] *Note the standard theological parallelism of power and knowledge.*

[228] Bk. 3, 387. a) The comment reflects the thinking of Ludwig Feuerbach (1804-1872) whom Freud revered when he was about twenty (see letter to E. Silberstein, March 1874). The comment is also condensed in the metaphor in the line below: "Der Mensch ist sozusagen eine Art Prothesengott geworden…" b) Freud's approach to the question of 'religion' paralleled the analytic observational and causal-reductive structure of psychoanalytic therapy. This may partially explain why Karl Jaspers, the psychiatrist and philosopher of Existenz, called Freud's psychoanalysis 'a violaton of human dignity.' Jaspers's critique reflected his own 'psychology of world-views' and his conviction that "the totality of man lies way beyond any conceivable objectifiability." Writing in the 1950's, he found Freud "dated." (See "Philosophical Autobiography" in The Philosophy of Karl Jaspers, The Library of Living Philosopers, edited by Paul Arthur Schilpp (Open Court Press, 1957), p. 19, 25). b) Like classical Marxism, psychoanalysis attempted to explain too much and too neatly. However, Jaspers did not appreciate Freud as a literary artist of the human condition. Also, he may not have known about Freud's close noetic and personal bonds with L. Binswanger, the major intellectual force in the development of existential therapy. c) Freud overgeneralized and claimed too much for core ideas. The Oedipus complex, for example, has value as an experimental type hypothesis useful in some contexts, but it fails as an inclusive truth-claim about human Dasein. Totem and Taboo was done before B. Malinosky's research on the Trobriand Islands, but by 1929 Malinosky had rebutted the universality of the Oedipus complex. Freud also made clinical mistakes and refused responsibility for them. On the other hand, his assertion that symptoms were sometimes 'over-determined' suggests a non-dogmatic perspective on causality. Diagnosis and dogma aside, the method of deep listening, a form of empathy, to complaints may often assist healing. It also may constitute a form of "tacit knowledge" (M. Polanyi).

[229] This resembles a slogan of some of the European Enlightenment thinkers. It is not a complete sentence in German or in our translation.

[230] a) Humor based on personal experience, but with a tragic quality. Freud is probably also referring to the painful and clumsy prosthetic device he wore for years because of cancer of the palate (he endured 13 operations on his jaw). Prosthetics in his time were painfully crude. [In the 21st century these devices, some using computors, will gradually turn the body into a hybrid of the human and machine.] b) The sentences following this

ud

himself that this development will not exactly end with the year 1930 A.D. Future ages will bring with them new and probably unimaginable great progress in this field of culture and will further increase man's likeness to God. But in the interest of our research we will not forget that present-day human beings do not feel happy in their Godlikeness (*Gottähnlichkeit nicht glücklich fühlt*).

We recognize, then, that countries have attained high points of culture if we find that in them everything is cultivated and functional (*gepflegt und zweckmäßig besorgt wird*), the human exploitation of the earth and protection from the forces of nature; in short, [when] everything is useful to him (*ihm nützlich ist*).[231] In countries like these, rivers which threaten to flood are regulated, their water directed (*hingeleitet*) through canals to places short of it. The soil is carefully cultivated and planted with vegetation which it is suited to sustain, and the mineral wealth underground industriously raised to the surface and fashioned into the required instruments and utensils (*verlangten Werkzeugen und Geräten verarbeitet*).[232] The means of communication are ample, swift and reliable (*reichlich, rasch und zuverlässig*),[233] wild and dangerous animals have been killed, and the breeding (*Zucht*) of domestic animals flourishes (*Blüte*).[234] But we have other demands and hope (*Anforderungen zu stellen und hoffen*) from culture and it is remarkable that we hope to find them realized in these same countries.[235] As though we were embarassed by the first demand we raised, we welcome it as cultural (*begrüßen wir es auch als kulturell*) if we see people also directing their care to things that formally appeared completely useless (*ganz und gar nicht nützlich sind, eher unnütze*

---

one sound like a comment on Fichte (1742-1814) but without the optimistic belief in progress found in his lectures Die Grundzüuge des gegenwärtigen Zeitalters (Characteristics of the Present Age (1806). In Bk. 3 Freud expressed hope that 'future ages' would bring 'great advances' in civilization, but his conclusions in Bk. 8 strike a far different note.

[231] A difficult sentence. Note the complementary parallelism. Contemporary eco-psychologists would disagree.

[232] Note the synonymous parallelism.

[233] Note the 'r' alliteration.

[234] Bk. 3, 387. '*Zucht*' can mean animal breeding and human manners. On the term, see Raymond Geuss, *Morality, Culture, and History. Essays on German Philosophy* (Cambridge, 1999), pp. 45-6, fn. 11. '*Blüte*', like '*Trieb*', is a botanical term. Hence the constant translation of *Trieb* by 'instinct' is a serious mistake.

[235] Standard phrasal complementary parallelism. "*Anforderungen stellen*" translates as 'make large demands and expectations.'

ud

erscheinen);[236] for example in city playgrounds and fresh air areas (*Spiel platze und Luftreservoirs*) unnecessary flower beds (*Blumenbeete*) are laid out, or the windows of the houses are decorated with flower pots (*Blumentöpfen*).[237] We soon observe that the useless thing which we expect culture to value is beauty; we require that cultural persons revere beauty where they encounter it in nature and to create it in the objects of their handiwork in so far as they are able (*soweit seiner Hände Arbeit es vermag*). But this is far from exhausting our demands on culture. We demand besides to see the marks (*Zeichen*) of cleanliness and order (*Reinlicheit und Ordnung*).[238] We don't think highly of the culture of an English country town of Shakespeare's time when we read that there was a high heap of manure in front of his father's house in Stratford; we are indignant and call (*ungehalten und schelten*)[239] it 'barbarous', the opposite to civilized, when we find the paths in the Wiener Waldes littered with paper. Dirtiness of any kind appears incompatible with civilization;[240] also, we extend our demands for cleanliness to the human body, we are astonished (*erstaunen*) when we learn of the bad odour which emanated from Roi Soleil,[241] and we shake our heads on the Isola Bella[242] when we are shown the tiny wash-basin for Napoleon's morning toilet. Yes, we are not suprised if someone proposes the use of soap as a direct measure of culture (*Kulturmesser*).[243] It is similar with order (*Ordnung*): it, like cleanliness (*Reinlichkeit*), relates only to the work of human beings (*Menschenwerk bezieht*).[244] But while cleanliness is not expected in nature, order is derived (*abgelauscht*)[245] much more from it; the observation of the

---

[236] **JS (p. 77) ignores "*eher unnütz erscheinen.*"**
[237] **Note the assonance and alliteration of the '*Blumen*' words.**
[238] **Note the parallelism of 'cleanliness and order'. A defining mark of the cultural order of Viennese middle-class Victorian culture, they were evident in the highly organized routine of Freud's daily life.**
[239] **Near-synonymous parallelism. '*schelten*' here = 'call' in the sense of 'call out' or 'scold, rebuke, reprimand.'**
[240] **"*Wiener Waldes*" refers to the wooded hills outside Vienna. This is another (rare) case where *Kultur* should be rendered 'civilization.' JS (p. 77) makes three sentences out of one.**
[241] **Louis XIV.**
[242] **An island in Lake Maggiore which Napoleon visited before the battle of Marengo.**
[243] **Freud was not a wealthy person but he paid close attention to his appearance including frequent use of a barber.**
[244] **Bk. 3, 388. JS (p. 78) has 'the same'; he ends the sentence after *Ordnung*, and follows with '...applies solely to the works of man.'**
[245] **Idem. Not 'imitated' as in JS (idem).**

ud

great astronomical regularities not only furnished human beings (*Menschen*) with a model, but also the first beginning points (*ersten Anhaltspunkte*) for the introduction of order in his/her life (*in sein Leben gegeben*.[246] Order is a form of repetitive compulsion (*Wiederholungszwang*) which through unique arrangements decides when, where and how something should be done so that in each similar circumstance one is spared doubt and hesitation (*Zögern und Schwanken erspart*).[247] The benefit of order is undeniable (*unleugbar*): it enables human beings the best use of space and time (*Raum und Zeit*) [248] while conserving their psychic force. One should have a right to expect (*Man hätte ein Recht zu erwarten*) that it [order] would have taken its place from the beginning and without opposition (*zwanglos*) in human activities and one can be astonished that this is not the case, that human beings, on the contrary, have a natural inclination to negligence, irregularity and untrustworthiness in their work (*Hang zur Nachlässigkeit, Unregelmäßigkeit und Unzuverlässigkeit in seiner Arbeit*), and a difficult training is needed before learning to follow the example of their celestial models (*himmlichen Vorbilder*). [249]

Beauty, cleanliness and order obviously take a special position among the requirements of civilization. No one will contend that they are as important for life (*lebenswichtig*) as control of the forces of nature and other factors that we have yet to learn about, and yet no one would willingly put them in the background as unimportant (*gern sie als Nebensächlichkeiten zurückstellen wollen*). That civilisation is not exclusively concerned about what is useful (*auf Nutzen bedacht ist*) is already shown by the example of beauty, which we do not want to omit (*nicht vermissen wollen*) from the interests of culture.[250] The usefulness of

---

[246] **The specific reference here is not clear. The Babylonians, Egyptians and some of the 'pre-Socratics' were the first to be mindful of astronomical regularities. Astrology and astronomy assumed a Ptolemaic model of a concentric circled finite universe until the 17th century. b) The beginning point for order in ordinary lives was not through observation of astronomical regularities but through the time-ordering schemas of the great religious systems. c) JS (p.78) has 'man' for *Menschen* and 'him' for *sein* (poss. pron. 'his, her, it').**

[247] **Note the synonymous parallelism.**

[248] **Bk. 4, 388. The complementary parallelism here was used earlier in Bk. 4. This ancient contrast of space and time has been common in ordinary language and in elaborations by philosophers.**

[249] **Idem. The last clause is difficult because of the colloquial "*an den Tag legt*."**

[250] **Idem. "*nicht vermissen wollen*" is rendered by JS (p. 79) as 'decline to omit.' *Kultur* is**

ud

order is completely obvious, whereas with cleanliness we have to consider what is demanded of us by hygiene and we may presume (*vermutten*) that a connection between hygiene and scientific prophylaxis was not entirely foreign to people of this time. But utility does not explain these strivings completely; something else must have been at play (*anderes im Spiele sein*).[251]

However, no other alleged factor (*Zeug*) characterizes (*kennzeichnen*) culture better than the appreciation and care (*Schatzung und Pflege*) of the higher mental activities, the intellectual, scientific and artistic achievements, and the leading role it assigns to ideas in human life. Foremost among those ideas are the religious systems, whose complex structure (*verwickelten Aufbau*) I have tried to throw light on elsewhere, next come the philosophical speculations, and finally, what one might call formations of ideals (*Idealbildungen*) of human beings, ideas of a possible perfection of the individual or peoples, of the whole of humanity (*Menschheit*) and the demands set up on the basis of those ideas.[252] That these creations are not independent of one another, but rather are closely interwoven, increases both the difficulty of describing them and [tracing]

---

used three times in these three sentences. 'Civilization' is best for the first two uses, but 'culture' is better for the third because the central meaning is 'cultivate'.

[251] Bk. 3, 388-389. Freud may have been thinking of the greater hygiene from the diet and bath rituals of orthodox Jews. b) That 'utility does not explain these strivings completely' ("*Aber der Nutzen erklärt uns das Streben nicht ganz*") qualifies the assertion by P. Rieff that "everything in the psyche is produced for use", *Freud: The Mind of the Moralist* (third edition, 1979), p. 351. However, because of his explication of the jest and the joke and the tendenious joke, Freud did not seem to grasp that play is often for its own sake. This reflects the psychoanalytical tendency to understand phenomena not in and for themselves but within a model or *Vorbild*.

[252] Bk. 3, 389. a) Initially I had 'ideal-images' for *Idealbildungen* but N. W. Warren suggested 'formation of ideals.' These *Idealbildungen* resemble Max Weber's ideal types but are used in a different context. b) Note the synonomous parallelism of "*Schatzung und Pflege*". c) The 'religious systems' which he 'tried to throw light on elsewhere' refers to his *The Future of an Illusion* (1927). In *DUK* Freud acknowledged the 'complex structure' of those religious systems. However, in *The Future of an Illusion* he gave less attention to their differences and internal complexities: 'we are concerned here with European Christian culture' ("*europäisch-christliche Kultur*"). Islam and the Mongul, Ottoman, Safavid empires are not mentioned in that text or in *DUK*. d) In the sentence in the text above, the phrases 'possible perfection' and 'the whole of humanity' reminds one of Second Isaiah and the late works by Kant (but Kant would not have agreed with the assertion on 'psychological derivation' in the sentence following). e) JS (idem) divides this long sentence into two and translates '*Idealbildungen*' as 'ideals' enclosed in quotation marks, but those marks are not in the German text.

ud

their psychological derivation (*psychologische Ableitung*). If we assume generally that the driving force (*Triebfeder*)[253] of all human activity is the striving after the confluent goals of utility and gaining pleasure (*zusammenfließenden Zielen, Nutzen und Lustgewinn*), we must also assume that this takes in the manifestations of culture (*angeführten kulturellen Äußerungen*) we have been discussing here, although it is easily visible (*leicht ersichtlich ist*) only for scientific and artistic activities. But one cannot doubt that these other strong needs, perhaps some of which are developed only by a minority, correspond [to those activities].[254] Also, we must not allow ourselves to be led astray (*beirren lassen*) through value judgments of individual religious [or] philosophical systems and their ideals (*und dieser Ideale*); whether one seeks in them the highest achievements of the human mind (*Menschengeistes*) or if one laments (*beklagt*) them as aberrations, one must recognize that their presence (*Vorhandensein*), especially when dominant, implies (*bedeutet*) a high level of culture.

The last, certainly not unimportant, characteristic trait of culture we have yet to evaluate, is the way in which people relate to one another; [how] their social relationships are regulated (*geregelt sind*), relations which impact (*betreffen*) a person as a neighbor, as a source of help, as another's sexual object, as a member of a family, of a state. It is especially difficult here to remain free of particular ideal standards (*Idealforderungen*) and to grasp (*zu erfassen*) what is cultural in general. Perhaps we may begin with the explanation (*der Erklärung*) [255] that the cultural element becomes a factor with the first attempt to regulate these social relationships. If such an attempt were not made (*Unterbliebe ein sucher Versuch*), these relationships would be subject to the arbitrary will (*Willkür*) of the individual, that is, the physically stronger would decide them in the direction of his own interests and desire-impulses (*Interessen und Triebregungen*).[256] Nothing of this would be changed if the stronger person

---

[253] **Idem. On '*Triebfeder*': '*Trieb*' has the sense of motive power. '*Feder*' is 'feather', also 'spring'. '*Triebfeder*' looks like a coinage, but it is in common use. JS (p. 80) has 'motive power' for '*Trieb*', a rare case of him not using the misleading 'instinct.'**
[254] **Note the parallelism of "*Nutzen und Lustgewinn*". The phrase "*vielleicht solchen*" refers to the 'other activities' (*Tätigkeit*) of the previous sentence. b) The image of needs as manifestations of culture is not unique to Freud but was developed by Marxist thinkers.**
[255] **Noun, not JS's 'explaining'.**
[256] **Bk. 3, 389. Freud used the noun [n] form "*Unterbliebe*" of the ir. v. a. *unterbleiben* =**

ud

for his part met someone even stronger. Human life in common is only possible when a majority (*Mehrheit*) finds that together they are stronger than any single individual and when held together (*zusammenhält*) against all separate individuals.[257] The power of this community is then set up as "right" against the power of the individual which is judged as "brute force." This replacement of the power of the individual by the community is the decisive cultural step. Its essence consists in the fact that the members of the community restrict their possibilities of satisfaction, whereas the individuals knew no such restrictions. The first cultural requirement is therefore that of justice (*Gerechtigkeit*), that is, the assurance that a legal order (*Rechtsordnung*) once given will not be broken in favor of an individual. With this nothing is decided about the ethical value of such a law (*Recht*). The further course of cultural development appears to tend toward making the law no longer the expression of the will of a small community—caste, section of the population, a tribal group (*Volksstammes*) —which, in turn, behaves like a violent individual toward other, and perhaps larger, masses of people. A rule of law should be the end result for all—at least those able to enter a community—who have contributed by a sacrifice of their desires, and leaves no one—again with the same exception (*Ausnahme*) —a victim (*Opfer*) of brute force. [258]

'omission'. b) Note the synonymous parallelism of "*Interessen und Triebregungen*". JS (p. 81) has 'own interests and instinctual impulses'. c) Perhaps Hobbes and the Plato of the *Republic* are in the conceptual background of these sentences. The theme (rejected by the Socrates of Plato) that the stronger would decide on the basis of his interests was developed in the first four books of the *Republic*.

[257] Idem. Hobbes is an influence here; also Plato whom Freud had studied as a young man.

[258] Bk. 3, 390. These powerful sentences on the rule of law as the end for all defend a theory of democratic politics opposed to the use of 'exception' by Carl Schmitt (1888-1985) who justified dictatorial rule through "the concept of leadership." Schmitt, the leading constitutional theorist of the Weimar period, joined the Nazi party on May 1, 1933 and became a Crown Jurist of the early Nazi regime. Freud was opposed to dictatorship and rejected the far-Right (fascism, Nazism) and the far-Left (Soviet Marxism). His greatest fear was of the Germanic form of fascism because its dream of world-domination evoked (*aufrief*) anti-Semitism, Bk. 4, 402-3. There was complexity here because he had mixed feelings about the masses and yet some sympathy for social democracy. In a letter to Martha of Aug. 29, 1883, he reflected upon "the poor, the common people" and how "*das Volk*" believes and hopes and works differently "than we do." This recognition of class difference is infused by cultural elitism and empathy: the "common man" has more "feeling of community than we do." The concerns and some of the motifs in this letter reappear many years later in *DUK*. However, the reflections on Eros as a mytho-poetic force of unity confused the clarity needed for a democratic theory of social contract.

ud

The liberty of the individual is not a cultural good (*Die individuelle Freiheit ist kein Kulturgut*).[259] It was greatest before any culture, although at that time mainly without value because the individual was scarcely in a position (*kaum instande war*) to defend it. Through cultural developments it experiences restrictions, and justice demands (*Gerechtigkeit fordert*) that no one be spared them. What makes itself felt in a human community as a drive toward freedom (*Freiheitsdrang*) may be a revolt against some existing injustice and hence favorable (*günstig*) to a further development of culture; but, it may remain friendly with culture (*mit der Kultur verträglich bleiben*). However, it [the drive toward freedom] may also emerge from the remains (*Rest*) of their original personality which is still untamed by culture (*von der Kultur ungebändigten*), and thus may become the basis of hostility to culture. The drive for freedom is also directed against the specific forms and demands of culture (*Formen und Ansprüche der Kultur*) [260] or against culture in general. It does not appear that any influence could bring a person to change his nature into a termite's, so he will probably always

---

[259] **Idem. This sentence expresses the basic libertarian belief in a natural right of self-ownership, an assumption that conflicts with collective interests. Political libertarianism stems from Hugo Grotius (1583-1645), John Locke (1632-1704), and John Stuart Mill's classic interpretation of liberty as the freedom or negative liberty to do what one wants. However, there are formative texts by Marx, Engels, Rosenburg; Trotsky -- hardly political libertarians -- which contained the libertarian assumption that the state should be an organ of civil society and that ultimately the state would 'wither away.' Freud's image of community and the individual stresses the community above [a view of] self-sufficient individuals: 'The liberty of the individual is not a cultural good.' Freud, like George Orwell, thought the deepest split was not 'left' vs. 'right', but libertarian against authoritarian. In *DUK* he tried to evaluate the claims of libertarians and communitarians ('claim of the individual and the cultural claims of the masses'). The hope inherent in his view that the development of culture tends toward the expansion of law was questioned by the low morality of the nation-states and the brutality of the Great War (*Thoughts for the Times on War and Death*, 1915[b] in *S. E.*, 14, 274-300) and the shock of the rise of political anti-Semitism in Austria in the late 19th century. By 1930 he sensed that despite the rule of law, justice as fairness within Europe would soon fracture under the reign of 'brute force'. We detect this in the predictive pessimism of the last sentence added to *DUK* in 1931.**

[260] **The preceding sentence is vague: it seems to posit an 'original personality' before culture. Note the lexical-conceptual parallelism of "*Formen und Ansprüche*".**

ud

oppose his demands for individual liberty to the will of the masses (*Willen der Masse verteidigen*). A good part of the struggles of humanity focus around the task of finding a suitable (*zweckmäßigen*) balance, i.e. one that will bring happiness (*beglückenden*) between this claim of the individual and the cultural claims of the masses; it is one of their [humanities] fateful problems (*Schicksalsprobleme*) whether this balance between a particular form of culture can be reached or if the conflict is irreconcilable (*ob dieser Ausgleich durch eine bestimmte Gestltung der Kultur erreichbar oder ob der Konflikt unversöhnlich ist*).

By allowing common feeling (*gemeinen Empfinden*) to be our guide in deciding what features of human life are civilized, we have obtained a clear impression of the general picture of culture (*deutlichen Eindruck vom Gesamtbild er Kultur bekommen*); but so far we have discovered nothing that is not universally known (*was nicht allgemein bekannt ist*). At the same time, we have been on guard not to concur (*beizustimmen*) with the prejudice (*Vorurteil*) that civilization is the same as perfecting, that it is the ordained way to perfection for human beings (*sei der Weg zur Vollkommenheit, die dem Menschen vorgezeichnet ist*).[261] But now a point of view impresses itself which may lead in another direction. The development of culture appears to us as a peculiar process (*eigenartiger Prozeß*) which humankind undergoes and in which many things appear strange (*anmutet*).[262] We may characterize this process through the

---

[261] Bk. 3, 389-390. SF's inquiry on a possible balance between the claims of the individual and cultural claims and his avoidance of equating civilization with *Vollkommenheit* are Wisdom type motifs, quite different from reductive psychoanalytic dogma, a few of which are in *DUK*. Moreover, the German '*Vollkommenheit*' and the English rendering as 'perfection' do not translate into the luminous type of 'emptiness' (*Shūnyatā*) in Mahāyāna thought as elaborated by Nāgājuna, the 'second Buddha' who taught "emptiness is not different from form, form is not different from emptiness." See David B. Griffiths, *Buddhist Discursive Formations: Keywords, Emotions, Ethics* (2004).

[262] The assumption that underlies this theory of development is sometimes stated as a biogenetic law: "Ontogeny recapitulates phylogeny" (from Ernst Haeckel, 1834-1919). The stages of individual development parallel those of the species. This assumption has poetic force and might have some connection to current theories of language learning and development stages, but if so, without the overly specific mechanisms and stages posited by Freud. His postulate of a phylogenetic instinct, a counter to a *tabula rasa* environmental empiricism, lacked a sound factual basis. He accepted the Lamarckian assumption that acquired characteristics are passed on by way of hereditary transmission; but, at least, he did not appropriate them into an optimistic 'best of all possible worlds' vision. He believed the decisive step in cultural development was the replacement of the power of the individual by the power of the community (Bk. 3, 389-90), but this did not negate the

ud

changes it brings about in the familiar drive-dispositions (*Triebanlagen*) of human beings, the satisfaction of which is, after all, the economic tasks of our lives (*ökonomische Aufgabe unseres Lebens ist*). [263] A few of these drives are used up (*aufgezehrt*) in such a way that something else takes their place, and in an individual this is what we describe as a character trait (*Charaktereigenschaft*). We have found the most remarkable example of this process in the anal eroticism of young human beings. Their original interest in the excretory function, its organs and products (*Organen und Produkten*) is changed in the course of their growth into a group of traits known to us as thriftiness (*Sparsamkeit*), a sense of order and cleanliness (*Ordnung und Reinlichkeit*) [264] and these, though in themselves valuable and welcome (*wertvoll und willkommen*), [265] may be raised into a striking predominance (*auffälliger Vorherrschaft steigern*) and produce (*ergeben*) what one calls the anal character. How this happens we do not know, but there is no doubt about the correctness of the view (*dieser Auffassung kein Zweifel ist*). [266] Now, we have found that order and cleanliness are important demands of civilization (*Kulturansprüche*), although their necessity for life (*Lebensnotwendigkeit*) is not always exactly apparent, any more than their suitability as sources of pleasure. At this point we must above all be struck (*zuerst aufdrangen*) by the similiarity of cultural

---

somber pessimism found in *DUK*.

[263] 'Drive-dispositions' is our coinage for '*Triebanlage*'. Satisfaction of drives, even though Freud acknowledges the so-called higher ones (*Idealbildung*), is two narrow a concept and task to provide a normative theory of the Good within Western ethics. It is even more difficult for Buddhist and Jaina ethics because their goal is the extinction of desire in *nirvāna* and realizing the trans-ethical condition of liberation or *mokṣa*. More specifically, the Good in Sōtō Zen is seeing "one's original face" and the "dropping [away] of body and mind", so Dōgen (1200-1255). b) As stated before, and with awareness of the etymological fallacy, the term 'economic' is from a Greek word relating to household management and stewardship. Hence, it differs from modern English and German usage. Freud uses '*ökonomische*' to specify the tendency to preserve mental energy within the tasks of our lives, and to satisfy the drive-dispositions.

[264] A favorite lexical parallel. That 'drives' can be 'used up' reflects a problematic reductive mechanistic dimension. Another question is on how drives can change, for instance, how anal eroticism can be transmuted into consciousness of order and cleanliness? On this, see Freud's footnote at the beginning of Bk. 4, and our fn. 266.

[265] Rare adjectival parallelism.

[266] Bk. 3, 391. Freud's footnote: "S. "*Charakter und Analerotik*" (1908b) and numerous other contributions by E. Jones (1918) u.a. (et al.)." '*Auffassung*' is a keyword with the basic meanings of "comprehension, apprehension, interpretation; conception, view." *Cassell's German-English Dictionary*, p. 36. JS (p. 83) has 'finding' for '*Auffassung*.'

ud

process with individual libido development. Other drives are induced (*veranlasst*) in order to shift (*zu verschieben*) the conditions for their satisfaction so as to move them into other paths, in most cases this coincides with the well-known *sublimation* (*Sublimierung*) of drive aims (*der Triebziele*) but can be differentiated in other cases.[267] Sublimation of drive is an especially conspicuous trait of cultural development: it makes it possible for higher psychic activities, scientific, artistic, and ideological,[268] to play an important role in cultural life. If one yields to the first impression, one is tempted to say that sublimation may generally be the fate awaiting our human drives, as forced upon us by culture (*Wenn man der ersten Eindruck nachgibt, ist man versucht zu sagen, die Sublimierung sei überhapt ein von der Kultur erzwungenes Triebschicksal*).[269] But it would be better to reflect upon this longer.[270] Finally, in the third place, and this

---

[267] **Idem. "*der Triebziele*" is in brackets. a) Sublimation was a theme in Freud long before *DUK*. Perhaps the first major exploration was in "*Die kulturelle Sexualmoral und die moderne Nervosität,*" (1908d) in *G.W.*, 7 (translated as "*Civilized Sexual Morality and Modern Nervous Illness,*" *S.E.*, 9, pp. 179-204). The third cultural stage was characterized by sublimation. Only a small number of people were capable of it. Sublimation was defined "as the capacity to exchange the originally sexual aim for another one, which is no longer sexual but which is psychically related to the first aim"; as cited by Westerink, p. 76, fn. 74. b) JS breaks this sentence up into two sentences; has 'displace' rather than 'shift', 'lead' instead of 'move', and 'instinctual aims' for '*Triebziele*'. In Bk. 3, 391, '*Sublimiergung*' is in italics and is followed by '*der Triebziele*' enclosed in brackets.**

[268] **Idem. Note the triad: "*wissenschaftliche, künstlerische, ideologische*", the latter is from the Greek *logia*, 'idea', plus *logie*, 'speaking'. The term, in indicating an idea or position one opposes, often carries more feeling than precision. In Freud's perspective, an ethics based upon 'religion' is an ideology. Freud's '*ideologische*' in the sentence above follows '*wissenschaftliche*' ('scientific') and '*künsterische*' ('artistic'), and read along with the phrase "*intellektuellen, wissenschaftlichen und künstlerischen Leistungen*" (Bk. 3, 389) refers to higher (*höheren*) philosophical-intellectual activities (*Tätigkeiten*). JS (p. 84) inserts an 'or' between 'artistic' and 'ideological', thus ruining the sentence.**

[269] **It was unclear to me how '*Triebschicksal*' works in this sentence. Freud coined this term in 1917 and it is part of the German lexicon. I thank N. W. Warren and M. Edlich for discussion of this sentence. If '*sei*' is taken as a subjunctive, 'may be' is better than the imperative 'is.' JS (p. 84) has 'vicissitude which has been forced upon the instincts entirely by civilization.'**

[270] **Idem. This modesty toward thinking as process reflects his deep interactional experiences and many years of reflection, e.g. in Bk. 8, 419 he comments that a proposition (*Satz*) may be worthy of our interest ("*verdient er unser Interesse*") even if it is only an average approximation. b) Initially psychoanalysis was largely scorned, it soon became dogmatic and hence schismatic, and later was so famous that it was absorbed into the vocabularies of ordinary people. The movement had some recognition by 1922, but for many years, Freud was on the defensive. He believed that psychoanalysis was a 'science' and that the early dissenters (Adler, Jung, Stekel) had seized upon only one fragment within its spectrum of thought. However, late in his life he acknowledged that some of the**

ud

appears the most important, it is impossible to overlook the degree to which culture is built upon the renunciation of drive (*auf Triebverzicht aufgebaut ist*), nor how much it exactly presupposes the non-satisfaction, suppression, repression, or something else? of powerful drives (*Unterdrückung, Verdrängung oder sonst etwas? von mächtigen Trieben zur Voraussetzung hat*). [271] This frustration by culture ("*Kulturversagung*") dominates the large field of social relations between human beings; as we already know, it is the cause of the hostility to culture (*Ursache der Feindseligkeit*) against which all cultures have to struggle (*zu kämpfen haben*).[272] It will also place severe demands on our scientific work, and here we have much to explain (*viel Aufklärung zu geben*). It is not easy to understand how it is possible to take away the satisfaction of a drive (*Triebe die Befriedigung zu entziehen*). Doing so is not without danger; if one is not economically compensated [for the loss], serious disorders will result (*ernste Störungen gefaßt*

---

psychoanalytical concepts might be provisional. In an essay never finished and published two years after his death on September 23, 1939) he said that it was hard to say whether the basic claims of psychoanalysis "should be regarded as postulates or as products of our researches" (John Hunter Pader in *The Oxford Companion to The Mind* (p. 270). But there is evidence that Freud was unrelenting and often unforgiving about deviation from his views. In some cases he appeared to value friendship less than agreement with his views and he ignored Nietzsche's saying that "convictions are greater enemies of truth than lies." However, the Frued of *DUK* is generous of mind toward intellectual critics, e.g. Rolland, Jung, Klein.

[271] Bk. 3, 391. The text has "*Drittens endlich*", and the phrase 'suppression, repression or something else?' is in parenthetical marks. JS (p. 84) has an explanatory footnote: ["Freud had already mentioned two other factors playing a part in the 'process' of civilization: character-formation and sublimation."]. In the German text (*Unterdrückung, Verdrängung oder sonst etwas?*) are enclosed in parentheses.

[272] Bk. 3, 391. a) '*Kulturversagung*' is a basic concept in the treatise. The word has double quotation marks in the text. b) On "*zu kämpfen haben*": *Kampf, m.* "combat, fight, contest, engagement, battle, conflict, action, struggle, strife..." (*The New Cassell's German Dictionary*, p. 253). *Kampf* is a key word in this treatise. It was used the most in Bk. 6. Conflict characterizes human beings. Renunciation is necessary for the sexual drives. Their frustration creates resentment and hostility toward culture, but culture via sublimation is also the vehicle for the expression of desire. The renunciation of aggression is even more important than that of the sexual drives. c) Freud believed in cultural development but *Kultur* was two-faced: both a necessary means and an impediment to human development. In 1929-31 he was pessimistic about the protections of civilization or bourgeois culture from the destructive drives, and he was critical of utopian images of progress. This probably began with his disillusionment during the First World War and shortly after the period of *Totem and Taboo* (1912-13). In a letter to the Zurich based Pastor Oskar Pfister (1873-1956), founder of pastoral psychology, he said he found little that is 'good' about human beings in general. [The long correspondence, Pfister's letters have not survived, is very rich in insight on Freud as a person and his ideas].

ud

machen).

But if we want to know what value we can attach to our view of the development of civilization (*Kulturentwicklung*) as a special process comparable to the normal maturation of the individual;[273] we clearly must attack another problem, and ask ourselves to what influences the development of civilization owes its origin, and through what has its course been determined (*welchen Einflüssen die Kulturentwicklung ihren Ursprung dankt, wie sie entstanden ist und wodurch ihr Lauf bestimmt wurde*).[274]

IV

This task appears immense (*übergroß*), and toward it one can confess diffidence. Here is the little that I can guess (*erraten konnte*). After primal man had discovered that it—literally—lay in his own hands to improve his lot (*Los*) on earth through work, it could not be a matter of indifference to him (*ihm*) if another person worked with him or against him. The other acquired the value for him of co-worker (*Mitglieder*) with whom living together was useful. Even earlier in his ape-like prehistory (*Vorzeit*) man had formed the habit (*Gewohnheit*) of building families, and family members were probably his first helpers. Probably the founding of families had something to do with the fact that the need for genital satisfaction (*genitaler Befriedigung*) ceased to be like a guest who suddenly drops in and after his departure is heard of no more for a long time, but instead settled himself in as a long-lasting lodger. With that came a motive for the man to keep the woman, or speaking more generally, his sexual objects, near him; while the female (*Weibchen*), who did not want to be separated from her helpless young, must therefore in their interests remain with the stronger male (*stärkeren Männchen*).[275] In this primitive family (*dieser*

---

[273] The contrast here requires 'civilization' rather than 'culture.'

[274] This is not a strong version of historical determinism. Freud was aware of the role of human agency. [We now know that DNA is too complex to support a claim of determinism.] JS (p. 85) divides this sentence into three, and adds a footnote: ["Freud returns to the subject of civilization as a 'process' below, on p. 119 and again on p. 137. He mentions it once more in his open letter to Einstein, *Why War?* (1933b)".]

[275] Bk. 4, 392. a) The very long footnote by Freud is presented in JS's translation with a few changes and an effort to retain Freud's sentence structures. b) Many scholars have doubted Freud's main points, but one should note that Freud claimed he was presenting "only a theoretical speculation" and that his insights were formulated to suggest further research. "The organic periodicity of the sexual process has persisted, it is true, but its effect on psychic sexual excitation has rather been reversed. This change seems most likely

ud

primitiven Familie) one essential feature of culture (*einen wesentlichen Zug*

---

to be connected with the diminution of the olfactory stimuli by means of which the menstrual process produced an effect on the male psyche. Their role was taken over by visual excitations, which, in contrast to the intermittent olfactory stimuli, were able to maintain a permanent effect. The taboo on menstruation is derived from this 'organic repression', as a defence against a phase of development that has been surmounted. All other motives are probably of a secondary nature. (Cf. C. D. Daly, "Hindumythologie und Kastrationskomplex, *Imago*, XIII, 1927). This process is repeated on another level when the gods of a superseded period of culture turn into demons. The diminution of the olfactory stimuli seems itself to be a consequence of man's raising himself from the ground, of his assumption of an upright gait; this made his genitals, which were previously concealed, visible and in need of protection, and so provoked feelings of shame (*Schämen hervorruft*). The fateful process of civilization would thus have begun with the adoption of an erect posture. From that point the chain of events would have proceeded through the devaluation of olfactory stimuli, and the isolation of the menstrual period to the time when visual stimuli were paramount and the genitals became visible; and thence to the continuity of sexual excitation, the founding of the family and and thus to the threshold of human civilization. This is only a theoretical speculation, but it is important enough to deserve careful checking with reference to the conditions of life that obtain among animals closely related to man. A social factor is also clearly present in the cultural trend toward cleanliness, which has received justification after the fact [JS substitutes *ex post facto* here] in hygienic considerations, but these had manifested before their discovery. The incitement to cleanliness originates in an urge (*Drang*) to get rid of the excreta, which have become disagreeable to sense perceptions. We know that in the nursery (*Kinderstube*) things are different. The excreta arouse no disgust in the children; they appear valuable to them, a part of their own body, which has come from it. Here upbringing insists with special energy on hastening the developmental process which lies ahead, and which should make the excreta worthless, disgusting and abominable (*wertlos, ekelhaft, abscheulich und verwerflich machen soll*). Such a reversal of values (*Umwertung*) would hardly be possible if the expelled substances were not doomed by their strong smells to share the fate that overtook olfactory stimuli after man adopted the erect posture. Anal eroticism, therefore, succumbs in the first instance to 'organic repression', which paved the way to culture. The existence of the social factor which is responsible for the further transformation (*Umwandlung*) of anal eroticism is attested by the circumstance that, in spite of all developmental advances, man scarcely finds the smell of his own [JS puts 'his own' in italics] repulsive, but only that of others. The unclean, that is, the one who does not hide his excreta, is offending others, he is showing no consideration (*Rücksicht*) for them, and this is confirmed by our strongest and commonest terms of insult (*Beschimpfungen*). It would be incomprehensible (*unverständlich*) that human beings should use the name of their most faithful friend in the animal world as a term of abuse if the dog had not incurred their contempt through two characteristics: that he has no horror of excrement and that he is not ashamed of sexual functions." c) As a footnote to this footnote: the ancient Greek Cynics (literally, 'doggish ones' and/or 'those who live a dog's life') were reportedly not ashamed of excrement or sexual functions in public. d) The theme of 'erect' posture may have come to Freud through the writings in the 1890's of Edward Fuchs. According to Walter Benjamin, Fuchs linked "the threshold between human and animal…to that other threshold, of erect posture…" Walter Benjamin, *One-Way Street and Other Writings*, with an Introduction by Susan Sontag (Verso, 1979, the quote is from *Gesammelte Schriften*, Bd I-IV (Frankfurt 1974-1976).

ud

der Kultur) is still missing; the arbitrary will of its head, the father, was unrestricted. In *Totem and Taboo* [1912-13], I have tried to show how the way led from this family to the next stage of life together, in the form of the band of brothers (*Form der Brüderbünde führte*). In overpowering the father, the sons had discovered that a combination can be stronger than a single individual. The totemic culture is based on the restrictions the sons had to impose on one another in order to support this new state of affairs (*Aufrechthaltung des neuen Zustandes einander auferlegen mußten*). The taboo observances were the first "right" ("*Recht*").[276] Therefore the communal life of human beings had a two-fold foundation: the compulsion (*Zwang*)[277] to work, created by external need; and the power of love (*die Macht der Liebe*), which made the man unwilling to be deprived of his sexual object, the woman, and the woman unwilling to be deprived of that part of her that had become separated, her child. Eros and *Ananke* also became the parents of human culture.[278] The first result of culture was that

---

[276] Bk. 4, 393. JS (p. 88) adds 'or 'law' with a footnote saying that the German word means both 'right' and 'law.' *Totem and Taboo* (1913), ch. 1. Taboo as the first 'right' is distinct from religious and moral prohibitions. The taboo structures are based on fear of 'demonic' powers, a fear or anxiety that later develops into veneration or horror. Freud's analogy between neurosis and 'primitive man' ("*Menschen der Vorzeit*") is useful in understanding transgression, rooted within the taboo structure, and psychical fixations and ambivalence, e.g. the delight in the fall of the high and mighty. But the analogy is too weak to support the generalizations. The same holds for the contentions in the fourth essay on the 'primal horde' theory (from Darwin) and the slaying of the father by the band of brothers and the emergence of social organization from that event. The generalizations are too sweeping, the conclusions too confident. However, this does not mean that the application of psychoanalysis to social psychology has no intellectual value, e.g. the insight on the killing of the primal father has symbolical truth in relation to the struggle of the young against the authority of the father, father figures, as well as the boredom of modern adolescence.

[277] Bk. 4, 393. '*Zwang*,' ('compulsion') is an important word in *DUK*, and in the 1915 essay '*Zeitgemässes über Krieg und Tod*' (1915[b], *G. W.*, 10, 324. In this treatise, 'Thoughts for the Times on War and Death,' *S.E.*, 14, 275), he stated that during the life of an individual there is a constant replacement of external compulsion by internal compulsion. The significan of this rather commonplace thought relates to the necessity for renunciation of desire by culture and for culture. (This treatise was written at the time of the First World War. Freud was initially supportive and two sons were in the Austrian military, but he became extremely troubled when the early reports of victory turned into accounts of slaughter and mindless nationalism).

[278] The sudden jump from ethnology to Greek *mythos* is jarring. According to Hesiod, the Greek god of love ("Desire") was born out of chaos at the beginning of creation. "Desire"

ud

a larger number of people were now able to live together in community (*Gemeinschaft bleiben konnten*). And since these two great powers were at that time working together (*zusammenwirken*), one could expect that further development would smoothly take place, toward an even better domination of the external world and further extension of the number of people included in the community. It was not easy to understand how culture could act upon the participants without making them happy (*beglückend wirken kann*).

Before we go on to inquire about where a disturbance (*Störung*) might arise, this recognition of love as one foundation of culture (*einer Grundlage der Kultur*) may justify a digression that can close a gap (*Lücke*) left in an earlier discussion.[279] We said there that man's discovery that sexual (genital) love (*geschlechtliche (genitale) Liebe*) gave the strongest experiences of satisfaction, provided the prototype for all happiness, and must have suggested that he should continue to seek the realization of happiness in the domain of sexual relations,[280] and that he should place genital eroticism at the central point of his life (*auf dem Gebiet der geschlechtlichen Beziehungen zu suchen, die genitale Erotik in den Mittelpunkt des Lebens zu stellen*).[281] We continued by saying that in doing so he made himself dependent in a dangerous way on a portion of the external world, namely his chosen love-object, and exposed himself to extreme suffering if rejected by that object or lost it through betrayal or death. For that reason the wise ones of every age (*Die Weisen aller Zeiten*) have warned emphatically against this way of life, but in spite of that it has not lost its attraction for a great number of people.[282]

---

was also and more commonly held to be the son of Aphrodite and Ares. *Ananke* = 'necessity' < the Greek god *Ananke*, mother of Adrasteia who gave out reward and punishment. There is unclarity in *DUK* on this pair and their relationship to Eros. There is also unclarity on the death-drive and Eros as eternal adversaries (see end of Bk. 8). Freud's likely source for the Eros and *Ananke* binary was a Dutch novelist named Multatuli (Eduard Douwes Dekker) whom Freud read in translation and admired. Freud cites Multatuli on *Logos* and *Ananke* in a footnote in *Die Zukunft einer Illusion* X, p. 365. See H. Westerink, *A Dark Trace*, p. 244, footnote 75.

[279] The German text has no page reference to this *Lücke* ('gap'). JS (p. 83) refers to p. 63 which corresponds to p. 381 of Bk 2, *DUK*. The term *Lücke* is not used on that page, instead we find '*Unvollständigkeit*', 'incomleteness'.

[280] Bk. 4, 393. JS (p. 89) has 'along the path of sexual relations.'

[281] Idem. The generalization on genital eroticism 'at the central point of life' begs defense and needs individual and cultural examples.

[282] Idem. Use of "*die Weisen aller Zeiten*" needs specific examples. Epicurus (c. 341-270

ud

A small minority are enabled by their constitution to find happiness through the way of love, but before that, far-reaching mental changes in life-function are essential (*unerläßlich sind*). These people make themselves independent of the approval of their object (*Zustimmung des Objekts unabhängig*) by displacing what they mainly value from being loved (*Geliebwerden*) onto what they love;[283] they protect themselves against this loss (*Verlust*) of the object by directing their love not to single objects but in equal measure to all humans, and they avoid the variations and disappointments (*Schwankungen und Enttäuschungen*) of genital love by turning away from its sexual goal, and transforming the drive into a *goal-inhibited* emotion (*ablenken, den Triebe in eine zielgehemmte Regung verwandeln*).[284] What they bring about in themselves in this way is an evenly suspended, imperturbable, tender feeling (*gleichschwebenden, unbeirrbaren, zärtlichen Empindungs*) which has little external resemblance to the stormy movements of genital love, from which it nevertheless derives.[285] Saint Francis of Assisi went further perhaps in the

---

BCE) would be one: his 'hedonism' stressed moderation and his community accepted women and slaves. Diogenes of Sinope (the Cynic, died 320 BCE) is a possible counter-example. The culturally diverse Tantra traditions that celebrate sexuality as an instrument of enlightenment completely elude Freud's category.

[283] Bk. 4, 394. I take this to mean self-love rooted in the "I" ideal of the early childhood sense of having all power (omnipotence of thought). According to Christopher Lash, there is some affinity between Freud's self-love as leading to universal love and the insights of Jonathan Edwards (1703-58), the great Calvinist theologian and 'new birth' Puritan preacher. The text cited is Edwards' *The Nature of True Virtue* (posthumous). Christopher Lash, *The True and Only Heaven: Progress and Its Critics* (Norton, 1991), pp. 251 ff., and footnote (p. 252): Freud's "analysis of the ego ideal...can be read as a twentieth-century restatement of this [Edwards'] argument." But Freud regarded universal love as an extreme that devalued love, and he thought love was in tension with hate and not everyone was worthy of love ("*es sind nicht alle Menschen liebenswert*", Bk. 4, 394). Moreover, Freud had disdain for Puritan theology and praxis. However, he and Edwards were both intense reader of 'signs' and Freud in 1909 found a more appreciative audience in New England educated circles than he had in Vienna, the exceptions being his own inner circle, the Wednesday night meetings at his house, the Vienna Psychoanalytical Society, and the B'nai Brith lodge.

[284] Idem. Note the synonymous parallelism of "*Schwankungen und Enttäuschungen*". JS (p. 90) has 'uncertainties and disappointments'. In the text, "*zielgehemmte*" is in italics.

[285] Idem. a) This aetiological extension of 'genital love' as a non-dialectical causal structure is an engaging myth but is not credible if taken literally. The same holds for Freud's interpretation of the Oedipus myth as a developmental model and the basis of individual and cultural development. The analogy between them is shaky, and Freud's reading of the Greek text is defective in the partial erasure of women and silence on the infanticidal desire of the father. The conceptual presuppositions of the Oedipus complex

ud

utilization (*Ausnützung*) of love for the benefit of an inner feeling of happiness; what we recognize as one of the techniques (*Techniken*) for fulfilling the pleasure principle has in many cases been brought into connection with religion, connected with it in some distant regions where the distinction of the 'I' (*Ich*) from the object or between objects themselves is neglected (*vernachlässigt wird*).[286] In one ethical perspective (*ethische Betrachtung*), whose deeper motivation will become clear soon, this readiness for a universal love of humankind and the world represents the highest attitude (*Einstellung*)[287] which humanity can reach. Even this early we do not want to hold back our two main objections.[288] A love that does not discriminate (*die nicht auswählt*) seems to us to lose part of its value, in that it is unfair to its object. And further, not all humans are worthy of love (*es sind nicht alle Menschen liebenwert*). [289]

---

are a developmental view of sexuality, infantile sexuality, incest. The concept has specific uses on a hypothetical level but is far from a universal causal structure. b) There is also the problem of internal textual contradictions. Freud's inclusive claim for sexuality was modified by asserting that the 'I' is the original home of the libido. This, however, conflicts with the primal duality of Eros and *Ananke* as the mythical parents of *Kultur*. The brief narrative (end of Bk. 8) of Eros and *Ananke* has at least the advantage of dialectical motion. I suspect that Eros is a trope of how the 'I' connects with others and that *Ananke*, the mother of Adresteia, who distributed rewards and punishments, is a figurative expression of necessity (*ananke*). It is, however, unclear to me how this fits with 'genital love.' c) Freud's inclusion of the sexual instincts within libido reminds one of the dominance of Catholic discourses on sin and sex. A friend of James Joyce recommended psychoanalysis to him; but Joyce, who was ambivalent about Freud, replied: "Well, if we need it, let us keep to confession." Quoted by Richard Ellmann in *James Joyce* (1959, Galaxy Book, 1965), p. 486.

[286] Bk. 4, 394. a) '*Ausnützung*' can also be translated as 'exploitation' (so JS) but this makes Freud's comment on St. Francis (1181/2-1226) heavy-handed and insensitive. We had 'use', but N. W. Warren suggested 'utilization.' b) According to tradition, the love practiced by St. Francis included God, humans and non-humans, and it reflected humility, empathy, detachment from possessions. c) The vague clause on 'distant regions' wherein techniques for fulfilling the pleasure principle link up with 'religion' must refer to stages of infancy.

[287] Idem. '*Einstellung*,' n. *einstellen* 'to take a position… to have an attitude toward + nom. suffix - *ung*.'

[288] Bk. 4, 394. "*Wir möchten schon hier unsere zwei hauptsächlichen Bedenken nicht zurückhalten.*" JS (p. 91) has: "Even at this early stage of the discussion I should like to bring forward my two main objections to this view."

[289] Idem. a) It was known long before Freud that the varieties of love are correlated with varieties of person and situation, but this variety hardly justifies a quantitative view of love. Moreover, Freud did not formulate a general principle of justifiabilty for deciding who is and who is not worthy of love. He put love under the verdict of justice; but the same question of justifiability applies in that case, e.g. in classical rabbinical teaching, if justice conflicts with mercy, mercy should prevail. In our opinion, love and justice are

ud

That love which formed the family continues to operate in culture in its original form (*ursprünglichen Ausprägung*), in which it does not give up direct sexual satisfaction, and [it operates] in its modified form as goal-inhibited tenderness (*sowie in ihrer Modifikation als zielgehemmte Zärtlichkeit in der Kultur weiter wirksam*). In both forms it carries on its function of binding a large number of human beings together, and it does so in a more intensive way than can be done through the interests of work in common (*Interesse der Arbeitsgemeinschaft*). The careless way in which language uses (*Nächlassigkeit der Sprache in der Anwendung*) the word 'love' has its developmental justification (*genetische Rechtfertigung*). People call love the connection between a man and a woman who have founded a family on the basis of their genital needs, but also the positive feeling beween parents and children,[290] between bothers and sisters in the family, although we must describe this as goal-inhibited love or tenderness.[291] Goal inhibited love was originally fully sensual love (*vollsinnliche Liebe*) and it remains so in the human unconscious (*Unbewußten des Menschen*).[292] Both sensual and goal-inhibited love

---

co-dependent and interconnected. b) JS (p. 91) divides the sentence and uses the personal pronoun 'me'.

[290] a) On the point about "*genetische Rechtfertigung*", we should note that how the *Es* (It) influences the 'I' fails to distinguish 'cause of' from 'reason for.' b) On another dimension, it is important to recognize how Freud's work resulted in a profound change in the relationship between parents and children. This change was notable in Anna Freud's application of psychoanalysis to children, and in her Hampstead Clinic for children that she and Dorothy Tiffany Burlingham managed. c) Freud's views on developmental stages and infantile sexuality became widely accepted, but most of the crude mechanisms in the original model were gradually eliminated by 'neo-Freudians' of later generations. This revision is similar to the deconstruction of the Marxist-Leninist model by independent thinking European Marxists, e.g. Rosa Luxemburg, and later the so-called Frankfurt School (Horkheimer, Adorno, H. Marcuse, E. Fromm).

[291] Bk. 4, 394. JS (p. 91) puts 'we' in italics, and encloses his rendering of "*zielgehemmte Liebe*" and "*Zartlichkeit*" in single quotes. Freud points out the careless way in which the term 'love' is used in relation to developmental complexity. However, this is not done in the interest of a descriptive exegesis of differences and similarities, but to justify a genetic, causal, developmental explanation. Jung's essay translated as 'The Love Problem of a Student' (in *Civilization in Transition*, Vol. 10 of *The Collected Works*) is a relevant comparison. Jung asserts that how the word 'love' is used is an obstacle to a discussion of it. He mentions the many uses of the term in Christian texts, the *amor Dei* of Origen, the *amor intellectualis* of Spinoza, and he cites Goethe, and so forth.

[292] Idem. a) There is no substantial use of the concept of the Unconscious, a central category for Freud, in *DUK*. It is, however, presupposed. "*Was am Vater begonnen wurde, vollendet sich an der Masse*"; 'What began with the father is completed in the masses', (Bk. 7, 415) presupposes unconscious patterns that erupt in threshold or liminal situations. b)

ud

(*vollsinnliche und zielgehemmte Liebe*) extends outside the family and create new bonds with those who were strangers. Genital love leads to (*führt zu*) the formation of new families, goal-inhibited love to 'friendships' which become culturally valuable because they escape some of the restrictions of genital love, for example its exclusiveness.[293] But in the course of its development the relation of love to culture loses its unambiguity (*Eindeutigkeit*). On the one hand, love opposes the interests of culture; on the other hand, culture threatens love with painful restrictions (*empfindlichen Einschränkungen*). [294]

This rift appears inevitable (*unvermeidlich*); the reason for it is not immediately recognizable.[295] At first it expresses itself as a conflict between the family and the larger community to which the individual belongs. We have already surmised (*erraten*) that one of the principal endeavors (*Hauptbestrebungen*) of culture is to bring people together into larger unities (*großen Einheiten*). But the family will not free the individual. The closer the attachment of family members, the more often they tend to separate themselves from others, and the more difficult it is for them to enter larger life circles (*größeren Lebenskreis*). The phylogenetical mode of life in common, which is older, and only exists in childhood, resists being superseded (*abgelöst*) by the cultural mode [of life] acquired later (*später erworbenen*). Detachment from the family becomes a task for every young person, and society often helps through puberty and assimilation rites (*Pubertäts- und Aufnahmsriten*). [296] We get the impression that these are

---

The exploratory spirit of analysis of the unconscious in *DUK* differs from Schopenhauer's metaphysics of the unconscious Will but this alone does not make the concept compatible with a psychological naturalism; or, even less, a Jungian essentialistic 'collective' Unconscious of *ewige* (everlasting) archetypes. The logical challenge with the 'unconscious' is not to confuse psychological fact, e.g. desire, with object-based normative reason.

[293] Bk. 4, 394. a) Note the antithetical parallelism of "*vollsinnliche und zielgehemmte*". b) "*führt zu*" ('leads to') does not illuminate the distinction between cause of Y and reason for Y. c) This comment on 'exclusiveness' (*Ausschliesslichkeit*) conflicts with the claim made three pages later on an original bisexual disposition ("*bisexueller Anlage*").

[294] Bk. 4, 395. That 'culture threatens love with painful restrictions' is relative to time and culture, and inapplicable to sexualized postmodern cultures. b) JS (p. 92) has 'substantial' for '*empfinden*' but that term relates to feeling not quantity.

[295] Idem. JS (idem) turns this sentence into two.

[296] Bk. 4, 395. Note the complementary parallelism of *Pubertäts- und Aufnahmsriten*. Initially we had 'assimiliation rites' but 'initiation rites' is better. '*Aufnahme*' has the meaning of assimiliation, but 'initiation' is a better term in this context because in current English usage 'assimilation' relates more to foreigners and outsiders becoming part of

ud

difficulties fastened to all psychic [development]; and indeed, also at the basis of all organic development (*ja im Grunde auch jeder organischen Entwicklung anhängen*). [297]

Furthermore, women soon step into opposition to cultural trends (*Gegensatz zur Kulturströmmung*) and display their delaying and conservative influence (*entfalten ihren verzögernden und zurückhaltenden Einfluß*); [298] the same (*dieselben* [women]) who in the beginning through the claims of their love had laid the foundations of culture. Women represent the interests of the family and of sexual life; the work of culture has increasingly become more the affair of men (*Sache der Männer geworden*): it places more difficult tasks upon them, compels them to desire sublimations that women are no match for (*wenig gewachsen sind*). Since a man does not have unlimited quantities of psychic energy available, he must accomplish his tasks by making an expedient distribution of his libido (*zweckmäßige Verteilung der Libido erledigen*). What he expends (*verbrauch*) for cultural goals he withdraws in great part from women and sexual life: his constant being together with men, his dependence on his relationship to them, alienates him even further from his duties as a husband and father. Hence the woman finds herself forced into the background of culture and adopts a hostile attitude towards it (*Hintergrund gedrängt und tritt zu ihr in ein feindliches Verhältnis*). [299]

---

society. On this point, we thank N. W. Warren and M. Edlich.

[297] Idem. JS (p. 92) has 'inherent in' for '*anhängen*' ('hang on,' 'fasten to').

[298] Idem. Synonymous parallelism.

[299] Bk. 4, 395. These sentences, especially the one on women as a 'delaying' and 'conservative influence' on cultural trends, and as 'no match' for men in respect to certain sublimations, are biased in the sense of unfair. However, SF generally used descriptive not normative language (cf. Adorno's view of 'totality' (*Totalität*) as an essential concept but not something he endorses). Women laid the foundations of culture and were 'forced' into the background by male bonding and the division of labor. Moreover, men took a 'great part' of their energy from 'women and sexual life.' Recent evolutionary anthropological studies by Sarah Blaffer Hrdy, Adrienne Zihlman, Frances Dahlber and others have radically revised this view, but obviously Freud was not aware of this evidence. Freud's intellectual relationship to women was complex. He was not an advocate for feminist causes, but many women were attracted to psychoanalysis and became skilled in analysis and/or promotion of the psychonanalytic movement, e.g. Melanie Klein, Joan Riviere, Alix Strachey, and Anna Freud. The gender balance changed in 1912 with the participation of the gifted Lou Andreas-Salomé (a lover of Rilke and friends with Nietzsche, who sought in vain through an intermediary to marry her). [See Freud's letters to "*Liebe* Lou" (April 3, 1931, May 1931, May 16, 1935) in Appendix, Volume 3, *Life and Work* by E. Jones, pp. 452-3, and 461; and see her opening letter of 2 Sept. 1912 to Freud and his reply of 1 Oct.

ud

The tendency on the part of culture to restrict sexual life is no less evident (*nicht minder deutlich*) than the other tendency to expand the cultural circle (*Kulturkreises*). Already the first culture phase, the totemic, brings with it the prohibition of incest object-choice, perhaps the most drastic mutilation which human erotic life has experienced in the course of time. Through taboo, law and custom (*Gesetz und Sitte*) [300] further restrictions are imposed that relate to both men and women.[301] Not all cultures go equally far in this; the economic structure of society also influences the amount of sexual freedom that remains. We already know that culture follows the laws of economic necessity (*ökonomischen Notwendigkeit*) as a great amount of psychic energy that it uses for itself must be withdrawn from sexuality.[302] In this, culture behaves toward sexuality like a tribe (*Volksstamm*), or another stratum (*Schichte*) of its population does, which has subjected another one to its exploitation

---

1912 (*Sigmund Freud and Lou Andreas-Salomé Letters,* p.7)] And the balance changed later with Anna Freud's professional maturity, the presence and roles of Marie Bonaparte, who helped rescue Freud from Austria in 1938, the translations by Joan Riviere, Helene Deutsch's works, and the contributions of other creative women in the 'movement.' Freud's simplistic evolutionary model of culture, the penis and vagina binary, and an inclination toward sweeping judgments are all problematic. However, he was not uncritical of his own thinking: for instance in his 1932 lecture on "Femininity" he noted that what he had to say was "incomplete and fragmentary and does not always sound friendly…If you want to know more about femininity, enquire of your own experiences of life, or turn to the poets, or wait until science can give you deeper and more coherent information" Lecture 33, "The Psychology of Women" in *New Introductory Lectures on Psycho-Analysis* ([1932]1933a; English translation in *S.E.,* 22, 5-182).

[300] Idem. Observe the synonymous parallelism. On the word 'taboo', see *Totem und Tabu* (1913) Bk. 2, 4, pp. 77-78, Eng. translation by A. A. Brill (Barnes & Noble, 2005, 1913), pp. 60-61.

[301] Bk. 4, 395. This is one of the few cases where both women and men are explicitly specified.

[302] Idem. We think the distinction between the 'economic laws' of culture/civilization and the 'economics' of the libido needs clarification. The proposition that 'culture follows the laws of economic necessity' may sound vaguely Marxist but there is no real connection to a classical Marxist analysis. However, class exploitation does have a psychological parallel in the use of sexuality by culture to exploit other strata of the population. Marx and Engels are not mentioned in *DUK*, but in Bk. 5, SF asserted that he had no problem with a 'communist' critique of private property. However, he was convinced that the abolition of private property would not end the problem of violence or ensure human progress because of inherent tendencies toward sexual aggression. He also thought the idea of 'progress' in 'communist' discourse was as illusory as that posited by 'religion.' Psychoanalysis, however, psychoanalysis had its own view of progress, i.e. the undoing of neurotic patterns of repression. Late in his life, Freud realized that this progress was not fully effective or comprehensive, and therefore that the initial goals of psychoanalysis had been set too high.

ud

(*Ausbeutung unterworfen hat*). Anxiety about a revolt by the suppressed drives it to stricter precautionary measures.[303] Our western European culture has attained a high point in such a development. It is absolutely justified psychologically that it [a cultural community] start with the restriction of manifestations of the sexual life of children, for the control (*Eindämmung*) of the sexual lusts of adults would be impossible if the ground had not been prepared for it in childhood.[304] Nevertheless, in no way can a cultural community be justified in going so far as to deny (*zu leugnen*) these easily demonstrable (*nachweisbaren*), indeed, remarkable phenomena. [305] The object choice of a sexually mature individual is restricted to the opposite sex and most extra-genital satisfactions are forbidden as perversions (*außergenitalen Befriedungen als Perversionen untersagt*). The prohibitions set forth (*kundgegebenen*) in these requirements that there should be a single form for all kinds of sexual life

---

[303] Bk. 4, 396. a) '*Schichte*' is Austrian dialect: "layer, bed, course, stratum…" b) The clause and the comments that follow 'another stratum (*Schichte*) of its population' are clues to why W. Reich, Herbert Marcuse, and some Surrealists tried to syncretize Freud and Marx. Erich Fromm, using the 'humanist' Marx of the 1844 manuscripts, attempted the same; but without the pre-cultural biological factors that Marcuse considered essential. In *The Search for a Method* (*Question de méthode*, 1957) Sartre's existential psychoanalysis sought to unite aspects of Marx and Freud. The conceptual efforts to connect Marx/Engels with Freud, e.g. works by W. Reich, reflect the need to balance the sexual and bodily dimensions of life with economic forces and the political dimension. This attempt is warranted if both foci are integrated into a total perspective on *Dasein* (thrown human existence) as 'to-be', but I suspect that Freud would have regarded these attempts with ironical detachment. Nevertheless, it is said that he was very interested in the account of Chaim Weizmann on Galician Jews arriving in Palestine in the middle -1890's with only the clothes on their backs and two books: a copy of *Das Kapital* under one arm and *Die Traumdeutung* under the other (E. Jones, *Life and Work*, vol. 3, p. 30).

[304] Note that the argument is on the grounds of consequences rather than a principle of pure or practical reason, as in Kant. This raises the influence question: SF acknowledged Schopenhauer and Nietzsche and Spinoza but not Kant, the dominant intellectual presence in the German speaking lands during Freud's time. It is known (so Andrew Brook) that Freud owned and studied a copy of the *Critique of Pure Reason* and Brook suggests a close affinity between SF's tripartite structure of the psyche and Kant in his first Critique. We lack the knowledge to explore this; but in terms of ethics we think Freud in DUK was anti-Kantian, i.e. morality relates to desire and the tension between Eros and the Death-wish/drive and an 'ethical perspective' was 'unpsychological.' See DUK Bk. 4,394-5; Bk. 8,422. On the other hand, moral law for Kant as expressed in the Categorial Imperative with its affirmation of reciprocal recognition is the fundamental dimension of humanity.

[305] The referent is not clearly identified. It is the restrictions of the sexual life of children, not the reality of the manifestations of that life. JS puts 'disavowing' (his translation of '*zu leugnen*') in italics.

ud

disregards the dissimilarities (*Ungleichheiten*), both inborn and acquired (*angeborenen und erworbenen*)[306] in the sexual constitutions of human beings; it cuts off a fair number of them from sexual enjoyment, and hence becomes a source of severe injustice.[307] The result of these restrictive measures might be that to those who are normal, not prevented by their constitution (*könnte nun sein, daß bei denen, die normal, die nicht konstitutionell daran verhindert sind*), all their sexual interests would flow without loss into the open channels. However, heterosexual love which has remained free of proscription (*Ächtung frei bleibt*) is itself restricted by insistence upon legitimacy and monogamy (*der Legitimität und der Einehe weiter beeinträchtigt*).[308] It is clear that in contemporary culture only sexual relationships on the basis of a unique, irrevocable bond (*einmaligen, unauflösbaren Bindung*) between one man and one woman is allowed, and that sexuality as an independent source of pleasure is not liked and is only tolerated up to now because it is the unreplaced source (*unersetzte Quelle*) for the propagation of humanity.

This is, of course, an extreme. It is known that, even for a short time, it is unfeasible (*undurchführbar*) to put into operation. Only the weak have submitted to such a comprehensive invasion (*weitgehenden Einbruch*) of their sexual freedom, stronger natures have done so only under a compensatory condition,[309] about which we can speak later. Civilized

---

[306] **Antithetical parallelism. I thank N. W. Warren for help with this sentence.**

[307] **Freud's repudiation of injustice in the sexual sphere, relevant to current debates on 'gay rights' and 'gay marriage' challenged the normative status of heterosexuality. Both 'normal' and 'abnormal' sexuality are 'fables', and while fables are neither true nor false they negate a view of homogeneous sexuality. However, his view of the sequential stages of sexuality as presented in *Three Essays on the Theory of Sexuality* (1905d), and elsewhere, conflicts with full acceptance of non-normative sexuality. Freud expressed his own attitude toward homosexuality in a letter to an American mother who was despairing over a homosexual son. He wrote: "it is nothing to be ashamed of, no vice, no degradation, it cannot be classified as an illness; we consider it to be a variation of the sexual function produced by a certain arrest of sexual development…" He went on to call Plato, Michelangelo, Leonardo da Vinci homosexuals (April 9, 1935, quoted in E. Jones, *Life and Works*, vol. 3, pp. 195-196). There are tensions or even contradictions here. Freud wrote of himself that he stood for "an infinitely freer sexual life, although I myself have made little use of such freedom". (Letter to James J. Putnam, July 8, 1915).**

[308] **Freud, informed on the latest ethnological research, knew that 'monogamy' had high cultural variablity. Thus, the reference in this and the following sentence is to strict literalist forms of Christianity, orthodox and ultra-orthodox forms of Judaism. He later calls the description '*ein Extrem*'.**

[309] **The terminology of *Schwächlinge* ('weak'), *stärkere Naturen* ('stronger natures'),**

ud

society (*Kulturgesellschaft*) has been obliged to pass over in silence (*stillschweigend zuzulassen*) many transgressions (*Überschreitungen*) which according to its own statutes ought to have been prosecuted (*Satzungen hätte verfolgen mussen*). [310] But we must not go astray (*irregehen*) on the other side and assume that, because not all the aims are achieved such a cultural attitude is wholly innocuous (*überhaupt harmlos*). The sexual life of civilized humans is still severely impaired (*doch schwer geschädigt*); it gives, now and then (*mitunter*), the impression of a retrogression of function (*Rückbildung befindlichen Funktion*),[311] like our teeth and hair seem to be as organs. One probably has a right to assume that its importance as a source of feelings of happiness (*Glücksemfindungen*), as well as in the fulfillment of our life goal, has painfully diminished (*emfindlich nachgelassen hat*). [312] Sometimes one seems to believe that it is not only the pressure of civilization (*Druck der Kultur*) but something in the nature of the function itself which prevents full satisfaction and drives us on to other paths. This may be a mistake (*Irrtum*); it is difficult to decide. 313

Einbruch ('invasion') reminds one of F. Nietzsche.

[310] **Bk. 4, 396. This idea relates to the interplay of transgression and taboo. This phenomenon was analyzed by the anthropologist Michael Taussig, e.g. in *Walter Benjamin's Grave* (2006) who argued that students of religion have neglected the role of transgression within Christian traditions and also the Dionysian elements in Greek and Roman culture, and the 'left-handed' paths in Islamic, 'Hindu' and Buddhist traditions that use sensory excess as a means toward noetic/spiritual goals. This dynamic interplay of the sacred and the profane requires secrecy, hence the 'pass over in silence' (*stillschweigend zuzulassen*). b) For 'satzungen' JS (p. 95) has 'rescripts', a Latin-based term (*rescribere*, 'to write back'), first used in ecclesiastical and imperial contexts. According to the *OED*, the first attested use is 1817. Freud knew Latin but often prefered [Proto-] Germanic based terms. A preference for compounding new words from Old (High/Low) Germanic rather than Greek and Latin roots is wide spread in German and not peculiar to Freud. (I thank N. W. Warren for comment on this sentence). JS (idem) has 'punished' (*bestrafen*) for 'verfolgen.'**

[311] **Idem. More literally, '*Rückbuildung*' is 'reversion to type.'**

[312] **Bk. 4, 396. JS (p. 95) renders '*emfindlich*' with the ambiguous 'sensibly.' Freud's footnote: "Among the works of the sensitive English writer J. Galsworthy, who today enjoys general recognition, there is a short story called "The Apple-Tree." It shows in a penetrating way (*eindringlicher Weise*) how the life of contemporary civilized people has no more space for the simple natural love of two human beings." Galsworthy is no longer read much, but the citation helps explain what Freud means by 'something' in the nature of the function of civilization itself which 'prevents full sexual satisfaction' ("*eine volle Befriedigung verhindert*").**

[313] **Bk. 4, 397, a) JS has 'wrong' for *Irrtum*. b) The very long footnote by Freud is on**

ud

bisexuality. It is an extension of comments in *Drei Abhandlungen zur Sexualtheorie* III (1905). According to E. Kris, the term 'bisexual' (*bisexuell*) was current in the literature of the day. The first date given by the *OED* is 1859. Freud was indebted to W. Fliess for the theme of constitutional bisexuality but they differed in their interpretation of that condition. Freud rejected Fliess' "biological conditions excluded psychological explanations." (Moreover, in the footnote Freud states that the theory of bisexuality 'still lies in obscurity.') E. Kris, 'Introduction' to *The Origins of Psycho-Analysis*, cited above, p. 39, and p. 38, fn. 1 and 2. Freud's footnote (Bk. 4, 97): "The following comments support the view expressed above: man is an animal organism with an unmistakably bisexual disposition [JS adds 'like others']. The individual corresponds to a fusion of two symmetrical halves, of which, according to some researchers, one is simply male and the other female. It is equally possible that each half was originally hermaphrodite (*hermaphroditisch war*). Sexuality is a biological fact, which although of extraordinary importance for mental life is difficult to understand psychologically. We are accustomed to assert that every human being displays both male and female drive-impulses, needs, attributes (*Triebregungen, Bedürfnisse, Eigenschaften*), but though it is true that anatomy can point out the characteristics of maleness and femaleness, psychology cannot. [For psychology] the sexual contrast fades into one of active and passive, in which we far too readily identify activity with maleness and passivity with femaleness, a view by no means confirmed in the animal kingdom. The theory of bisexuality still lies in obscurity, and we feel it is a serious impediment to psychoanalysis that it has not yet found a link with the theory of the drives (*Triebelehre*). However this may be, if we assume as fact that each individual seeks to satisfy both male and female wishes in his/her sexual life (*sexualleben*) we are prepared for the possibility (*sind wir für die Möglichkeit vorbereitet*) that those demands are not fulfilled by the same object and that they interfere (*stören*) with each other, unless they can be kept apart and each impulse (*Regung*) guided into a specific channel suited to it. Another difficulty arises out of this, the association of the erotic relationship, above its own sadistic components, with an amount of direct inclination to aggression (*Aggressionsneigung*). The love-object will not always view these complications with the same understanding and tolerance offered (*entgegenbringen*) by the peasant woman (*Bäuerin*) who complained that her husband did not love her any more because he had not beaten (*bekagt*) her for a week. But the deepest conjecture (*Vermutung*) is the one which takes its start from my statement in the footnote on page 392 (*DUK* in vol. 2 of *Freud ZB*) that with the erect posture of humans and the depreciation (*Entwertung*) of the sense of smell, it was not only anal erotism which threatened to fall victim to organic regression, but the whole of his sexuality; so that the sexual function was accompanied by a repugnance (*Widerstreben*) which cannot be accounted for and which prevents full satisfaction and forces it away from the sexual goal into sublimations and libidinal displacements. I know that Bleuler ('*Der Sexualwiderstand*', *Jahrbuch für psychoanalyt. und psychopathol. Forschungen*, Bd. V, 1913) pointed to the existence of a primary repelling attitude like this toward sexual life. All neurotics, and many others, take exception to the fact that '*Inter urinas et faeces nascimur*' ['between urine and faeces we are born']. The genitals, too, have strong sensations of smell which many cannot tolerate and which spoil sexual intercourse for them. Thus we should find that the deepest root of the sexual repression which accompanies civilization (*Kultur*) is the organic defense of the new erect gait against his earlier animal existence, and this result of scientific research coincides in a remarkable way with commonly heard prejudices (*Vorurteilen*). Nevertheless, at present (*derzeit*) these are no more than unconfirmed possibilities, not substantiated by science (*Wissenschaft*). We should also not forget that in spite of the undeniable depreciation of olfactory stimuli (*Geruchsreize*) there are peoples (*Völker*) in

ud

V

Psychoanalytic work has shown us that it is just these frustrations (*Versagungen*) of sexual life that the so-called neurotics cannot tolerate (*nicht vertragen werden*). They create substitute satisfactions (*Ersatzbefriedigungen*) which either cause suffering or become sources of suffering by causing difficulties in the environment and society (*Umwelt und Gesellschaft*).[314] The last is easy to understand, the former presents us with a new problem. But civilization demands (*Die Kultur verlangt*) other sacrifices than that of sexual satisfaction.

We have treated the difficulty of cultural development as a general difficulty of development by tracing it to the inertia of the lidido, to its aversion (*Abneigung*) to giving up an old position for a new one. We are saying about the same (*ungefähr dasselbe*) when we derive the antithesis between culture and sexuality (*Gegensatz zwischen Kultur und Sexualität*) from the circumstances that sexual love is a relationship between two individuals in which a third party can be be superfluous or disturbing, whereas civilization depends on relationships between a considerably larger number of individuals. When a love relationship is at its height there is no interest remaining in the environment; a pair of lovers (*Liebespaar*) are sufficient to themselves, and do not even need the child they share to make them happy. In no other case does Eros so clearly betray (*verrät*) the core of his being, his purpose of making more out of one; but when he has reached this in the proverbial way (*sprichwörtlich geworden ist*) through the love of two human beings, he refuses to go further. [315]

We have come so far that we can well imagine how a cultural community consisting of double individuals like this, who, libidinally

---

Europe who highly prize the strong genital odours, so repellent to us, as sexual stimulants and refuse to give them up. (See the collections of folklore obtained from Iwan Bloch's 'questionnaire' ('*Umfrage*') 'on the sense of smell in sexual life' ('Über den Geruchssinn in der *vita sexualis*') in different volumes of Friedrich S. Krauss's *Anthropophyteia*).

[314] Synonymous parallelism.

[315] Bk. 5, 398. The presence of a Third may disturb sexual love but that observation is no basis for the claim that there is an antithesis between culture and sexuality. Elsewhere, Freud uses Eros as a mytho-poetic trope; here it is used to reinforce the descriptive narrative, and prepare it for the flat denial of 'love of neighbor' in the sentences that follow. In the sentence immediately following: "*Wir können uns…*" we note the parallelism of "*Arbeits - und Interessengemeinschaft*", 'shared work and common interests.'

ud

satisfied (*libidinös gesättigt*), are linked together through the bonds of shared work and common interests (*Arbeits - und Interessengemeinschaft*). In this case, civilization would not need to draw energy out of sexuality. But this desirable condition (*wünschenswerte Zustand*) does not exist and has never existed; reality shows us that civilization (*die Wirklichket zeigt uns, daß die Kultur*) is not content with the ties we have until now allowed it, that it also aims at binding the members of the community together in a libidinal way, and uses every means to that end; every way that establishes strong identifications is favored, and the largest scale of aim-inhibited libido is summoned up in order to strengthen the communal bond by relations of friendship (*Freundschaftsbeziehungen zu kräftigen*).[316] The fulfillment of these intentions requires the unavoidable restriction of sexual life. But what we are missing here is the insight into the necessity (*Uns fehlt aber die Einsicht in die Notwendigkeit*) of what drives culture along this path and which causes its antagonism to sexuality. It must be a matter (*handeln*) of some disturbing factor that we have not yet discovered. The so-called ideal demands of civilized society may show the clue (*die Spur zeigen*). According to it: "You should love your neighbor as yourself"; it is world famous, certainly older than Christianity, which displays (*vorweist*) it as its proudest claim, but it certainly is not very old; even in historical times it was still strange to humanity (*Menschen noch fremd*). We will take a naïve attitude toward it as if we had heard if for the first time.[317]   Then we

---

[316] Bk. 5, 398. a) Note how *Kultur* is reified through attribution of causal agency, and note the ontological confidence that 'reality shows us...' That 'confidence' probably reflects the influence of F. Brentano, one of his early teachers. Brentano was steeped in Aristotle, and is often called the father of phenomenology. b) The keyword 'libido', used by Augustine, resembles Schopenhauer's '*Wille*', but not Kant's volition as the autonomy of practical reason. Through Proto-Indo-European, the Old Latin *lubido* may be cognate with 'love'; but, of course, the origin of a word does not establish its meaning. Freud identified libido with the sexual energies and only them (*An Autobiographical Study*, p. 60). However, sexuality and emotion need to be distinguished; and sexuality, which in itself explain nothing, must be viewed in embodied form and social context. c) This heavily clausal sentence is one of the longest in the treatise. It is not obscure but JS (p. 99) divides it into three or four sentences.

[317] Idem. a) As a very young person, Freud probably heard this command in Hebrew and German (and perhaps also in the Galician Yiddish of his mother Amalie Nathansohn). The "love your neighbor as thyself" is *Leviticus* 19:18, and "love your enemies" is in the New Testament, e.g. "Love your enemies, Be good to your haters,.." is Luke 6: 27. If one granted the claim that the 'ideal demands of civilized society' center around this commandment or *mitzvah* to 'love your neighbor as yourself', it would illustrate the gap between ideal and fact in history. This perhaps explains Freud's comment that the

ud

become unable to resist a feeling of surprise and consternation (*Überraschung und Befremden*).[318] Why should we do it? What good (*helfen*) will it do us? But above all, how can we achieve it? How can it become possible? My love is something valuable to me which I cannot throw away without reflection (*Rechenschaft verwerfen darf*). It imposes duties (*Pflichten*) on me for whose fulfillment I must be ready to make sacrifices (*Opfern zu erfüllen bereit sein muß*). If I love someone he must in some way deserve it. (I leave out the use that he may be to me, and his possible importance as a sexual object, for neither of these forms of connection concern the precept of love for one's neighbor (*der Nächstensliebe nicht in Betracht*). He deserves it, if he is so like me in important ways that I can love myself in him; and he deserves it, if he is so much more perfect than myself that I can love my ideal of my own self in him;[319] I must love him if he is the son of my friend because the pain my friend would feel if any harm came to him would also be my pain, [i.e.] I would have to share it. But if he is a stranger and cannot attract me through any value of his own *(keinen eigenen Wert)* or significance obtained earlier for my emotional life *(Gefühlsleben)* it would be difficult for me to love him. It would even be wrong (*unrecht*) to do so, for my love would lose all meaning as preferential treatment (*als den Bevorzugung geschätzt*), and it is an injustice to them [one's own people] if I treat a stranger equally (*wenn ich den Fremden ihnen gleichstelle*). But if I love him with this universal love (*Weltliebe*), simply because he is an entity (Wesen) on this earth, like the insect, the earthworm, or a grass snake (*wie das Insekt, der Regenwurm, die Ringelnatter*), then I fear that only a small amount of my love will be his share; impossible [to be] so much (*unmöglich so viel*) as I, according to the judgment of reason (*dem Urteil der Vernunft*), am entitled to retain for myself. What is the point of a precept (Vorschrift) if its fulfillment cannot be recommended as reasonable (*wenn ihre Erfüllung vernünftig empfehlen*

---

command was 'still strange to humanity.' He was writing hundred of years after the religious wars, the Crusades, the Inquisitions, the Mughals, and the horrible carnage of the First World War. b) 'We will take a naïve attitude…' illustrates the vaguely Socratic style of heuristic tentativeness that recurs in *DUK*.

[318] Note the conceptual parallelism. JS (idem) renders '*Befremden*' as 'bewilderment', but that term requires '*Verwirrung*'.

[319] The influential mirror-image view of 'love'—'*love myself in him*'— needs a focus on language; the bond between 'I' and Other, and the formative context for the emergence of self.

ud

kann)? [320] If I look at this closer, I find still more difficulties. Not only is this stranger not worthy of my love, but I must also confess that he has more claim on my hostility, even my hatred. He appears to have minimum love for me and shows me not the least consideration. If it is useful for him he has no hesitation in harming me, nor does he ask himself if the amount of advantage (*Nutzen*) he gains corresponds (*entspricht*) to the quantity of his harmfulness. Indeed, he does not even need an advantage from it; if only he can satisfy a certain pleasure by it, he thinks nothing of jeering at me, insulting me, slandering me (*zu verspotten, zu beleidigen, zu verleumden*),[321] to show his power; and the more secure he feels and the more helpless I am, the more certainly I can expect him to behave (*Benehmen*) against me like this. If he behaves differently, if he shows me as a stranger consideration and indulgence (*wenn er mir als Fremden Rücksicht und Schonung erweist*) [322]; I am ready, and without any precept (*Vorschrift*), to repay (*zu vergelten*) him in the same way. Indeed, if this great commandment had read: 'Love your neighbor as your neighbor loves

---

[320] **Bk. 5, 399. a) In these long passages, the German terms behind 'recommend', 'reasonable', 'fulfillment' remind one of Kant's lexicon, but the project of bringing an unknowable unconscious into the logos of language is not Kantian. One might say that Freud's attack on the love precept could be phrased in Kantian terms as an example of the hypothetical imperative as opposed to a categorial imperative. However, Freud's view of 'love' as a quantity subject to social duties and choices of distribution is anti-Kantian. His discourse on love has poetic charm — "*das Insekt, der Regenwurm, die Ringelnatter*", and it is reasonable to oppose formulating a precept in a categorial form when it cannot be fulfilled. An example is how the five basic moral rules (*pancha-sīla*) in Theravāda Buddhism become modified by cultural practices. b) However, Freud does not give a precise definition of 'love' or distinguish it in terms of continuum and types. Freud's protest against the futility of a commandment relates to his insistence that 'love' is needed as a defense against aggression. The need for that defense may explain the fusion of myth and philosophy in the postulation of the Eros-Death duality. I think, however, that the image of ascent in Plato's *Symposium* and in South-Asian noetic discourses is better than a love-death dualism unless that is reconfigured as a dynamic dialectic. (The best formulation would be 'co-dependent arising'.) This dialectic is hinted at in Bk. 7, 419 and in the last two sentences of *DUK*.**

[321] **Note the rhythmic trust and poetic power. The statement on being 'worthy' of love reminds one of Aristotle in *Nicomachean Ethics* 1166a 1-5 and 1166b 25-30. But what is gained by this 'stranger' versus 'neighbor' polemic? It seems as if Freud in *DUK* became somewhat obsessed by verses in the New Testament (Mt. 5: 44; Luke 6: 27) and this distracted him from the topic of culture and suffering. The focus on culture and suffering do not recommend let alone command 'love' unless 'love' is understood as respect and empathy for persons as self-conscious, volitional beings. Perhaps Freud's extreme polemic against 'love' is really aimed at pity as disguised cruelty, i.e. 'I love my neighbor' is a form of self-congratulation, whereas authentic love requires a measure of distance.**

[322] **Synonymous parallelism.**

ud

you' I would not oppose it (nicht widersprechen).[323] There is a second commandment (*Gebot*) that I find even more incomprehensible, and creates greater opposition in me. It is: Love your enemies *(Liebe deine Feinde).*[324] However, if I think it over *(Wenn ich's recht überlege)* I realize I am wrong (*unrecht*) as it is not a greater imposition *(eine noch stärkere Zumutung abzuweisen).* Fundamentally it is the same thing *(Es ist im Grunde dasselbe).* [325] I believe I can now hear a dignified voice of admonition

---

[323] This passage is SF at his philosophical worse. He failed to distinguish 'precept' from 'commandment', replaced unconditional love with a hypothetical form of the 'golden rule': "love your neighbor as your neighbor loves you." While this is too compressed, it does require that one imagine the situation of the other and that can increase moral impartiality. Kant, however, thought the conventional formulation of the golden rule was 'trivial' and dependent upon the contingency of situations, e.g. see his comment in the *Groundwork of the Metaphysics of Morals*: "for on this principal (assumption of a golden rule) the criminal might argue against the judge who punishes him, and so on." However, Kant was mistaken in restricting the maxim only to desires, e.g. the formulation of 'Do to others, as you would be done by them" is close to his 'Formula of Universal Law'(which according to D. Parfit "has been the world's most widely accepted fundamental moral idea" (*On What Matters*, 2011, vol. 1, 321-330). While the phrase 'golden rule' is modern, the maxim in both positive and negative formulations is found in several of the world's scriptures and is attested in several ancient civilizations. The key texts within Western traditions are Mt. 7: 12, Luke 6: 31. It is phrased in negative form in the Western text (variant readings found in Greco-Latin manuscripts) of Acts 15:29; and the saying was attributed to Hillel, an influential Jewish teacher at the time of Jesus, and it is found in *B. Shabbath*, 31a of the Talmud. In Buddhist canonical texts, the major witness is the *Dhammapada*, 129-130. On 'golden rules', see D. Griffiths, *Buddhist Discursive Formations* (2004), pp. 303-4.

[324] Bk. 5, 399. '*Gebot*', a keyword in *DUK,* would be translated by the Biblical Hebrew '*mitzvah*(*ot*)'. In some passages it is used along with *Vorschrift,* in the sense of precept and rule. *Gebot* is also paired with *Verbot* (prohibition) and is used in a 'religious' context, but also as the command of the *Über-Ich.* JS (p. 102) puts this in single quotation marks. The German text has no quotation marks.

[325] Idem. a) 'wrong' is used here in the belief-relative sense. In Bk. 7, 410, '*Unrecht'* is used in the sense of relative to belief and evidence. Freud reinterpreted 'love your neighbor' to conflate it with 'love your enemy.' This, in Freudian terms, is a repressional and compensational theory of moral judgment which reflects Nietzsche's analysis of slave-morality (crudely put, 'cover the hate by profession of love'). It reflects, to some degree, Freud's experience of Judaeophobia. According to E. Jones, Freud's first visit to Rome in 1901 "betokened …his willingness to take appropriate steps to circumvent the clerical anti-Semitic authorities who had for so many years denied his well-earned entry into the ranks of University professors" (*Life and Works*, one vol. edition, p. 246). Also, in a letter of 1883 to his fiancée Martha Bernays he told her how he had been called "a dirty Jew" while riding in a third-class train compartment. Freud knew the verbal and physical pain of anti-Semitism, but he escaped the worse. He reached London in June 1939. He died in September, before knowing the fate of his sister Adolfine, who died of starvation in Theresienstadt, and the other three sisters who were murdered in the camps in 1942. d) His experiences explain the footnote on and citation by Heine, the gifted Jewish pariah who satirized Germanic sentimentality. Freud: "A great poet may permit himself to

ud

(Stimme die Mahnung): 'It is precisely because your neighbour is not worthy of love, and is your enemy, you should love him as yourself.' I then understand that this case is like that of *Credo quia absurdum.*[326] It is now very likely that my neighbor, if he enjoined *(aufgefordert wird)* to love me as he loves himself, will answer exactly as I have and will reject me on the

---

express, at least jokingly, psychological truths that are severely forbidden (*schwer verpönte*). Hence Heine confesses: 'I have a peaceful disposition. My wishes are: a modest cottage with a thatched roof, but with a good bed, good food, milk and butter, very fresh, flowers before my window, and a few beautiful trees before the door, and if God wants to make my happiness complete, he will allow me the joy of seeing six or seven of my enemies hanging from those trees. I shall be moved in my heart, before their death, to forgive them all the wrong they did me in their lifetime—indeed, one must forgive one's enemies but not before they have been hanged' (Heine, *Gedanken und Einfälle*). JS (p. 102) adds "Section I".

[326] *DUK*, Bk. 5, 400. a) Freud met and talked with William James in the fall of 1909. His *The Varieties of Religious Experience* (1902) had passages on love for one's enemies that would have balanced Freud's critique (see citations in our Bibliography). b) The textual situation was more complex than Freud acknowledged. Love of neighbor and love of the stranger were merged on the basis of the image of God's love as selfless (*agape*): see Mt. 5: 43-48. c) *Crēdō*, the first word of the Apostles or Nicene Creed, means 'I believe.' The Latin phrase cited by Freud and attributed to Tertullian is famous in the form: "I believe because it is absurd." The irony in this reaches absurdity of a non-Surrealist type, but it was balanced within Christian thought by Anselm's '*credo ut intelligam*'. The maxim on love was intended to check aggression, but was wholly inadequate on a psychological level. He cited "*Credo quia absurdum*" in *Die Zukunft einer Illusion* (1927c, in *Freud ZB*, pp. 346-347), *The Future of an Illusion*). d) His footnote in that text on p. 346 reads "*Tertullian zugeschriebener Satz: 'Ich glaube, weil es widersinnig ist.'*" Tertullian was a North African Church father, c. 160 —c. 225, who wrote mainly in Latin. It is unclear how the context of that quotation relates to Freud's usage, but what Freud means is that rational argument is impossible with faith-based propositions that defy our bio-psychological constitutions, e.g. "*Es gibt keine Instanz über der Vernunft*" (There is no appeal beyond reason.) e) The post-Freudian 'interpersonal' therapists (e.g. Harry Stack Sullivan) and the 'existential' therapists (e.g. Rollo May) corrected one imbalance in psychoanalysis but the price was a downplaying of commitment to scientific rationality and Freud's sense of the tragedy in finitude with its innate aggression. The Euro-Enlightenment dimension in Freud coexisted with a strong conviction of the power of feeling, hence his love of Goethe, Schiller, Nietzsche, and his close intellectual friendship with Ludwig Binswanger.

ud

same grounds. [327] I hope he will not have the same objective foundation (*objektiven Recht*) for doing this, but he will have the same idea as I have. After all there are differences in the behaviour of human beings, which ethics, overlooking (*Hinwegsetzung*) that those differences are determined, classifies as 'good' or 'bad' (*als "gut" und "böse" klassifiziert*). As long as those undeniable differences (*unleugbaren Unterschiede*) are not overcome, the meaning of adherence to (*bedeutet die Befolgung*) [328] high ethical demands damages the aims of civilization by putting a direct premium on being evil (*direkte Prämien für das Bösesein aufstellt*). [329] One is reminded here of an event in the French Chamber during a debate on capital punishment: a member had been passionately supporting its abolition and to loud applause, when a voice from the hall called out *'Que messieurs les assassins commencent!'* [330]

The element of truth here, which people are so glad to deny, is that men are not gentle beings who want to be loved (*liebebedürftiges*), and at the most when attacked can defend themselves; but there is to be reckoned

---

[327] **This and the previous sentences are opposed to an ethics of 'pure practical reason' and the dignity of persons as mutually respecting autonomous wills. It is also clear in later passages that Freud rejected a Kantian model of moral autonomy because humans have strong aggressive tendencies. One might still say that by internalizing external authority, the *Über-Ich* (super-ego) appears to take over one role of Kant's categorial imperative; but not all the maxims of the *Über-Ich* are appropriate to become moral laws, and Kant distinguished maxims, precepts, moral law and his 'pure practical reason' was not a psychological or metapsychological concept.**

[328] *DUK*, **Bk. 5, 400. JS (p. 103) has 'obedience.'**

[329] **Idem. JS (idem) has 'positive' for "*direkt-e*". Without attempting his own definition, Freud was critical of 'ethics' for not recognizing that behavior is determined. Freud did not self-describe as a 'moralist' and was critical of Nietzsche for so doing. However, he was a 'moralist' in his critique of a good-bad duality that elicited trangression. One can agree that there are differences in behavior that are determined, and agree that 'ethics' should not classify them as 'good' or 'bad.' However, Freud goes on to contend that if those differences in behavior are not overcome, 'high ethical demands' will damage the goals of civilization by 'putting a preminum on being evil.' This does not follow. One, it confuses a taboo-trangression dialectic, a fact about behavior, with ethical norms. Two, it makes 'ethics' (and   the semantic range of the term is not specified) depend upon a set of natural facts. Three, not all 'undeniable differences' can be overcome, and the fact of differences is not relevant to the status of some ethical truths. The normative is not determined by the descriptive, or to express it better: while an 'ought' should consider factual differences in behaviours it is not determined by them. Hence, the example of the French Chamber debate misses the point that 'murder' and 'capital punishment', the gibbet and "*les assassins*", should both be condemned.**

[330] **'The murderers should make the first move.'   Freuds fn. (in square brackets) is "*Dem Sinne nach: Mögen die Herren Mörder vorangehen.*" His gift as a fictocritical writer is shown in this vivid polemical passage.**

ud

among their desire endowments a powerful share of aggressive tendencies (*Triebbegabungen auch einen mächtigen Anteil von Aggressionsneigung rechnen darf*). As a result, a neighbor is for him not only a potential helper and sexual object, but also a temptation (*Versuchung*) to satisfy his aggression on him, to exploit his capacity for work (*Arbeitskraft*) without compensation, to use him sexually without his consent (*Einwilligung*), to seize his possessions (*Besitz seiner Habe*), to humiliate him, to cause him pain, to torture and to kill him (*Schmerzen zu bereiten, zu martern und zu töten*).[331] *Homo homini lupus*: who, in the experience of life and history, has the courage to dispute this sentence? (*diesen Satz zu bestreiten?*). [332] As a rule this cruel aggression waits upon provocation or puts itself in the service of another purpose whose goal might have been attained with milder means (*mit milderen Mitteln zu erreichen wäre*). Under circumstances favourable to it, when the mental counterforce which usually inhibit it are out of action, it manifests itself spontaneously and reveals humans as a wild beast (*Menschen als wilde Bestie*) to whom consideration of his own kind is foreign (*Schonung der eigenen Art fremd ist*).[333]   One

---

[331] **Note the rhythmic energy in the '*zu*' phrases.**

[332] **Bk. 5, 400. Freud's footnote 3: "*Der Mensch is des Menschen Wolf*", nach Plautus."**
'Man is a wolf to man', also drawing on Plautus'. JS adds 'Derived from Plautus, *Asinaria* II, iv, 88'. In his text, he quotes the Latin phrase and ends the sentence with it. The phrase is also found in Hobbes and attested in Schopenhauer.

[333] **Idem. There is a question of agreement for '*Menschen*' (plu.) and '*Bestie*' (s.). b) This comment [and others] in *DUK* establish that Freud did not have confidence in a simple image of progress based on a 'positivist' world-view. There was progress in some areas of life, but cultural strivings (*Kulturbestrebung*) had so far not achieved very much (idem, 401). Darwin's influence was real and Freud believed in evolution from 'primitive' social forms to *Kultur,* and he thought psychoanalysis was a progressive 'science' within psychology. However, that he soured on an image of the 'progress' of humankind is evident in his enumeration of atrocities in the preceding and following passages. In his essay *Thoughts for the Times on War and Death*, first published in 1915, he quoted the Latin phrase: 'If you desire peace, prepare for war." But this attitude changed. He had been deeply shocked by the violence and mendacity of the First World War, and the rise of the anti-Jewish political movements in Austria. After *DUK* was published, he endured the knowledge that his books were burnt in Berlin in May 1933; he endured the shock of the confiscation of his *Verlag* by the Nazis in March 1938, the interrogation of Anna by the Gestapo, and the reign of terror in Vienna. c) In the context of Freud's pessimism**

ud

who calls to mind (*Wer*)[334] the atrocities of the racial migrations (*Völkerwanderung*), or the invasions of the Huns (*Einbrüche der Hunnen*), the so-called Mongols under Genghiz Khan and Tamerlane, the capture of Jerusalem by the pious Crusaders (*frommen Kreuzfahrer*), yes, even the horrors of the recent World War, anyone who calls these thing to mind must bow humbly before the reality of this view (*der Tatsächlichkeit dieser Auffassung demütig beugen müssen*). [335]

The existence of this inclination to aggression (*Aggressionsneigung*), which we can detect in ourselves, and correctly assume exists in others, is the factor which disturbs our relations with our neighbor, and compels culture to its expenditure [of energy] (*Aufwand nötigt*).[336] As a consequence of this primary hostility of human beings against one another, civilized society stands under constant threat of disintegration (*Zerfall bedroht*). The interest of work in common would not hold it together, [and] instinctive passions (*triebhafte Leidenschaften*) are stronger than reasonable interests. Culture must muster (*aufbieten*) all means to set limits to the aggressive strivings of human beings and to keep

---

about human relations (*Kulturpessimismus*) and his belief in an inherent inclination to aggression, it is difficult to understand key parts of his 1932 letter to Einstein. In the letter he affirmed the indirect methods of sublimation and asked rhetorically: "And how long shall we have to wait before the rest of mankind become pacifists too?" (*Warum Krieg?*, Sept. 1932 letter to Einstein, in *Freud ZB*, vol. 2, pp. 483-493; *S.E*, XXII, pp. 203-215). The sentence was sincere but also utopian given SF's pessimistic view of the human death-drive.

[334] '*Wer*' is not an interrogative here (we thank N. W. Warren for his correction). It is a relative pronoun, so: 'One who...'/ 'he/she who...' JS has 'anyone', as is implied by the final verbal phrase: "*in seine Erinnerung ruft*".

[335] Bk. 5, 400. The term '*beugen*' is also used as '*Verbeugung*', p. 406; '*beugt*', p. 410, and '*beuge*', p. 424. JS (p. 104) has 'truth' for '*Tatsächlichkeit.*'

[336] Bk. 5, 400-401. a) It is puzzling why Freud was not content with this statement on 'inclination to aggression.' Sadly, it is easy to verify. The eternal (*ewige*) power of a death drive in struggle with Eros adds a mythograpical poetic layer and a trans-cultural critical standard to the awareness of this aggression. However, it is beyond the canons of empirical evidence and in Bk. 4 the death-drive is confused with 'necessity' or *Ananké*. b) Incidentally, the term '*Thanatos*', does not occur in the text and in this regard, H. Westerlink makes a mistake (p. 247). The use of the term is widespread, e.g. H. Marcuse has an entire chapter entitled "Eros and Thanatos". Freud used the term *Thanatos* in conversation, but not in his writings. It was used first by W. Stekel in 1909 in terms of a death-wish, and P. Federn introduced it in relationship to Eros (E. Jones, *Life and Works*, vol. 3, p. 273).

ud

down the manifestations of them by psychic reaction-formations (*psychische Reaktionsbildungen niederzuhalten*). That, also, is why [there is] the use of methods intended to entice (*antreiben*) people into identifications and goal-inhibited love relationships; hence also [there is the] restrictions of sexual life, and also the ideal commandment (*Idealgebot*) to love the neighbor as one loves oneself, a commandment really justified by the fact that nothing else is so contrary to the original nature of human beings (*der ursprünglichen menschlichen Natur so sehr zuwiderläuft*).[337] Through all this trouble, these strivings of culture (*Kulturbestrebung*) have so far not achieved very much. They hope to prevent (*hofft sie zu verhüten*) the crudest excesses of brutal violence by assuming the right to use violence, but the law is not able to lay hold (*Gesetz nicht zu erfassen*) of the more cautious and refined expressions of human aggressiveness.[338] The time comes when each one of us must give up as illusions (*als Illusionen fallenzulassen*) the expectations which he held in his youth (*die er in der Jugend*), and which he pinned on his fellow humans (*Mitmenschen geknüpft*), and when he may realize how much difficulty and pain has been added to his life by their malevolence (*wie sehr ihm das Leben durch deren Übelwollen erschwert und schmerzhaft gemacht wird*).[339] At the same time, it would be unfair to reproach culture

---

[337] Bk. 5, 401. The 'ideal' commandment of love is not from Deity or a sacred text, but from the demands of *Kultur* to restrict human aggressive tendencies. This passage, an impressive use of paradox as argument, is a key to Freud's image of the human being. His confidence in knowing 'the original nature of human beings' reflects an Enlightenment sensibility; but his belief in innate aggression undercuts a simple identification of 'reason' and optimism. However, he trusted that reason could deconstruct the naïve and ingenuous optimism of 'religion', and its secular substitute image of human goodness. One should add that his own postulate of the Oedipus complex and the primal slaying of the father was as filled with illusion as the 'religion' he critiqued.

[338] Idem. This is perhaps a psychological interpretation and critique of Hobbes (1588-1679). The direct form of address that follows resembles a moralistic father talking to a son or daughter (cf. Qohelet: 11:9). Freud's image of the body differed from Hobbes, but he shared with him an image of desire as sequential, non-static, and unlimited ("a perpetuall and restlesse desire of Power after power…" *Leviathan*, chap. 11, 161). But this perspective must avoid a component theory of the self, as found in different forms in Plato and Freud. The Theravāda Buddhist theory of 'no-self' is a useful corrective to an image of the self that reifies the complexity of desire. The 'no-self' doctrine can also complement the NT image of agape via *kenosis* or emptying out of self.

[339] Bk. 5, 401. The sentence is dependent upon the pronouns (*uns, er, ihm* [dat. sing. of *er*] *deren* [gen. sing. or plural]). Note the tone of personal bitterness and the synonymous parallelism of 'difficulty and pain' ("*erschwert und schmerzhaft*").

ud

with attempting to eliminate disputes and competition (*Streit und Wettkampf*) from human activity. These are definitely indispensable, but opposition is not necessarily hostility; it is merely made an occasion for abuse (*Anlaß für sie mißbraucht*).[340]

The communists believe they have found the way to deliverance from evil (*Erlösung vom Übel gefunden zu haben*). Man is clearly good, well-disposed (*wohlgesinnt*) toward his neighbour, but the system of private property has corrupted his nature (*hat seine Natur verdroben*). The possession of private goods (*Gütern*) gives the individual power, and with it the temptation to maltreat his neighbor, while the individual excluded from possession is bound to rebel in hostility against his oppressor. [341] If one overcame private property (*Wenn man das Privateigentum aufhebt*), shared all goods in common, and everyone allowed to share in the

---

[340] Idem. a) The softening or qualification in this sentence of the previous generalization shows the dialectical rather than dogmatic dimension of Freud's thought. b) 'These' (*Diese*) refers to 'disputes and competition.' The 'it' in 'it is only an occasion for misuse' also refers to the near-synonymous parallelism of 'disputes and competition.' JS (p. 105) expands "*wird nur zum Anlaß für sie Mißbracht*" into 'it is merely misused and made an *occasion* for enmity.' c) This paragraph contains the premise for the subsequent critique of the illusory assumptions about human nature attributed by Freud to the 'communists.'

[341] Idem. a) In the opening paragraph of chapter two of *The Future of an Illusion*, Freud recognized the reality of the materal factors of wealth and distribution of wealth, and the mental or psychical factors of civilization (*seelische Besitz der Kultur*). The material dimension was not enough. An unnamed Marxist criticized Freud for implying that Marxism attributed social change only to economic factors. Freud's modest reply was that he lacked a 'thorough knowledge', and was glad to learn that neither Marx nor Engels "has denied the influence of ideas and super-ego factors" (E. Jones, *Life and Work*, vol. 3, pp. 344-345). b) He did not use the word 'communist' in *The Future of an Illusion*, although the Bolshevik attempt at new cultural organization is commented upon in chapter 1. In *DUK* the term *Kommunismus* is synonymous with *Bolschwismus* and a vague phrase about overcoming private property (*Privateigentum*) is used. But the Bolskeviks opposed private ownership of the means of production and land, not individual possessions of goods or 'personal rights over material goods.' JS has 'ownership of private wealth', but 'wealth' would be '*Reichtum*' not '*Gütern.*' c) Freud was interested in the 'communist' issue because he thought that 'communism' and 'religion' were both powerful illusions. The image of 'man' in communist anthropology was a product of a naïve utopianism because human beings were subjects of repressed unconscious forces. Freud's footnote on p. 401 of *DUK* shows empathy for 'the miseries of poverty' and disdain for inequality of wealth. In general sensibility, he was more sympathetic to 'socialism' than to 'religion.' However, his distrust of the masses sits uneasily with comments on 'change in relation to possessions' and the need for 'virtue' to be rewarded on earth as opposed to reward/punishment in an afterlife. His focus on the here and now as counterposed to systems of supernatural reward and punishment reveals a timid approval for a vague type of top-down socialism. See Bk. 5, 422.

ud

enjoyment, ill-will and hostility (*Übelwollen und Feindseligkeit*)[342] would disappear among human beings. Inasmuch as all needs were satisfied, there would be no reason (*keiner Grund*) to regard another as an enemy, and all would be willing to undertake the necessary work.[343] I have nothing to do with any economic criticisms of the communist system, and I cannot inquire into whether the abolition of private property is expedient and advantageous (*zweckdienlich und vorteilhaft ist*).[344] But I am able to recognize that its psychological premise (*psychologische Voraussetzung*) is a rootless illusion.[345] With the overcoming (*Aufhebung*) of private property we deprived the human love of aggression of one of its instruments (*Werkzeuge*), certainly a strong one, though certainly not the strongest. But we have not altered the differences in power and influence (*Macht und Einfluß*) which aggression misuses for its own aims, nor have we altered it in its essence (*Wesen*).[346] It [aggressiveness] is not created through property, it reigned almost without limits in primitive times (*Urzeiten*) when property was still very scanty (*Eigentum noch sehr armselig war*), and it already shows itself in the nursery almost before property has given up its primal, anal form (*anale Urform*); it forms the basis (*bildet den Bodensatz*) of all tender and loving connections (*zärtichen und Liebesbeziehungen*) among people, perhaps with the single exception of a mother's relation to her male child.[347] If one removed (*räumt*) personal

---

[342] **Note the synonymous parallelism.**

[343] **This socialist communitarian image is present in some of the early Marx, the 'utopian' socialists, and Trotsky's *Literature and Revolution*. It differs factually and morally from the Soviet Marxism.**

[344] **Bk. 5, 401. Note the reinforcing lexical parallelism. Freud has a footnote at the end of this sentence: "Anyone who has experienced the miseries of poverty in his youth, and the indifference (*Gleichgültigkeit*) and arrogance (*Hochmut*) of the well-to-do, should be free from the suspicion that he has no understanding and no sympathy for the striving against the inequality (*Besitzungleichheit*) of humanity and what it leads to. Of course (*Freilich*), if an attempt is made to ground this fight on an abstract demand, in the name of justice for the equality of all, there is an objection close by, that nature through extremely unequal physical attributes (*körperliche Ausstattung*) and mental gifts (*Begabung*) has introduced injustice, against which there is no remedy (*keine Abhilfe gibt*)." But the point of 'no remedy' confuses the issue of equality as a human right issue with the factuality of innate disparities and contingencies of birth.**

[345] **Idem. JS (p. 106) adds 'on which the system is based.'**

[346] **Bk. 5, 402. Note the synonymous parallelism. JS (idem) leaves out '*für ihre Absichten*' and joins this sentence with the previous one. This sentence turns the human inclination toward aggression ('*menschlichen Aggressionslust*') into a comprehensive ontical power.**

[347] **Bk. 5, 402. a) Note the synonymous parallelism. At this point, Freud cites his earlier**

ud

rights to material goods (*dingliche Güter*), there still would remain the prerogatives of sexual relations which are the source of the strongest dislike and the most violent hostility among otherwise equal human beings (*sonst gleichgestellten Menschen*). If one also removed this factor [prerogatives of sexual relations] through the full satisfaction of sexual life, and hence abolished the family, the germ-cell of civilization (*Keimzelle der Kultur*), we cannot easily forsee what new paths of development culture could take (*einschlagen kann*); but one thing we may expect is that this indestructible trait of human nature will also follow it there (*ihr auch dorthin folgen wird*).[348]

It is obviously not easy for humans to give up the satisfaction of this inclination to aggression: they do not feel good without it. The advantage of a comparatively small cultural circle (*Kulturkreises*) in allowing this drive (*Trieb*) an outlet in the form of hostility against outsiders is not be scorned (*geringzuschätzen*). It is always possible to bind together a considerable number of people in love for one another, if there are other people left over to receive the expression of their aggression (*Äußerung der Aggression übrigbleiben*).[349] I once devoted attention to the phenomenon that it is precisely communities close to one another, and related in other

---

work *Massenpsychologie und Ich-Analyse* (1921, S.A. vol.9; *Group Psychology and the Analysis of the Ego*, S. E. vol.18). Suddenly, aggression, in the absence of the countervailing power of Eros, becomes over-determined and over-extended, e.g. the only evidence presented is a reference to early anality. b) Freud recognized the aggressive dimension of human animals; but he put too much emphasis on it in *DUK*; perhaps because of the focus of social Darwinism on conflict and competition, but also and more deeply by his experience of the war and violence of European history. P. Kropotkin's *Mutual Aid* (1902) presented a counter-image to innate aggression, and recently there is primatological evidence, e.g. by Franz de Waal, on lack of innate violence. c) Freud's realism about aggression could lead to resignation, as vividly illustrated in the Georg Fuchs case. Fuchs wrote *Wir Zuchthausler* ('We Convicts') a protest against conditions in prison, and he asked Freud to endorse the book's protest against that treatment as a disgrace to civilization. Freud refused to help, and with numbing irrelevance replied that it was not a disgrace because the brutality accorded with the cruelty of civilization (Letter to Georg Fuchs, 1931f, *S.E.* 22, 251).

[348] This generalization might be supported by the failure of the democratic socialist kibbutzim (Heb. *qibbûs*) in Israel.

[349] a) JR has 'smaller communities' for *Kulturkreises*, JS has 'small cultural group'. (b) The verb '*verzichten*' and noun '*Verzicht*' are keywords in *DUK*. The term is often, but not in this sentence, confined to males who must renounce sexual gratification. c) '*Liebe*' is too strong a word here, especially so because Freud used it in the context of the comandment to love others. This insight on binding together through an Other is an interpretative key to most forms of nationlism, especially those of the 'exceptionalist' and victim-based types.

ud

ways, that are always feuding and mocking one another (*befehden und verspotten*),[350] like the Spaniards and Portuguese, North and South Germans, the English and Scotch, and so forth.[351] I gave it the name, 'the narcissism of small differences' ("*Narziβmus der kleinen Differenzen*"), a name which does not contribute much of an explanation.[352] We can see that it is a mild and relatively harmless satisfaction of an aggressive inclination, by means of which the cohesion of the members of the community is made easier (*erleichtert wird*). The Jewish people, scattered everywhere (*überallhin versprengte*), have in this respect rendered the most useful services to the cultures of their host countries where they had settled (*Wirtsvölker erworben*); unfortunately, all the massacres of the Jews in the Middle Ages did not make the period more peaceful and secure for their Christian comrades (*friedlicher und sicherer für seine christlichen Genossen zu gestalten*).[353] After the Apostle Paul had made universal love the foundation of his Christian community, extreme intolerance of Christendom (*äuβerste Intoleranz des Christentums*) against those who remained outside it became the inevitable result (*unvermedliche Folge geworden*); [but to] the Romans, who had not founded their communal life (*Gemeinwesen*) as a State upon love, religious intolerance was foreign (*religiöse Unduldsamkeit fremd gewesen*), although religion was a concern of the State and it was permeated by it (*und der Staat von Religion durchtränkt war*).[354] It was also not a chance event (*unverständlicher Zufall*) that the dream of Germanic world domination evoked anti-Semitism as its complement (*Weltherrschaft zu seiner Ergänzung den Antisemitismus*

---

[350] Not the lexical near-synonymous parallelism.

[351] Freud's footnote cites *Massenpsychologie und Ich-Analyse, unten*, S. 450f. [This refers to vol. 2 of *Freud ZB*, p. 450ff.]

[352] Bk. 5, 402. The phrase has become fairly well-known.

[353] Note the use of lexical synonymous parallelism in this attack on anti-Semitism. The term '*Genossen*' was adopted by members of fascist and communist groups. Freud's sarcastic wit is displayed in this sentence.

[354] The contrast between 'the Romans' and Paul's 'Christian community' and 'extreme intolerance' needs qualification. Many Christian preachers, writers and Church fathers from the early 2nd century were Judaeophobic. The polemical treatise *Adversus Judaeo* by St John Chrysostom (c. 347-407) was a major force in the negative homilies within a sub-genre of early Christian literature. Some Romans had respect for the ethical dimension of Judaism, but the historian Tacitus wrote of Jews with scorn and Josepheus was subject to criticism for his positive image of them in the *Jewish Antiquities*. The discussion of 'this nation' in the Babylonian Talmud, *Shabbat* 33b expressed Jewish animosity and distrust toward the Romans.

ud

aufrief), and it is understandable that the attempt to establish a new, communist culture (*Kultur*) in Russia should find its psychological support in the persecution of the bourgeois (*in der Verfolgung der Bourgeois seine psychologische Unterstützung findet*). One only asks with concern what the Soviets will begin to do after they have eliminated their bourgeois (*sie ihre Bourgeois ausgerottet haben*).[355]

If culture imposes such great sacrifices not only on sexuality, but also on human tendencies of aggression, we can understand better why it is hard for humans to be happy in that civilization. Prehistoric man (*Urmensch*) was better off in knowing no restrictions on his drives (*Triebeinschränkungen kannte*). In compensation (*zum Ausgleich*), his prospects of enjoying this happiness for any length of time were very restricted. Civilized man (*Der Kulturalmensch*) has exchanged a part (*ein Stück*) of his possibilities of happiness for a portion (ein *Stück*) *of* security.[356] But we must not forget, however, that in the primal family (*Urfamilie*) only the head of it had enjoyed such freedom of desire; the others lived in slavish oppression. In that primal period of culture, the contrast between the minority who enjoyed the advantages of culture, and the majority who were robbed (beraubten) of them, was therefore carried to extremes (*aufs Äußerste getrieben*). Concerning the primitive people of today (*heute lebenden Primitiven*), we have through careful inquiries (*Erkundung*) shown that their instinctual life (*Triebleben*) can by no means

---

[355] **Bk. 5, 403. a) In a single sentence Freud attacked the far Right in the form of a Germanic dream of world dominance which had anti-Semitism as its complement, and the Soviet 'Marxists' in the persecution of the bourgeois. In this sentence on the Soviets, Freud unleashes his moralistic wit. Several British intellectuals and poets, e.g. Louis MacNeice, George B. Shaw, thought that Soviet Marxism was a valuable secular alternative to capitalism. b) The Soviet regime banned psychoanalysis in the early 1930's. Trotsky, who preferred Freud to Pavlov, vainly opposed the move. There may have been some connection between the banning and the radical pro-sexuality lectures that W. Reich, who sought a synthesis of Freud and Marx, gave in the country around this time. E. Jones quotes the official 'communist' line: "Freudism" is defined [as] "a reactionary idealistic trend widespread in bourgeois psychological science...now in the service of imperalism..." (Jones, *Life and Work*, vol. 3, pp. 345-6). Freud had a deep interest in Russia and Russian literature.**

[356] **Bk. 5, 403. Note the rhythm of *ein Stück ... ein Stück* in *"Der Kulturmensch hat für ein Stück Glücksmöglichkeit ein Stück Sicherheit eingetauscht."* In *DUK*, the implicit social contract is that, assuming all do it, one gives up unfettered rights to happiness in exchange for social stability. b) The use of *Urmensch* and 'primal family' illustrate the troubled relationship between useful poetic prototypes and factual claims, i.e. Freud seemed to assume that *Urmensch* was an actual person and *Urfamilie* a factual beginning.**

ud

be envied for its freedom (*Freiheit beneidet werden darf*); it is subject to restrictions of a different kind but perhaps more severe than those of modern civilized man (*des modernen Kulturmenschen*).

If we correctly object to the current state of our culture, for its insufficiency in fullfilling our plans for an order of life (*Lebensordnung*) that will make us happy, and for allowing so much suffering (*wieviel Leid*) that was probably avoidable (*zu vermeiden wäre*), when we strive with unsparing criticism (*schonungsloser Kritik*) to uncover the roots of its imperfection (*die Wurzeln seiner Unvollkommenheit aufzudecken*) we are certainly practicing a proper right (*gutes Recht*), and are not showing ourselves as enemies of culture (*und zeigen uns nicht als Kulturfeinde*). We may gradually expect to carry through (*durchzusetzen*) such changes of our culture that will better satisfy our needs and will avoid our criticism (*die unsere Bedürfnisse besser befriedigen und jener Kritik entgegen*). But perhaps we should also familiarize (*vertraut*) ourselves with the idea that there are difficulties inherent in the nature of culture, and that will not yield to attempts at reform (*Reformversuch weichen werden*).[357] Apart from the tasks of restricting the desires, which we are prepared for, our attention is forced on the danger of a state of things which might be called 'the psychological poverty of the masses' ("*das psychologische Elend der Masse*" *benennen kann*). This danger threatens the most where the bonds of a society (*gesellschaftliche Bindung*) are chiefly constituted through the identification of members with one another while leaders with individuality (*Führerindividualitäten*) do not have the importance they should in the formation of a group *(Massenbildung zufallen sollte).*[358] The present

---

[357] In the previous sentence, note the lovely balance of 'better satisfy our needs' and 'escape our criticism.' E. Jones thought that Freud wrote in "a vein of tempered optimism" about the future of society, but this sentence (which Jones quotes) does not support that conclusion. It would be better to say that he wrote in 'a tempered distrust of civilization with a cautious degree of hope.' The style of thinking in *DUK* was often ironical, e.g. note the phrase: 'there are difficulties inherent to the nature of culture'. It was also lucid, tight and yet analogical, and it avoided the facile polarity of 'optimism' and 'pessimism'. After the horrors of the Great War, Freud wrote to Max Eitingon that generally he had a "cheerful pessimism" but now "the second element occasionally becomes the more prominent one" (E. Jones, Vol. 3, p. 6).

[358] Freud's footnote: "*Siehe: Massenpsychologie und Ich-Analyse, 1921[c].*" The term '*mass-en*' can be 'mass-es' or 'the people', but 'group' is the standard English rendering. This indictment of the masses set over against "leaders with individuality" combined with the extreme contrast between 'religion' and 'science' has troubling proto-fascist and scientistic- technocratic implications. However, Freud may be only suggesting the need for

ud

cultural situation of America could give us a good opportunity to study this fearful damage to culture *(befürchteten Kulturschaden zu studieren)*. I avoid the temptation to do a critique of American culture, I will not give the impression of wanting to use American methods *(amerikanischer Methoden bedienen)*. [359]

---

exemplary leaders who are respected. "American culture" is his example of 'fearful damage to culture.' This is exaggerated. '(T)he present cultural situation' of America in the 1920's was vital and lively in the arts, but the national executive branches were mediocre and scarcely rational. Freud's belief that Americans preferred 'religious belief' to the 'scientific spirit' was expressed in his comment in *The Future of an Illusion* on the "monkey trial in Dayton" (see fn. following).

[359] Bk. 5, 403. According to Freud, the 'psychological poverty of the masses' is especially problematic in a society in which people identify with one another and lack respect for leaders with individuality. (This comment recalls Tocqueville.) b) JS (p. 110) has 'American civilization' for "...*amerikanischen Methoden bedienen*". Freud's 'American methods' can refer to several things: the prestige of the so-called pure sciences, his sense that a focus on changes of behaviour may dominate focus on psychic changes (which proved to be the case), and that religious belief in America had blocked the progress of the *wissenschaftliche Geist* (scientific mind). A decisive example of this was the controversy over evolution in the trial in Dayton, Tenn. in 1925. Freud mentioned this in the text and in a footnote in *Die Zukunft einer Illusion*, Bk. 7, 354. Freud had a deep interest in England but was not really interested in America. He made his single trip, with Jung and Ferenzi, in 1909 to give five lectures at Clark University (he gave them in German and without any notes) and to receive an honorary degree. (His letters to O. Pfister are a source on this). Freud remained grateful for that experience. It was probably the first public audience for an expression of his ideas that he had known. The Clark lectures were the basis for *The Origin and Development of Psycho-Analysis* (1910, translated by Harry W. Chase), also published under the title "Five Lectures on Psycho-Analysis," (1910a, in *S.E.*, 11, 3-55). He was not optimistic about psychoanalysis in America and on January 17, 1909, wrote Jung that "once they discover the sexual core of our psychological theories they will drop us. Their prudery and their material dependence on the public are too great." *F. J. Letters*, p. 196. A cultural anti-American bias based on an association with money, vulgarity, prudism, competition was widespread among German and French speaking intellectuals at this time (profound changes came in the 1940's and early 1950's with the realization of the profound contrast between totalistic regimes and a constitutional nation-state with a Bill of Rights). Freud was ambivalant about America. He was delighted that there was an eager audience for his ideas, still widely rejected in Vienna, but he later complained that the cuisine had damaged his intestines and even damaged his handwriting. These odd complaints led E. Jones to comment that Freud's anti-Americanism "'actually had nothing to do with America itself.'" Freud wrote his elder daughter Mathilde (1887-1978) that he was glad he was "away from it, and even more that I don't have to live there", but it was "extremely interesting and probably highly significant for our cause. All in all one can call it a great success." Freud had a long talk with William James. James was interested in Freud's ideas but critical of his hostility to religion, and on that point favored Jung. James' great two-volume study *Principles of Psychology* (1890) anticipated some themes and shared some sources with Freud, e.g. the role of the unconscious within the flow of consciousness. Freud's psychoanalysis had definite pragmatic, as defined by James, dimensions. For instance, in *Future of an Illusion* he wrote that psychoanalysis was a *Forschungsmethode*

ud

VI

Never in my previous work have I had so strong an impression that what I am describing is common knowledge and that I am using up paper and ink, and later, typesetter and printer's work, to expound things that are essentially self-evident (*um eigentlich selbstverständliche Dinge zu erzählen*). That's why if it were to appear that the recognition of a special, independent aggressive drive means a modification of the psychoanalytical theory of the drives (*Abänderung der psychoanalytischen Trieblehre bedeutet*) I would gladly seize the point.

We shall show, however, that this is not so and it is merely a matter of bringing into sharper focus a turn of thought effected long ago (*eine Wendung, die längst vollzogen worden ist*) and of following out its consequences (*Konsequenzen zu verfolgen*). [360] Of all the slowly developed pieces of analytical theory, the theory of the drives (*Trieblehre*) groped its way forward the most laboriously (*mühseligsten vorwärtsgetastet*). And yet that theory was indispensable to the whole, so that something had to be put in its place.[361] At first, in my complete perplexity (*vollen Ratlosigkeit*), I took as my starting point a saying by the

---

('method of investigation'), an impartial instrument, somewhat like the infinitesimal calculus (vol. 2 of *Freud ZB*, VII, p. 352). Freud also had intense discussions with James Jackson Putnam (1846-1918), a neurologist and professor at Harvard Medical School. Putnam was an early and eager defender of psychoanalytical method. Freud wrote a moving thank you letter to him at the end of 1910. It is fascinating that this and other New England Brahmins, mental descendents of the Puritans, should have embraced Freud. However, while the optimistic-minded Putnam remained loyal to psychoanalysis, he thought Freud's views were too psychogenetic and "too *negative* to be fully satisfactory." See P. Roazan, *Freud and His Followers,* pp. 374-80, quoted phrase, italics in the original, p. 376; Peter Gay, *Freud* (1988), pp. 206-213.

[360] This type of dialectical ('dialectic' < Greek, "art of conversation") set-up piece is used several times in the treatise. In a letter to an unnamed 'Marxist', Freud thanked him/her for making clear that Marxism did not deny the role of an *Über-Ich,* but he said he still could not understand 'dialectic'. As used in that exhange, 'dialectic' represented Marxist historical materialism. Our use of 'dialectical' refers to a statement of humility, e.g. 'complete perplexity' before a situation, followed by bringing an earlier expression of thought 'into sharper focus'.

[361] a) Freud has a footnote to '*Trieblehre*': [Vgl. Den Abschnitt 'Die Triebe' in Bd. 1 der *Werkausgabe*.] b) The reasoning here seems to be that until one theory was fleshed out, another had to be operating in its place, but the truth in this is relative to the level of abstraction.

ud

poet-philosopher, Schiller: 'hunger and love' (*Hunger und Liebe*) drives the world and holds it together (*das Getriebe der Welt zusammenhalten*).[362] Hunger could be considered as representative of the drives which aim at preserving the individual, love strives after objects; and its main object, favoured by nature in every way, is the preservation of the species (*Erhaltung der Art*). So at first the 'I'-drives and Object-drives (*Ichtriebe und Objekttriebe*) [363] confronted one another. I introduced the term 'libido' (*den Namen Libido*) to denote the energy of the latter, and only it; always with it [there is] the contrast (*Gegensatz*) between the 'I'-drives, and the libidinal drives of love, in the widest sense, directed to an object (*aufs Objekt gerichteten, 'libidinösen' Trieben der Liebe im weitesten Sinne*). One of these object-drives, the sadistic, stood out from the others in that its aim was very far from loving (*daß sein Ziel so gar nicht liebevoll war*), also it was obviously in some ways attached to the I-drives: it could not hide (*verbergen*) its close affinity with the drives of mastery (*nahe Verwandtschaft mit Bemächigungstriebe*) which have no libidinal purpose (*libidinöse Absicht*), but these discrepancies were overcome; after all, sadism was clearly a part of sexual life, in the activities of which affection (*zärtliche*) could be replaced by inhuman sport (*grausame Spiel*).[364] The neuroses appear as an outcome of a struggle between the interests of self-preservation and the demands of the lidido, a conflict in which the 'I' had won (*in dem das Ich gesiegt hatte*), but at the price of severe pain and renunciation (*Leiden und Verzichte*). [365]

---

[362] **Bk. 6, 404. Freud quoted Schiller's '*Hunger und Liebe*' phrase and then gave his own gloss. JS (p. 112) has 'hunger and love are what moves the world' in single quotation marks. Freud has a footnote: [I*n dem Gedicht 'Die Weltweisen'.*]**

[363] **Idem. JS (idem) has 'ego-instincts and object-instincts.' In the treatise *On Narcissism: An Introduction* (1914[c] *S.E.*, 14, 69-102), Freud separated the 'I' libido and the 'object libido'. He also presented an early critique of Jung's view of the nonsexual libido, and a critique of Adler.**

[364] **Bk. 6, 404. A long and complex sentence. JS (idem) breaks it into three, has 'antithesis' for *Gegensatz*, and 'cruelty' for *grausame Spiel*. I find SF's analysis of sadism inadequate. Without a very strong concept of neurosis, it is impossible to grasp how 'activities' of 'affection' can be 'replaced by inhuman sport.'**

[365] **a) Conceptual parellism. b) Freud assigns sadism to both the drives of mastery and of sexual life, but this does not clarify how it relates to neurosis. Moreover, a neurosis may reflect not only the struggle between the 'I' and the 'demands of the libido' but the 'I' and an external oppressive Other. c) Also as claimed in *Totem und Tabu* (1912-1913, III, 4, 84-5), the neuroses have a deep reaching correspondence (*teifreichenden Übereinstimmungen*) to the great social productions of art, religion, and philosophy (*der Kunst, der Religion und***

ud

Every analyst will admit that even today this has the sound of a long-obsolete error (*ein längst überwundener Irrtum klingt*). Still, alterations in it became essential because our inquiries advanced from the repressed to the repressing (*als unsere Forschung vom Verdrängten zum Verdrängenden*),[366] from the Object-drives to the 'I.' Decisive here was the introduction of the concept of narcissism; that is, the insight that the 'I' itself is connected with libido (*daß das Ich selbst mit Libido besetz ist*);[367] that the 'I', indeed, is the libido's original home and to a certain extent remains its headquarters (*Hauptquartier bleibe*).[368] This narcissistic libido turns towards objects, and thus becomes object-libido, and it can change back again into narcissistic libido (*narzißtische Libido zurückverwandeln*). The concept of narcissism made it possible to obtain an analytic understanding of the traumatic neuroses and of many of the emotional states (*Affektionen*) bordering on the psychoses, as well as [an analytic understanding of] these themselves (*und diese selbst analytisch zu erfassen*).[369] The interpretation of the transference neuroses (*Übertragungsneurosen*) as attempts of the 'I' to defend itself against sexuality did not have to be given up, but the concept of the libido came into danger (*geriet*). Since the 'I'- drives, too, were libidinal, it appeared inevitable (*unvermeidlich*) for awhile, that we should make libido coincide

---

der Philosophie), but they were also a distortion and caricature of them. It is unclear if and how this relates to art and philosophy, but Freud was explicit on 'religion' being a caricature (*Zerrbild*) of compulsion neurosis.

[366] Note the conceptual and lexical parallelism.

[367] Bk. 6, 404. JS (p. 113) uses the coinage 'cathexis' here, i.e. 'cathected with libido.' JR has 'libido cathects the ego itself'. The term 'cathexis' became standardized in the analytical vocabulary and translations, including the letters. Freud, however, used the simple term for 'possession.' 'Cathexis' (dated, 1922) is from Greek *káthexis*, 'holding,' 'retention,' < *katekhein*, 'to hold fast.' The core idea in the psychoanalytic context is the investing or investment of libidinal energy in a project, person, concept or con cepts.

[368] That the 'I' is the original home of the libido refutes the popular cliché or Freudian soundbite that he reduced everything to sexuality. Logically: if sexuality is everywhere, it cannot be anywhere. As Maurice Merleau-Ponty expressed it, Freud thought sexuality was a symbol of existence, and existence a symbol of sexuality. But Freud also looked for the meaning of the future in the past and the meaning of the past in or toward the future. He was aware of the circular rhythms of life. [This awareness was basic to the Heb. book *Qohelet/Koheleth*; and to various concepts of karma/kamma, unfortunately formulated in terms of before and after lives, rather than within this embodied, lived project.]

[369] Bk. 6, 405. In this sentence, '*Affektionen*' means 'disturbed emotional states'; hence, JS's (p. 113) 'affections' is misleading. JR has 'diseases.' The central text underlying this pericope is *On Narcissim: An Introduction* (1914[c] cited in our fn. 482.

ud

with drive energy (*Triebenergie*) in general, as C. G. Jung had already advocated earlier.[370] Nevertheless, there remained [for me] a certainty for which reasons were not yet established (*noch nicht zu begründende Gewißheit*), that the drives could not all be of the same kind.[371] I took my next step in *Jenseits des Lustprinzips* (1920[g]), when the repetition compulsion and the conservative character of the life-desires first struck my attention (*Wiederholungszwang und der konservative Charakter des Trieblebens zuerst auffiel*). Starting from speculation about the beginning of life and from biological parallels, I drew the conclusion (*zog ich den Schuß*) that besides the drive to preserve living substance (*außer dem Trieb, die lebende Substanz zu erhalten*) and to join it always into larger units (*Einheiten*);[372] there must be present another, contrary drive (*ihm gegensätzlichen, geben*), seeking to dissolve those units and return them to their primeval, inorganic state (*uranfänglichen, anorganischen Zustand zurückzuführen strebe*). Therefore, apart from Eros there is a death-drive (*Todestrieb*); from the concurrent or mutually opposing action (*Zusammen-und Gegeneinanderwirken*)[373] of these two drives the phenomena of life could be explained. Now it was not easy (*Nun war es nicht leicht*) to demonstrate the activity of the supposed death-drive. The manifestations of Eros were striking and noisy enough (*auffällig und*

---

[370] **Freud's 'libido' became Jung's 'life-force' and this is a fair-minded mention of Jung in a short piece of intellectual autobiograhy. Many years earlier, Freud had applied the German terms for 'mysticism' and 'obscurity' to Jung's thought. On Jung and mysticism see Richard Noll, *The Jung Cult. Origins of a Charismatic Movement* (1994). While based on primary sources, the Jung family and 'Jungians' attacked the book and Noll.**

[371] **The phrase 'remained in me' is inserted by JS. It is implied in the text, but not stated.**

[372] **a) Another source for the 'death-drive' (*Todestrieb*) was Goethe's *Faust*. See fn. 583. b) Why a tendency 'to preserve living substance' entails another and contrary instinct that seeks to dissolve those units of living substance is not substantiated, but note Freud's hope that it would prove useful. His footnote: "The opposition which thus emerges between the ceaseless spreading trend of Eros and the general conservative nature of the drives is striking (*auffällig*), and it may become the starting point (*Ausgangspunkt*) for study of further problems."**

[373] **This is an important example of antithetical parallelism. That the phenomena of life can be explained by the concurrent or opposing action of these two drives relies upon a theological causal type of explanation which Freud had rejected in his critique of 'religion'. We should add that in *Jenseits des Lustprinzips (Beyond the Pleasure Principle* (1919-1920[g], *S.E.*, 18, 3-64) he argued that the ruling tendency of psychic life was reduction. He called this tendency the Nirvana-principle and proposed it as one basis for believing in the death-instincts. The terminology here was unfortunate given that thee range of meanings of *nirvāna* in Hindu and Buddhist thought does not include reduction but another mode of consciousness.**

ud

geräuschvoll genug);[374] one could assume that the death-drive operated silently within the living being towards its dissolution, but that naturally was no proof (*daß der Todestrieb stumm im Inneren des Lebewesens an dessen Auflösung arbeite, aber das war natürlich kein Nachweis*). An idea that led further was that a portion of the drive was diverted against the external world and then comes to light as a drive of aggression and destruction (*zur Aggression und Destruktion zum Vorschein komme*).[375] Thus the drive could be forced into the service of Eros, in that the living being was destroying something other than itself, whether animate or inanimate (*Belebtes wie Unbelebtes*).[376] Conversely (*Umgekëhrt*) any restriction of this aggression directed outwards would necessarily increase the self-destruction (*Selbstzerstörung*), which is increasing anyhow (*ohnehin*). At the same time, one can suspect from this example, that both drives seldom—perhaps never—step forth in isolation from one another (*voneinander isoliert auftreten*), but are bound together (*legieren*) in varied, very different proportions, and hence become unrecognizable to our judgment (*unserem Urteil unkenntlich machen*). In sadism, long recognized as a component drive of sexuality (*Partialtrieb der Sexualität bekannten*), we have before us a particularly strong alloy (*Legierung*) of this kind [of alloy] of love striving and the destructive drive (*Liebesstrebens mit dem Destruktionstrieb*);[377] while masochism, its counterpart (*Widerpart*), would be a union (*eine Verbindung*) between destructiveness directed inwards and sexuality,[a union] through which the otherwise imperceptible striving becomes striking and palpable (*durch welche die sonst unwahrnehmbare Strebung eben auffällig und fühlbar wird*).[378]

---

[374] *DUK*, Bk. 6, 405. Note the parallelism of 'striking and noisy.' JS (p. 114) translates '*auffällig*' with 'conspicuous.'

[375] Synonymous parallelism.

[376] Bk. 6, 405. Antithetical parallelism.

[377] Idem. Antithetical parallelism. The '*isoliert*' (v.a.) in the previous sentence was a keyword for Hegel.

[378] a) There seem to be two kinds of union or strong alloy (*Legierung*) here: love and the destructive drive (sadism) and inwardly directed destructiveness and sexuality (masochism). Freud seemed to shy away from the topic of sadism, but his 'A Child is Being Beaten': A Contribution to the Study of the Origin of Sexual Perversions' (1919[e]) in *S.E.*, 17, 175-204) is an important analysis of obsessional neurosis originating in repression of phantasies of being beaten by an adult. In the most important phase, this was by a father. Masochism originates from sadism, which is masochism turned around. The problem with this analysis is that it does confront the difference between actually being beaten and a phantasy of being beaten. Secondly, masochism may be more complex, e.g. in *The*

ud

The assumption of a death or destruction drive has encountered resistance even in analytical circles; I know that there is a frequent inclination rather to ascribe all that is dangerous and hostile (*gefährlich und feindselig gefunden wird*) [379] in love to an original bipolarity in its own essence (*ihres eigenen Wesens zuzuschreiben*). To begin with I had only presented my views as an experiment (*versuchsweise vertreten*), but in the course of time they had such power over me that I can think in no other way.[380] I think (*Ich meine*) they are more theoretically useful than all possible others; they provide that simplification (*Vereinfachung*), without either ignoring or doing violence to the facts (*Vernachlässigung oder Vergewaltigung der Tatsachen her*), [381] that we strive for in scientific work. I know (*Ich erkenne*) that in sadism and masochism we have always seen before us manifestations of the destructive drive (directed outwards and inwards), strongly linked with erotism; but I can no longer understand how we could have overlooked and neglected (*übersehen und versäumen konnten*) the ubiquity of non-erotic aggression and destruction, and can have failed to give it its due place in our explanation of life (*ihr die gebührende Stellung in der Deutung des Lebens einzuräumen*). (Of course, the desire for destruction (*Destruktionssucht*) when turned within, mainly escapes our perception (*Wahrnehmung*) [382] unless colored with erotism

---

Economic Problem of Masochism (1924[c] in *S.E.*, 19, 157-170) Freud distinguished three forms: erotogenic, feminine, moral. The 'feminine' form is based upon an [unacceptable] assumption about 'feminine nature', the erotogenic form is the basis of the other two, and 'moral masochism' has loosened its connection to sexuality. b) Note the near synonymous parallelism of 'striking' and 'palpable'.

[379] Bk. 6, 405. Note the synonymous parallelism in a passage that acknowledges the opposition at the time, e.g. by Ernest Jones, to the theory of a death-drive. Jones is not identified in this passage but he opposed Freud both on this and other concepts: "I differed completely from Freud in many matters…Lamarckism, telepathy, child analysis, lay analysis, the "death instinct," the origin of anxiety…." Ernest Jones, *Life and Work*, Vol. 3, xii. There may be some exaggeration here.

[380] Another example of his style: posit, qualify, retract, and affirm. This and following passages contain valuable intellectual autobiography.

[381] Bk. 6, 406. The implication of 'ignoring or doing violence' to the 'facts' is not convincing because the concept of the death-drive is not the only explanation of sadism and masochism. Also if the death-drive is only a drive toward dissolution how can it have an erotogenic dimension?

[382] Bk. 6, 406. The parenthetical markers are in the Ger. text. JS (p.115) has 'inwards' in italics for '*innen*'. This is textual intrusion. On '*Wahrnehmung*', a keyword in *DUK*, JR has 'perceptions' but '*Wahrnehmung*' is fem. singular. It is translated in *Cassel's German-English Dictionary*, p. 551, as "perception, observation; maintenance; protection". See also Bk. 8, 418.

ud

(*nicht erotisch gefärbt ist*).[383] I remember my own resistence (*Abwehr*) when the idea of a destruction-drive (*Destruktionstriebes*) first entered psychoanalytical literature, and how long it took before I became receptive to it (*empfänglich wurde*). That others show and still show the same rejection (*Ablehnung*), surprises me less. For 'little children when they hear it, do not like it',[384] [that is] when there is talk of the inborn tendency of humans toward 'evil,' aggression and destruction, and so to cruelty [when] mentioned (*erwähnt wird*). God has made them in the image of his own perfection; no one wants to be reminded (*gemahnt werden*) of how difficult it is — in spite of the protestations of Christian Scientists — to reconcile the existence of evil with his omnipotence and all goodness combined (*Allmacht oder seiner Allgüte zu vereinen*).[385] The devil would be the best way out as an excuse for God (*zur Entschuldigung Gottes die beste Auskunft*), in that way he would be playing the same economic, exonerating (*entlastende*) role that the Jew does in the world of Aryan ideals (*wie der Jude in der Welt des arischen Ideals*).[386] But even so one can call God to

---

[383] This is overstated and ignores the close link between severe depression and suicide.

[384] Idem. On the phrase (not under quotes in the text): "*Denn die Kindlein, sie hören es nicht gerne*", Freud cites Goethe's poem, '*Die Ballade vom vertriebenen und heimgekehrten Grafen.*' Freud's next footnote cites *Faust* I. Teil, 3. On the destruction drive of Mephistopheles; he begins, however, with line two and not "*Ich bin der Geist, der stets verneint*"/.

[385] Idem. It seems odd that the Christian Scientists are the only denomination specifically named in this text. [They are also mentioned in *The Future of an Illusion*]. This is probably because of their view of 'evil' as an error or illusion of thought. Freud writes '*oder*' but it should be read as '*und*' because the problem of evil in classical theism was how evil could exist if God were both all-powerful <u>and</u> all-good. This escaped the Mind-only ontological idealism of the Christian Scientists. However, they were not a major representative of the problem of 'God' and the existence of evil in Ancient Near East and Western cultures. That problem derives from the early Church fathers and varied 'gnostic' speculations. JS (p. 116) errs in: 'His all-powerfulness or His all-goodness.' The dilemma only arises within monotheistic traditions because both are predicated of Deity. No choice, no dilemma. For instance, the problem of evil is reconfigured if the goodness of the Deity was infinite but the power of Deity was, in some relevant way, finite. Or if the problem was that of a God of love set in contrast to a creator god or Demiurge, as in Marcion, the 'heretic' (d. *c.* 160 CE).

[386] *DUK*, Bk. 6, 406. a) In this attack on anti-Semitism, Freud subtly shifts from the ontic-theological to the social-economic-historical. As a simplified contextual note: in the 17th-18th centuries, central and western European Jews were barred from almost all professions. They were driven into the roles of suppliers to the various armies, and creditors of the states, and in some cases used as hired tax collectors. They were exploited by power elites and were expelled or robbed when things went wrong. They knew no protection of the person until well into the 18th century. b) One notes the sarcastic analogy

ud

of the devil as an excuse for God and the economic role of Jews in the world of 'Aryan ideals.' Freud also mentioned the Aryan 'illusion' in *The Future of an Illusion.* The term is from the Vedic and Avestan "*arya*" (noble, lord) < * "*aryo-* with * PIE *ar-* "to assemble". Racialist uses began in the 19th century and increased in the 20th century. c) Freud wrote the above passage in 1929 or early 1930, about three years before the National Socialist law of April 6th-7th 1933 restricting civil service jobs to "Aryans" — defined as Germans whose parents and four grandparents were Christians and "members of the white race." [Some linguists still use "Aryan" in a technical sense as referring to a language branch of the Proto-Indo-European family, i.e. "Indo-Aryan."].   d) JS (p. 116) has 'the Aryan ideal', but the term is in the plural. e) There is another attack on anti-Semitism in the discussion of 'the narcissism of small differences' in Bk. 5, 402. f) Freud attributed some of the opposition to psychoanalysis to Judaeophobia. The Nazis banned it as a 'Jewish science' and Freud's books were burned in Berlin, the center of the psychoanalytical movement in the early 1920's, at the end of May 1933. However, credibility is sorely strained by an explanation of anti-Semitism through the constructs of the Oedipal complex, circumcision and castration anxiety, with their 'uncanny impression'. [On the 'uncanny' see '*Das Unheimlicheit*' (1919[h], 'The Uncanny', *S.E.*, 17, 218-252).] The resentment toward 'chosenness' discussed in the late *Der Mann Moses* has more explanatory substance. Given the major motifs in *Der Mann Moses* and the timing of the work (1939) the question of Freud and Jewish self-hate (*selbsthass*) was raised. (The charge of 'self-hate' was also raised about Hannah Arendt after her book on the Eichmann trial.) We don't think the question has any merit. His relationship to Judaism was complex but he always identified himself as Jewish (as did Arendt). g) However, it is possible that Freud may have had a degree of bias toward *Ostjuden.* That attitude was widespread among educated Jewish middle-class German and English speakers (but not true of Sir Moses Haim Montefiore (1784-1885) the British-Jewish philanthropist) and it persisted into the 1980's in the feud between Bruno Kreisky, the first Jewish chancellor of Austria, and Simon Wiesenthal. While Amalie Freud spoke Galician Yiddish in preference to standard High German, her son seemed to downplay Yiddish and often pretended not to know Yiddish words. However, according to Y. H. Yerusalimi in *Freud's Moses* (1991) there are 13 Yiddish words in his correspondence (I don't know how this word-count was obtained). In his autobiographical account (1925) he basically invented German origins ('my father's family were settled for a long time on the Rhine (at Cologne)...'). Then they moved East. But the evidence is mixed. He refused to accept royalties on books translated into Yiddish or modern Hebrew, and in 1897, the year that the anti-Semitic Karl Lueger was elected mayor of Vienna, he joined the B'nai B'rith and resigned membership of other organizations. h) The rise of Judaeophobia did not lead to Zionist identity or Jewish praxis or conversion to Christianity. On the issue of conversion, a fascinating contrast is the experience of Franz Rosenzweig, the German-Jewish philosopher, who was contemplating conversion when he attended a Day of Atonement ceremony in Berlin in 1913 and deeply moved by the experience chose to fully embrace Judaism on ritual and conceptual levels. Freud, however, was proud of his atheism. He was also proud that 'the Jewish people' had kept monotheism alive. This inconsistency, one of many, is not alarming. a) It might be suggested that his intense opposition to 'religion' implies an earlier intense bond. But this is reductive reasoning, and one might suggest to the contrary that his love of figurines of god figures from diverse cultures expressed a 'sublimated' attachment to images of divinity. b) According to his son Martin, Jewish festivals were not celebrated at home. Martha Bernays was much closer to orthodox Jewish practice than her family (there were six children, Martin, Oliver, Ernst, Sophie, Anna, Martha). It has been reported that Martha Bernays would not write on Shabbat, although that may have been out of

ud

account (*Rechenschaft*) for the existence of the devil, just as well for the wickedness which he embodies (*wie für die des Bösen, das er verkörpert*). In view of these difficulties, it is advisable (*ratsam*) for everyone on suitable occasions to bow low to the deep moral nature of humankind (*eine tiefe verbeugung vor der tief sittlichen Natur des Menchen zu machen*), it will help us to be generally liked and much will be forgiven us for it. [387]

The name 'libido' can again be used for the manifestations of the power of Eros (*Kraftäußerungen des Eros*) in order to distinguish them

---

deference to her mother. On the role of power within the family: Freud controlled family habit and religious observance, while his wife managed the household details and protected him from domestic worries. Martha did not like psychoanalysis or allow the children to be asked about it at supper. Apparently she had her way, although Anne followed her father's devotion to *die Sache* (the 'thing' = psychoanalysis). In letters of 1887-1902 to W. Fleiss, I noticed that Freud often mentioned Christmas and Easter but not the Jewish holidays, but according to Y. H. Yerusalimi his letters to Martha reveal a close knowledge of Jewish festivals. For discussion and bibliographical notes, see Yosef Hayim Yerushalmi, *Freud's Moses* (Yale Univ. Press, 1991) and Michael Billig, *Freudian Repression* (Cambridge, 1999), pp. 224-235.

[387] Bk. 6, 406. A powerful example of his sarcastic irony. It is footnoted by a citation and comment on the declamation of Goethe's Mephistopheles in *Faust*, I, Scene 3. His introductory sentence was: "The identification of the principle of evil with the destruction-drive in Goethe's Mephistopheles is exceptionally convincing." "*Denn alles, was entsteht,*

> *Ist wert, daß es zugrunde geht.*
> ....
> *So ist denn alles, was Ihr Sünde,*
> *Zerstorung, kurz das Böse nennt,*
> *Mein eigentliches Element.*"
> [For all things, from the Void
> Called forth , deserve to be destroyed...
>   Thus, all which you as Sin have rated---
>   Destruction, ----aught with Evil blent,-----
>   That is my proper element.]

Then Freud writes: "The Devil himself names as his opponent, not the holy, the good; but the power of nature to create, to multiply life, that is, Eros." Then:

> ....
> "*Der Luft, dem Wasser, wie der Erden*
> *Entwinden tausend Keime sich,*
> *Im Trocknen, Feuchten, Warmen, Kalten!*
> *Hätt' ich mir nicht die Flamme vorbehalten,*
> *Ich hätte nichts Aparts für mich.* "
> [From Water, Earth, and Air unfolding,
> a thousand germs break forth and grow,
> In dry, and wet, and warm, and chilly:
> And had I not the Flame reserved, why, really,
> There's nothing special of my own to show.] (Bayard Taylor's translation)

ud

from the energy of the death-drive (Todestriebs zu sondern). [388] It must be conceded that we have much greater difficulty grasping the last one (letzteren, [i.e. Todestriebs]), we can only guess that it is something in the background of Eros, and evades (*entzieht*) detection unless betrayed by its link to Eros (*durch die Legierung mit dem Eros verraten wird*).[389] It is in sadism, where it [the death-drive] bends the erotic goal in its own sense (*seinem Sinne umbiegt*), and yet fully satisfies the sexual striving, that we succeed in obtaining the clearest insight into its nature and its connection to Eros.[390] But even where it is present without any sexual purpose, in the most blind fury of destructiveness (*blindesten Zerstörungswut*), we cannot fail to recognize that its satisfaction is tied to an extraordinarily high degree of narcissistic pleasure, because the 'I' is presented with fullfillment of its old wish for all-power (*indem sie dem Ich die Erfüllung seiner alten Allmachtswünsche zeigt*). The destruction-drive, moderated and tamed (*Gemäßigt und gebändigt*);[391] and, so to speak, goal-inhibited (*gleichsam zielgehemmt*) must, if directed toward objects, provide the 'I' with the satisfaction of its vital needs (*Lebensbedürfnisse*) and the control over nature. Since the assumption of the existence of this drive rests essentially upon theoretical grounds, one must admit that it is not fully secure from theoretical objections (*Einwendungen nicht voll gesichert ist*). But so it appears to us now, in the present state of our understanding (*gegenwärtigen Stand unserer Einsichten*);[392] future research and reflection (*Forschung*

---

[388] Bk. 6, 407. Freud's footnote 1: "Our present assumption can be roughly expressed in the statement that libido participates in everything, but not everything is libido." This statement counters the cliché that for Freud 'all is sexuality'. It should be in the text.

[389] Note the 'en' assonance: *erraten, entzieht, verraten.*

[390] *DUK*, idem. a) The existence of sexual sadism or the twisting of the death-drive in an erotic way, an insight most fully realized in de Sade's merger of death and the sexual climax, is terribly evident in experience, but it is difficult to understand how there can be a full satisfaction (*voll befriedigt*) of *sexuelle Streben* (sexual striving) in sadistic erotism. There may be sadistic impulses within obsessional neurosis (as in the case of the Rat Man) which produce a sense of guilt, but one doubts that sadism is an innate drive or invariably linked to autoeroticism. It arises only with narcissism. b) Freud found sadism 'puzzling' (*Introductory Lectures*, p. 306) and claimed it was only detected when a link with eroticism was established. This view probably reflects Freud's belief that human beings had an innate tendency toward aggression. c) H. Westerink wrote: "there seem to be no sadists in Freud's published works." He did not do a case study or analyze cases of sadism (*A Dark Trace*, pp. 156-7, and fn. 86).

[391] Note the synonymous conceptual parallelism. Both the destructive-drive and the sexual-drive are subject to goal-inhibition.

[392] Bk. 6, 407. JS (p. 418) has 'knowledge' for '*Einsichten.*'

ud

und Überlegung) will certainly bring decisive clarity (*entscheidende Klarheit bringen*). [393]

In all that follows, I therefore adopt the standpoint that the *aggress*ion tendency is an original, self-dependent (*selbständige*), drive-disposition of human beings (*Triebanlage des Menschen ist*), and I return to my view that in civilization it finds its strongest obstacle (*Hindernis*). At one point in the course of this investigation, I was pushed to the judgment (*Einsicht aufgedrängt*) that culture is a special process which humankind undergoes (*die Menschenheit abläuft*), and we are still under the constraint of that idea (*unter dem Banne dieser Idee*).[394] We may now add that it is a process in service of Eros, whose purpose is to combine single human individuals, later families, then tribes (*Stämme*), peoples (*Völker*),[395] nations (*Nationen*) into a greater unity, the unity of humankind. Why this has to happen, we do not know; that is just the work of Eros (*das sei eben das Werk des Eros*).[396] These collections of men are to be libidinally bound to one another, necessity (*Notwendigkeit*) alone, the advantages of a working community (*Arbeitsgemeinschaft*) will not hold them together. This project of civiliation is set over against man's natural aggression-drive (*natürliche Aggressionstrieb*), the hostility (*Feindseligkeit*) of one against all and all against one. [397] This

---

[393] **Note the complementary conceptual parallelism, and the confidence about impending 'decisive clarity.'**

[394] **Bk. 6, 407. *Triebanlage* ('drive-dispositions') is an important keyword. The passage contains more intellectual autobiography. In this and the following sentence, JS (p. 118) has 'I' for '*wir*.'**

[395] **Idem. Freud used the term '*Volksstamme*' in Bk. 3, p. 390. JS (p. 118) has 'races,' not 'tribes,' for '*Stämme*.' On '*Volk*', "people, nation, tribe, race' soldier, troops…" < MidHG, *volc (k)*, OHG, *folc*; corresponding to Dutch *volk*, OSaz, *folk*, AS, *folc*, English, "folk" < OE, *foc*. * PIE, *pelǝ* 1, "to fill", derivatives include "fill, plenty, folk", etc. '*Volk*' was used by Herder in a patriotic way, revived and heightened in Fichte's lectures of 1807-08.**

[396] **Bk. 6, 407. Change "Eros" to '*Geist*' and this could be Hegel on the unfolding of history as the progressive realization of Mind or Spirit culminating in the great 'Yes.' The primacy of Eros distances Freud's 'greater unity, the unity of mankind' from Kant's image of a 'liberal' and peaceful world order in *Toward Perpetual Peace* (1795), and from the economic-historical dynamics of Marxist thought. Eros, a romantic tradition aesthetic term, adds poetic-philosophical dimension to the narrative, but its teleological role conflicts with Freud's critique of 'religion' and 'providence'.**

[397] **Use of *Kulur* in this passage, with one possible exception, requires 'civilization.' The hostility motif is probably based on Hobbes' distinction of the state of nature from the laws of reason, although those laws are very limited. According to Freud, self-preservation required giving up the rights of nature to avoid "the hostility of one against all and all against one." Freud's image of the social contract connects egoism and altruism through**

Page 104

ud

aggression-drive is the derivative and high representative of the death-drive (*Abkommling und Hauptvertreter des Todestribes*),[398] which we have found next to Eros and which shares world-domination with it (*Weltherrschaft teilt*). And now, I think, the meaning of cultural development is no longer obscure (*Kulturentwicklung nicht mehr dunkel*). It must present us (*muß uns...zeigen*) the struggle between Eros and Death, between the drive of life and the destruction-drive, as it works itself out in the human species (*Menschenart vollzieht*). This conflict is everywhere the essential content of life, and the evolution of civilization (*Kulturentwicklung*) may therefore be plainly described as the struggle for life of the human species (*Lebenskampf der Menschenart*).[399] And our *nurse-maids (Kinderfrauen) wished to appease us about this battle of the giants (*Streit der Giganten*) with their lullaby of heaven ("Eiapopeia vom Himmel!").* [400]

VII

Why do our kin, the animals, have no such cultural struggle (*Kulturkampf*)? Oh, we do not know. Very probably some among them, the bees, the ants, the termites, strove (*gerungen*) for thousands of years before they arrived at the state institutions, the distribution of functions, the restrictions (*Einschränkung*) on the individual, that we wonder at today (*die wie heute bei ihnen bewundern*). It is characteristic of our present condition

---

the benefit that altruism bestows on egoism. The image is at variance with Hegel's image of the momentum and movement of *Geist*, the Marx-Engels historical dialectic, and ethical-noetic traditions, e.g. the Jains, that seek liberation from desire itself.

[398] **Bk. 6, 407. Conceptual lexical parallelism. It is not clear to me how the aggressive drive represents and derives from the death-drive and how the latter shares world-domination with Eros. In terms of academic and library classification, *DUK* would be subsumed under 'psychology of religion and theory of culture.' In this case, the term 'metapsychology' should also be used. In my view, *DUK* seeks scientific status and is a wisdom text, e.g. in the mytho-poetic postulate of Eros and the death-drive.**

[399] **Freud's footnote: "*Wahrscheinlich mit der näheren Bestimmung: wie er sich von einem gewissen, noch zu erratenden Ereignis an gestalten mußte*" was difficult, and I suggest: 'For a closer explanation, we may probably add, how he had to develop (*gestatten mußte*) from a specific still to be discovered event.' [We thank Marion Edlich for help with this sentence.] This 'still to be discovered event' probably refers to our ignorance, comcealed by the lullaby of heaven, of the origins or causality of the struggle for 'world-domination' between Eros and death. Freud's search for 'origins' distracted him from comparative research, and in formal terms the discourse on Eros-Death is as 'religious' as the one the *Kinderfrauen* tell the children.**

[400] **Double quotation marks are in the German. This is a line from H. Heine's poem *Deutschland; Ein Wintermärchen*, Caput I.**

ud

that we say of our own feelings (*Empfindungen*) that we should not consider (*schätzen*) ourselves happy in any of these animal states or any of the roles assigned (*zugeteilten*) within them to individuals.[401] With other animal species it may be that a temporary balance (*zeitweiligen Ausgleich*) has been reached between the influence of the environment (*Umwelt*) and the contending drives within it, and that therefore a cessation of development has occurred (*Stillstand der Entwicklung gekommen sein*). With primal man (*Urmenschen*) it may be that a new thrust of libido stimulated a new struggle of the destructive-drives (*neuer Vorstoß der libido ein neuerliches Sträuben angefacht haben*). There are a great many questions here, to which as yet there is no answer. [402]

Another question is nearer. What means (*Mittel*) does civilization use to restrain the aggression that opposes it (*entgegenstehende Aggression zu hemmen*),[403] to make it harmless, perhaps to remove it (*veilleicht auszuschalten*)? We have already become acquainted with some of these methods, but not yet with the one that appears the most important (anscheinend wichtigste aber noch nicht). We can study this in the history of the development of the individual (*der Entwicklungsgeschichte des einzelnen studieren*).[404] What happens in him (*mit ihm*) to make his desire for aggression harmless (*unschädlich zu machen*)? Something very

---

[401] Bk. 7, 408. Although the issue is obvious, the sentence is methodologically important in that it appeals to the evidence of how people speak about their own condition. It is especially significant because of the objections to psychoanalysis at this time (1929) for lacking a 'public' standard of verification. There was a rigidity of interpretation in certain clinical and literary cases and I suspect that Freud was not open about his clinical mistakes; however, the idea that he invented data to prove his theories is absurd. He generally refused to reduce complex phenomena to a single cause, and insisted on multiple causal factors. It was only in the mid-1940's that psychoanalysts began to confront the experimental and statistical standards of 'academic psychology', and the problem of verification is relative to text, problem, scope. The postulate of an Oedipus complex or of *Kultur* as having an innate erotic impulsion functions on a much higher level of abstraction than with the problems analyzed in *The Psychopathology of Everyday Life* (1901): checking out slips of word and slips of pen, cases of forgetting, and mistakes as "portals of discovery" (J. Joyce).

[402] Idem. JS (p. 120) has 'burst' for '*Sträuben*'. It is a botanical term: 'bunch (of flowers)', and used poetically it has the sense of "strife, struggle, combat, conflict" (*The New Cassel's German Dictionary*, p. 456). Freud raised the 'questions' about 'primal man'; but his male-only focus did not help with an 'answer', i.e. he missed the primary role of women as caregivers.

[403] '*Mittel*' is used often, usually in compounds, e.g. '*Mittelpunkt*'. The keyword '*hemmen*' (v/t) "check, stop, hamper" is used as a noun on p. 417, and as a modifier on p. 418.

[404] Cf. the whole-part methodology in this passage with Plato's method in the *Republic*.

ud

remarkable (*sehr Merkwürdiges*) that we would not have have quessed, but yet is so obvious (*das doch so naheliegt*). Aggression is introjected, internalized (*introjiziert, verinnerlicht*), essentially returned to where it came from (*zurückgeschickt*), thus turned against his own 'I' (*also gegen das eigene Ich gewendet*).[405] There it becomes taken over by a part of the 'I' (*einem Anteil des Ichs übernommen*), which sets itself over against the rest of the 'I' as Über-Ich, and which now in the form of 'conscience' ('*Gewissenheit*') is ready to practice the same harsh aggression (*strenge Aggressionsbereitschaft ausübt*) which the 'I' would have liked to satisfy upon other, foreign individuals. We call the tension (*Spannung*) between the harsh Über-Ich and the 'I' that is subjected to it (*dem ihm unterworfenen Ich*) the consciousness of guilt (*Schuldbewußtsein*); it expresses itself as a need for punishment (*Strafbedürfnis*). Civilisation, therefore, obtains mastery over the dangerous lust for aggression of the individual (*Aggressionslust des Individuums*) by weakening and disarming it (*schwächt, entwaffnet*) and through an authority (*Instanz*) within it, to watch over it, like a garrison in an occupied city (*wie durch eine Besatzung in der eroberten Stadt, überwachen läßt*). [406]

---

[405] **The use of maculine pronouns correlates with a male-dominated view of evolution. His footnote refers to "*Die Strukture der psychischen Persönlichkeit*" in the first volume of *Freud ZB* (*der Werkausgabe*), this section includes *Das Ich und das Es* and other works, pp. 369-429.**

[406] **Bk. 7, 408. a) This beautiful and lyrical passage is a key to his psychoanalytical theory of *Kultur*. The metaphor of 'garrison in an occupied city' is brillant. In this important pericope, '*Kultur*' should be understood as 'civilisation.' b)The analysis of conscience and guilt, which Freud continues in the next section, invites comparison with Heidegger's analysis in *Sein und Zeit* (1927). We have found no evidence of connection but Freud probably knew of Heidegger through Ludwig Binswanger. Freud and Binswanger were close friends and read each other's works, and Binswanger read Heidegger and met him in 1929.   b) On the problem of conscience, Heidegger was not operating on what he considered a 'psychological' level, a level which he regarded as derivative. Hence there is no connection with Freud's 'need for punishment.' Heidegger attempted an ontological analysis of conscience and the question of guilt (*Schuld*) and he did not generalize conscience beyond the sphere of everydayness. Hence it remained almost monadic or certainly not dialogical. The motifs of guilt and conscience, urge and care and repression, were important for Freud and Heidegger, but they confronted them on very different dimensions. In Freud's analysis, desire/drive and repression were interconnected. Conscience was connected to an ideal of the "*Ich*" (ego), constructed because of an unwillingness to forgo the narcissistic satisfactions of infancy, and it was related to the *Über-Ich's* process of internalizing external aggression. That development turns the *Über-Ich* into a functional equivalent, without the correlative institutional structures, of the confessional and penitential structures of the Catholic Christian faiths. '*Schuld*' for Heidegger is 'lack' (*Mangel*), lack with the sense of debt as something owed. This analysis**

ud

The analyst (*der Analytiker*) thinks differently than other psychologists about the origin of the feeling of guilt; but even he does not find it easy to give an account of it (*darüber Rechenschaft zu geben*). At first, if one asks how someone came to have a sense of guilt we receive an answer which one cannot oppose (*nicht widersprechen kann*): one feels guilty (pious people say: sinful) if one has done something that one recognizes as 'evil' ("*böse*").[407] But then one notices how little this answer gives us. Perhaps after some hesitation (*Schwanken*) one should add that even when *someone* has not actually done the evil thing, but only recognized an intention to do it, he may regard himself as guilty, and then the question arises of why the intention becomes regarded as equal to the doing (*die Absicht der Ausführung gleichgeachet wird*).[408] But both cases presuppose that one already recognizes that what is evil is bad, is something not to be carried out. How does one come to this decision (*Entscheidung*)? One may reject the existence of an original, as it were natural, capacity to distinguish good and evil (*sozusagen natürliches Unterscheidungsvermögen für Gut und*

---

of guilt is on an ontological level. It does not focus on day-to-day guilt as indebtedness or how an *Über-Ich* subordinates an 'I' (ego). Hence, being guilty for Heidegger is an ontological condition correlative to our status as thrown beings (*Geworfenheit*). See SZ, section 58: *Anrufverstehen und Schuld* (Understanding the Summons and Guilt), and see David B. Griffiths, *The Keywords of Martin Heidegger A Philosophical-Lexical Analysis of 'Sein und Zeit'* (The Edwin Mellen Press, 2006). c) Feud used the Gernan for 'sense of guilt' and 'consciousness of guilt' and they are not identical (despite JS's translation). Neither of them make the crucial distinction between authentic guilt in terms of a trans-cultural right-wrong standard, and guilt as unconscious psychic processes and neurotic formations. Freud did write, however, that ethics was 'a therapeutic attempt' to counter the inclination toward violence (Bk. 8). The idea that remorse (*Reue*) differs from a 'sense of guilt' because remorse relates to a past deed might be formulated to suggest the distinction between authentic and neurotic guilt. But, and we are in a murky circle here, because remorse presupposed conscience it is of no help in discovering the origin of conscience (Bk. 7).

[407] Bk. 7, 408. In this passage Freud comes close to an intuitionist theory of ethics, but he then slips away from it by discussing intention versus doing, and finally rejects any original capacity to distinguish good and evil (see the 2 footnotes following). b) This is one of the two cases in *DUK* where he distinguished the 'analyst' from the psychologist. The distinction may date to 1898 when he wrote W. Fliess that psychoanalysis 'went behind' the consciousness studied by psychology. c) The double quotation marks and lower case are in the German.

[408] On 'intention' as 'equal to the doing' or 'what he wills to do, that he also can do', see Kant's *Kritik der praktischen Vernunft*, I. 37. But as the sentences following show, Freud rejected Kant's view that moral rules, as distinct from maxims and precepts, are based only on practical reason, e.g. Freud says that 'external influence' determines 'what is called good and evil.' d) JS puts 'done' and 'intention' in italics.

ud

Böse). What is evil is often not injurious or dangerous (*Schädliche oder Gefährliche*) to the 'I', on the contrary it is ready to be desirable and enjoyable (*erwünscht ist, ihm Vergnügen bereitet*).[409] An external influence is shown here, and this determines what is called good and evil. As a person's own experiences (*eigene Empfindung*) would not have led him along this path, he must have had a motive to submit to this external influence (*fremden Einfluß zu unterwerfen*). It is easy to discover this in his helplessness and dependence on others (*von anderen leicht zu entdecken*), and it can be best designated as anxiety before the loss of love (*als Angst vor dem Liebsverlust bezeichnet werden*).[410] Loss of the love of others, on whom he is dependent, is also the loss of protection from many dangers, above all the danger that this stronger person (*dieser Übermachtige*) will demonstrate his superiority in the form of punishment (*der Bestrafung seine Überlegenheit erweist*). Therefore, at the beginning, evil is that which threatens one with the loss of love; on account of anxiety of that loss, one must avoid it (*aus Angst vor diesem Verlust muß man es vermeiden*). Therefore, it makes little difference if one has already done the evil or only intends to do it (*oder es erst tun will*); in both cases the danger only happens if the authority discovers it, and the authority would behave in the same way in either case. [411]

One calls this condition (*Zustand*) a 'bad conscience' ("*schlechtes Gewissen*"), but essentially it does not deserve this name; because at this

---

[409] a)Two sets of conceptual pairs. b) Freud may be correct in denying the existence of an innate moral capacity, or that we know moral truths directly rather than through inference based on experience; however, his comments on what is 'injurious or dangerous' to the 'I' confuses the distinction between 'evil' (*das Böse*) and well-being (*das Wohl*). c) The point about 'external influence' is relevant to the variety and range of social-historical influences; but these are not fixed facts in the sense that they cannot and should not be changed.

[410] a) The keyword '*Emfindung*' is often used in compounds, e.g. '*Emfindungsleben.*' Note the synonymous parallelism of "*Hiflosigkeit und Abhängigkeit.*" b) On the Kant-Freud point: the statement that 'evil' at the beginning is what threatens one with the loss of love gives priority to a psychological image of the good over a moral principle to which any rational agent is committed to by virtue of her/his autonomy. Freud did not work out the relationship between the good and the right as fairness. Instead he universalized a psychological image of love and this led in Bk. 4 to his splendidly hysterical attack on 'univeral love' as a form of injustice.

[411] Bk. 7, 409. By Kant's standard of universalizability, this image of 'evil' is totally inadequate. b) '(T)he authority' (*Autoritäst*) is not in the last clause, but indicated by '*diese*.' c) JS (p. 123) breaks up both of these sentences into two, and renders '*wenn*' as 'if and when.'

ud

stage the consciousness of guilt is obviously only anxiety of loss of love, 'social' anxiety (*"soziale" Angst*). [412] With small children it cannot be any other way, but also in many adults it has only changed in that the larger community has taken the place of the father or both parents. As a result, such people allow (*gestatten*) themselves regularly to do any evil thing which promises them enjoyment, as long as they are certain that the authority will not know about it or hold it against them; and their anxiety is only a concern about discovery (*und ihre Angst gilt allein der Entdeckung*). [413] Contemporary society has to give an account in general (*im allgemeinen zu rechnen*) of this condition.

A great change happens only when the authority (*Aufrichtigkeit*) is internalized (*verinnerlicht wird*) through the establishment of an *Über-Ichs*. With it, the phenomena of conscience then reach a higher stage (*Gewissensphänomene auf eine neue Stufe gehoben*), basically one should only now speak of conscience and guilt-feeling (*Gewissen und Schuldgefühl sprechen*). [414] Now the anxiety of being found out falls away (*entfällt auch die Angst vor dem Entdecktwerden*); moreover, the distinction between doing evil and willing to do it disappears completely (*vollends der Unterschied zwischen Böses tun und Böses wollen*), because nothing, not even thoughts, can be hidden from the *Über-Ich*. The real seriousness of the

---

[412] **Idem. a) JS (idem) has 'state of mind' for '*Zustand*', a key word in *DUK*. b) The German for 'bad conscience' and 'social' have double quotation marks. c) This use of 'social anxiety' is more complex than the usage in *Massenpsychologie und Ich-Analyse* (Vienna, 1921; translated by James Strachey as *Group Psychology and Analysis of the Ego*): "It has long been our contention that "dread of society" (*soziale Angst*) is the essence of what is called conscience." The phrase 'social anxiety' in this more general sense is integral to the current psychiatric vocabulary.**

[413] **Bk. 7, 409 Freud's footnote 1: "One thinks of Rousseau's mandarin." The standard reference of the term 'mandarin' (< Sanskrit, 'counsellor') is to 'state functionary'. I could not find the reference in Rousseau. Freud is probably repeating the widespread saying "*tuer mon mandarin*" attributed to H. de Balzac in his novel *Le Père Goriot* (1834-5). The saying was based on a dialogue in that novel, and he may have obtained the reference from Chateaubriand's *Genius of Christianity* (*Gènie du christianisme*). Freud was fond of Balzac and according to P. Gay, Balzac's *La Peau de chagrin* (1831) was the last book he read.**

[414] **Idem. Synonymous parallelism. JS (idem) divides this into two sentences. b) Freud's footnote 2 reads: "Of this summary description, people of discernment will recognize and take account the fact that in reality these sharply delimited events occur by slow transitions, and that it is not only a question of the existence of a *Über-Ich* alone, but of its degree of strength and range of influence (*relative Stärke und Einflußsphäre*). All that has been said until now about conscience and guilt is, indeed, common knowledge and almost undisputed (*unbestritten*)".**

ud

situation is anyway past (*allerdings vergangen*) because the new authority of the *Über-Ich* has no motive that we know of for ill-treating the 'I', with which it is intimately bound (*das Ich, mit dem es innig zusamengehört zu mißhandeln*).[415] But genetic influence (*Einfluß der Genese*), which leads to the survival of the past and [has been] overcome (*das Vergangene und Überwundene weiterleben läßt*),[416] manifests itself in the fact that fundamentally things remain as they were at the beginning (*daß es im Grunde so bleibt, wie es zu Anfang war*).[417] The *Über-Ich* torments the sinful (*sündige*) 'I' with the same feeling of anxiety and watches for opportunities (*lauert auf Gelegenheiten*) of getting it punished by the outside world.

At this second stage of development, the conscience shows a peculiarity (*zeigt das Gewissen eine Eigentümlichkeit*) absent from the first stage and which is now no longer easy to explain. Indeed, the more virtuous a man is (*je tugendhafter der Mensch ist*), the more severe and suspicious his behaviour, so that ultimately those who have carried holiness (*Heiligkeit*) the furthest, reproach themselves with the worst accusation of sinfulness (*sich der ärgsten Sündhaftigkeit beschuldigen*).[418] Virtue forfeits part of its portion of promised reward; the accomodating and chaste 'I' (*das gefügige und enthaltsame Ich*) does not enjoy the trust of its mentor, and

---

[415] Bk. 7, 410. The 'hidden' motif recalls Montaigne's essay "On Conscience." Note the antithetical parallelism of 'doing evil' and 'willing to do it', and the Hegelian style of 'falls away' and 'disappears'. JS (pp. 123-4) merges this sentence with the one following.

[416] Idem. a) This phrase, note the parallelism, is obscure. b) The determinism implied undercuts a philosophical justification for the clinical practice of freeing individuals from trauma and severe neurosis.

[417] Idem. Hence, while the *Über-Ich* has no motive for hurting the 'I', it does so because of the genetic push to keep things as they were. b) Freud may be using '*Grund*' in the sense of 'a principle of sufficient reason', as in Leibniz. However, if so, the 'reason' is insufficient, and incompatible with Freud's image of reason as "restless and disquiet" (Hume). '*Grund*' has several meanings, as used by German mystical theologians it can be dated to around 1400. Heidegger often used it centuries later. c) That 'things remain as they were at the beginning' might suggest Nietzsche's idea of eternal return; however, Freud's postulate of a death-drive as return to an original quietude is not a dynamic concept of recurrence.

[418] This generalization has a very restricted range. It might apply to the early Christian centuries but not to the Catholic form of humanism in the Renaissance period, or to the Protestant Reformers. It does not apply at all to classical Judaism, or to the Buddhist and Jaina traditions which function without creationist models with their images of sin and salvation. The correlation of 'holiness' with 'accusation' relates to the more extreme ascetic traditions within Catholic traditions. But ascetic 'reproach' was not an end in itself, it was preparation for union with the Deity. It is also odd that Freud adopts the terminology which he earlier identified with the 'pious.'

ud

seeks in vain, it would seem, to acquire it.[419] The objection will be made at once: these are already prepared artificial difficulties (*das seien künstlich zurechtgemachte Schwierigkeiten*).[420] The stricter and more vigilant conscience (*strengere und wachsamere Gewissen*) is just the characteristic trait of the moral person (*kennzeichnende Zug des sittlichen Menschen*), and when the saints call themselves sinners (*Heiligen sich für Sünder ausgeben*), they are not so wrong (*Unrecht*) considering the temptations to satisfaction of desire (*Versuchungen zur Triebbefriedigung*) that they are exposed to in a high degree;[421] as it is known that temptations are only increased by constant frustrations (*Versagen nur wachsen*), whereas an occasional satisfaction of them reduces them, at least temporarily (*zeitweilig nachlassen*). The field of ethics, so full of problems, presents us with another fact (*eine andere Tatsache*) namely that bad-luck (*Mißgeschick*), that is, external frustration, greatly enhances the power of the conscience in the *Über-Ich* (*die Macht des Gewissens im Über-Ich so sehr fördert*).[422] So long as things go well with a person, his conscience is gentle and lets the 'I' do all kinds of things, but when unhappiness comes upon him (*Unglück getroffen hat*) he contemplates himself (*er Einkehr in sich*), acknowledges his sinfulness, increases the demands of his conscience, imposes abstinences (*Enthaltungen*) on himself and punishes himself through penances (*Bußen*).[423] Whole peoples (*Ganze Völker*)[424] have

---

[419] **Note the conceptually reinforcing parallelism.**

[420] **Bk. 7, 410. '*einzuwenden*' (ir. v. a). '*Einwand*' (m. noun) and plural '*Einwendungen*' occur more often. JS (p. 124) joins this sentence with the long sentence following.**

[421] **Idem. a) Examples would include the later writings of Tolstoy and Mahātma Gandhi's dharma of nonviolence or *Satyāgraha* (Sanskrit, lit.: 'truth-holding'). The distinction implicit here between the 'I' and a moral self (*sittlichen Menschen*) which has a *Gewissen* (conscience) is compatible with what Freud called 'the field of ethics' (*der Gebiets der Ethik*). However, Freud did not develop the distinction, inherently ambiguous, probably because of his quantitative view of frustration and satisfaction. b) The role of adult conscience, within the *Über-Ich,* is the internalization of external authority and socially given norms of normalization. As the 'I' has no original unity the internalization may undercut or impede its status as a moral self. But if the 'I' becomes reasonably centered it can push back against the force of external authority internalized by the *Über-Ich*. This allows the 'I', with its fluid and porous boundaries, the minimal degree of autonomy for ethical status. c) Note the synonymous parallelism. JS (idem) cuts the sentence short.**

[422] **Conceding this role to 'bad luck' implies an open universe, but it is not totally open because of the role of genetic influence (*Einfluß der Genese*). However, genetic influence must be overcome to some extent or things will remain as they were at the beginning (*wie es zu Anfang war*).**

[423] **Idem. Freud's footnote 1. "The increase of morality as a result of bad-luck was shown**

ud

behaved in this way and still do. But this is easily explained by the original infantile stage of conscience, which is not given up after the introjection into the *Über-Ich*, but persists alongside and behind it (*sondern neben und hinter ihr fortbesteht*). Fate (*Schicksal*) is regarded as a substitute for parental agency (*Ersatz der Elterninstanz angesehen*), [425] if one has misfortune (*Unglück*) it means that he is no longer loved by this highest power (*höchsten Macht*); and threatened by this loss of love, he bows (*beugt*) once more to the parental representative (*Elternvertretung*) in the *Über-Ich*, which in days of happiness he wished to neglect (*vernachlässigen wollte*).[426] This becomes especially clear where fate is recognized in the strictly religious sense as only the expression of the divine will (*Schicksal nur den Ausdruck des göttlichen Willens erkennt*).[427] The people (*Volk*) of Israel had believed themselves to be the favorite child, and when the great Father threw upon them misfortune after misfortune (*Unglück nach Unglück*) [428] they were never wavering (*irre*) in their belief in his relationship or doubted God's power and justice (*Macht und*

---

by Mark Twain in a delightful little story *The First Melon I Ever Stole*. This first melon happened to be unripe. I heard Mark Twain tell this little story himself. After he gave out the title, he stopped and asked himself as if in doubt: '*Was it the first?*' With it, everything had been said. The first had not been the only one." [The last sentence was added in 1931. Freud heard Twain in Vienna].

[424] Bk. 7, 410. Two comments: the term '*Volk*' derives conceptually from '*demos*', '*populist*', and later '*natio*', and it has a meaning range from 'people' to 'nation' to the general distinction of us-versus-them. By Freud's maturity, or even by 1873 in Bismarck's address to the *Reichstag*, it had become politicized. Second: that 'entire peoples have behaved this way and still do' is attributed to the persistence of the 'original infantile stage of conscience.' This stage is not given up after its introjection into the *Über-Ich*. This broad generalization may reflect the neurological and biological reductionism of SF's 1895 *Project*, but his focus now is on the infantile stage as anxiety over the loss of love created by *Üngluck* or misfortune.

[425] Idem. '*Ersatz*' < *ersetzen* 'to replace, substitute.' As of 1875 and 1892, it (adj. and noun) was a permanent English loan word, see Pfeffer and Cannon, *German Loanwords in English* (Cambridge, 1994), p. 182. I thank R. Britto for the loan of this book.

[426] Bk. 7, pp. 410-11. a) The comments on 'fate', especially in connection with the concept of developmental stages, implies a weak form of determinism. In ordinary language usage, 'fate' often functions as a substitute term for Divine causality. b) According to Freud, the development of the individual recapitulates that of the culture (ontogeny recapitulates phylogeny). (See note below).

[427] Bk. 7. 411. Freud distinguished secular and religious uses of 'fate' (*Schicksal*). The use of 'fate' expresses one's attitude toward past and future, freedom and contingency. See Wittgenstein on 'the use of the word fate' in his *Vermischte Bemerkungen* (1977), translated as *Culture and Value* (1980), p. 61 and 61e.

[428] Synonymous parallelism.

ud

Gerechtigkeit);[429] but produced the prophets, who held up their sinfulness and produced out of their sense of guilt the overly strict religious rules of their priestly religion (*die überstrengen Vorschriften* [430] *seiner Priesterreligion*). It is remarkable how differently a primitive person (*der Primitive*) behaves! If he has met with misfortune, there is no guilt, rather he blames his fetish (*Fetisch*) who obviously has not done its duty (*Schuldigkeit*) and he thrashes it instead of punishing himself. [431]

Hence we recognize two sources of the feeling of guilt: one from the anxiety before authority, and the other, later on, from anxiety toward the *Über-Ich*. The first insists upon a renunciation (*verzichten*) of satisfactions

---

[429] **Biblically resonant complementary conceptual parallelism.**

[430] **Bk.7, 411. JS (p. 126) has 'commandments', but that requires '*das Gebote*'. The whole sentence (JS breaks it in two) requires 'religious rule'. A translation of this sentence into late Hebrew would probably use *hok* for *Vorschrift*, although in Psalms 74: 11 *hok* likely means 'bosom'. In other passages, *Vorschrift* (precept) is in apposition to *Gebot* (commandment). In this sentence, Freud probably did not have the Hebrew words in mind, but he would have known the difference between the specific rules of the Priestly code and the larger meaning range of *mitzvah* as interpersonal command. I thank M. Zaitzow for comment on this point.**

[431] **a) On the use of '*Primitive*' and '*primitiven*', see our Index. b) Freud's scattered comments on 'religion' in *Das Unbehagen* should be read along with *Der Mann Moses* (1939), the comments on latency and the return of the repressed in *Totem und Tabu* (1913), the very speculative claim in *Das Ich und das Es* (1923) that monotheistic religions are founded upon the imprint of a "father of personal prehistory," and the *The Future of an Illusion* (1927). Freud's critique of religion has recently won some favor in pro-atheist writings by R. Dawkins (1996), S. Harris (2004), C. Hitchens (2007), and D. C. Dennett (1995). Because these writers tend to identify complex religious traditions with mistaken propositions, one is reminded of the Yiddish saying "*Ateistn, zeit nisht fanatiker*" ('Atheists, do not be fanatics'). [In a different context, that saying is quoted by Yerusalemi (1991, p. 68.)] The writers mentioned do not agree on several points, but they all consider naturalistic and empirically based explanations superior to revelatory and intuitive ones. David Hume, whom Freud does not acknowledge, wrote some of the master texts behind this discourse. As mentioned before, Freud viewed 'religion' and 'science' as opposites. In *The Future of an Illusion* (1927) he wrote: "*Nein, unser Wissenschaft ist keine Illusion. Eine Illusion aber wäre es zu glauben, daß wir anderswoher bekommen könnten, was sie uns nicht geben kann*" ('No, science is no illusion. But it would be an illusion to suppose that we can get what it offers anywhere else'.) *Wissenschaft* was incompatible with undignified organized 'religion' and with 'spiritual' convictions like the 'oceanic feeling.' Freud began the 20th century by situating his own dreams and his analysis of the dreams of others within his view of psychoanalytical *Wissenschaft*. The value of that project remains, but so do conceptual problems with its method and basic concepts. There is little to no check on the reliability of the data assembled by a case study method. That method concealed the identity of the analysand, e.g. Little Hans was actually Herbert, and there is a spatial and mechanical image of energy and 'mind'. There are also the overgeneralized ideas on castration, penis envy, the Oedipus complex, the 'original infantile stage of conscience', and so forth.**

ud

of desire; the second, over and above this, presses for punishment because the continuation of forbidden wishes cannot be hidden (*nicht verbergen kann*) from the *Über-Ich*. [432] We have also learned (*gehört*) how the strictness of the *Über-Ich,* and thus the demands of conscience can be understood (*verstehen kann*). It is simply a continuation of the severity of the outside authority, which it has ousted and in part replaced.[433] We now see in what relationship the renunciation of desire has to the consciousness of guilt (*in welcher Beziehung der Triebverzicht zum Schuldbewußtsein steht*). Originally, indeed, renunciation of desire was the result of anxiety toward an external authority; in order not to lose its love one renounced one's satisfactions. If one has carried out this renunication; one is, so to speak, free of it, no feeling of guilt should remain (*quitt, es sollte kein Schuldgefühl erübrigen*). But with anxiety before the *Über-Ich* the case is different. Here the renunciation of desire is not enough because the wish still exists (*denn der Wunsch bleibt bestehend*) and cannot be concealed from the *Über-Ich*. Hence, in spite of the resulting renunciation a feeling of guilt comes about and this is a great economic disadvantage in the construction of an *Über-Ich,* or one could say, the formation of the conscience (*der Gewissensbildung*). Drive renunciation (*Triebverzicht*) now no longer has a fully liberating effect, virtuous abstinence (*Enthaltung*) is no longer rewarded with the security of love because a threatened external unhappiness—loss of love and punishment on the part of the outside authority—has been exchanged (*eingetauscht*) for a lasting inner unhappiness, the tension of the consciousness of guilt. [434]

These interrelations are so complicated and at the same time so important, that in spite of the danger of repetition, I want to handle them

---

[432] **The belief that culture requires the renuniciation of the drives is basic to the text. Complete renunciation as pure will-less contemplation was not possible; nor, unlike the ancient Jains, was it desirable. Freud also rejected any total affirmation of desire and drives and he was shocked by W. Reich (1897-1957), one of his most brillant students, who identified fulfillment with orgasmic fulfillment, wrote two influential books, became somewhat unbalanced, was persecuted and died in a US federal prison.**
[433] **Bk. 7, 411, Bk. 7: *"die von ihr abgelöst und teilweise ersetzt wird...."* Note how Freud's structure of the tripartite mind has transferred traditional religious functions to another dimension, e.g. the *Über-Ich* plays the role of God as 'searcher' of the 'wicked heart'.**
[434] **Idem. a) Freud's analysis of a 'lasting inner unhappiness' differs from classical virtue theory and Aristotle's perspective on 'happiness'. It also differs from the consequentialism of J. Bentham and John S. Mill. b) JS (p. 127) has 'instinctual renunciation' for *Triebverzicht*, and he breaks the sentence in two.**

ud

from yet another aspect (*noch von anderer Seite angreifen möchte*). The chronological sequence would then be: at first the renunciation of drive (*Triebverzicht*) owing to anxiety about aggression by the external authority—this is of course (*ja*) tantamount to anxiety of the loss of love, for love is a protection against this aggression of punishment (*Aggression der Strafe*)—, after that comes the formation of an inner authority (*der inneren Autorität*), and renunciation of desire because of anxiety toward it, that is, anxiety of conscience (*Triebverzicht infolge der Angst vor ihr, Gewissensangst*).[435] In the second situation, evil acts and evil intentions [are] equated (*Gleichwertung*), and from here [there is] consciousness of guilt, need of punishment (*daher Schuldbewußtsein, Strafbedürfnis*). The aggressiveness of conscience conserves (*konserviert*) the aggression of authority.[436] Thus far, things have become completely clear; but where does this leave space (*aber wo bleibt Raum*) for the reinforcing (*verstärkenden*) influence of misfortune (of renunciation imposed from the outside),[437] and for the extraordinary strictness of the conscience in the best and most agreeable [people] (*bei den Besten und Fügsamsten*)? [438] We have already explained both these particularities of conscience, but an unexplained residue remains because these explanations do not reach the foundation (*nicht bis zum Grunde reichen*). And here at last an idea comes in, which absolutely belongs to psychoanalysis, and is foreign to ordinary human thinking (*und dem gewöhnlichen Denken der Menschen fremd ist*). It is of a kind which enables us to understand why the subject must appear so muddled and obscure (*der Gegenstand so verworren und undurchsichtig erscheinen mußte*). Namely, it tells us that conscience at first (more correctly: the anxiety that later became conscience)[439] is the cause of the renunciation of desire, but that later the connection was reversed. Every renunication of desire now becomes a dynamic source of conscience, every new renunciation increases its severity and intolerance (*Strenge und*

---

[435] Bk. 7, 411. JS (p. 128) breaks the sentence up, puts one phrase in brackets, 'external' and 'internal' in italics, and has 'fear' for '*Angst*'.
[436] Idem. a) Freud talks here as if 'conscience' were an ahistorical, atemporal entity. b) JS (idem) has 'keeps up' for *konserviert* (tr.), and 'aggressiveness' for *Aggression*.
[437] The parenthetical marks are in the German text.
[438] Bk. 7, 412. Observe the synonymous parallelism.
[439] The parenthetical marks are in the German.

ud

Intoleranz),[440] and if we could only bring it into better harmony with what we already know about the history of the origin of conscience (*Entstehungsgeschichte des Gewissens*) we would be tempted to defend the paradoxical proposition (*Satz*): conscience is the result of renunciation of desire: or that renunciation of desire (imposed from the outside) creates conscience, which then demands further renunciation of desire (*das dann weiteren Triebverzicht fordert*).

The contradiction (*Widerspruch*) between this assertion and our accepted (*gegebene*) knowledge about the origin of conscience is essentially not so great, and we see a way of reducing it further. In order to make our description (*Darstellung*) easier, we take as our example the aggressive drive, and assume that it always acts in this connection [the origin of conscience] as a renunciation of aggression. Naturally, this should only be taken as a temporary hypothesis (*vorläufige Annahme sein*). The effect of the renunciation of desire on the conscience then is as follows (*geht dann so vor sich*): every part of aggression whose satisfaction the subject gives up is taken over by the *Über-Ich* (*übernommen wird*) and this aggression (against the 'I') [is] increased (*steigert*). This is not in accord with the view that the original aggressiveness of conscience is a continuation of the strictness of the external authority, and therefore has nothing to do with renunciation (*also mit Verzicht nichts zu tun hat*). This discrepancy (*Unstimmigkeit*) declines (*Schwinden*)[441] if we assume a different development for this first installment (*ausstattung*) of the aggression of the *Über-Ich*. The child must develop a considerable amount of aggression against the authority which prevents him from the first, but

---

[440] a) The later writings and actions of Tolstoy and the writings and personal addictions of Dostoevsky exemplify how new renunciation of desire increases the severity of conscience. In 1928, Freud wrote a study of *Dostoevsky and Parricide* (*S.E.*, 21, 175-196). He loved *The Brothers Karamazov,* and he thought Dostoevsky was a fascinatingly neurotic Russian Christian. b) Note the near-synonymous parallelism.

[b] *DUK,* Bk. 7, 412.   a) The parenthetical marks are in the German text.   b) This analysis of conscience, if I understand it, may apply to the socialization of handy rules and social norms but it is not adequate to conscience as moral agency which often resists the pressures of dominant groups and governing elites. c) The sentence is long and complex. JS (p. 128-9 divides it into two and ignores Freud's semantic markers.
[441] The n. noun '*Schwinden*' means "shrinking, shrinkage; drying up..." JS (p. 129) has 'removed.'

ud

not insignificant, satisfactions, regardless of the kind of desire renunciation (*Triebentsagungen*) demanded. The child is forced (*notgedrungen*) to renounce the satisfaction of this revengeful aggression. He is helped out of this difficult economic situation by the means (*Wege*) of well-known mechanisms: through identification (*durch Identifizierung*) he takes the unattackable authority into himself, the authority now becomes his *Über-Ich* and comes into (*gerät*) all the possession (*Besitz*) which a child would have liked to exercise against it. The 'I' of the child must acquiesce in (*begnügen*) the unhappy role of the humiliating (*erniedrigten*) authority—the father. [442] As so often, the situation here has been reversed (*Umkehrung*). "If I were the father and you the child, I would treat you badly." The relationship between the *Über-Ich* and the 'I' is a return, distorted by a wish, of the real relationships between the 'I,' still undivided, and an external object. That is also typical (*Auch das ist typisch*). But the essential difference is that the original strictness of the *Über-Ich* does not represent—or not so much—the severity which one has experienced from or expected (*zumutet*) from it [the object], rather it represents one's own aggression toward it. If that proves correct (*zutrifft*), one can really assert that conscience arises in the beginning through the suppression of an aggression (*einer Aggression*) and later becomes stronger through new suppressions of the same kind (*durch neue solche Unterdrückungen*). [443]

Which of these two conceptions is correct? The earlier one which genetically appeared incontestable (*genetisch so unanfechtbar erschien*), or the newer one which rounds off (*abrundet*) the theory in such a welcome way? Obviously, and also by the evidence of direct observations (*direkten Beobachtung*) they are both justified; they do not contradict each other (*sie widerstreiten einander nicht*), and even come together at one point, because the child's revengeful aggression will in part be determined by the degree of punitive aggression which he expects from his father. But experience teaches us (*Die Erfahrung aber lehrt*) that the strictness of the Über-Ich which a child develops corresponds in no way to the severity of treatment which he has himself experienced or met with (*die es selbst erfahren hat,*

---

[442] **Bk. 7, 412. JS (p. 130) and JR add a final clausal gloss on '*Vater*': 'who has thus been degraded.' The German text does not have this clause.**
[443] **Bk. 7, 413. JS (idem) translates '*Aggression*' (f. –*en*) with 'aggressiveness' = *Aggressivität*, and in the sentence following has 'aggressive impulse' for "*einer Aggression*". In *DUK*, Freud used '*aggressiven*' to modify *Triebe*; but, as far as I know, only on p. 419.**

ud

wiedergibt).⁴⁴⁴ It [the severity of the Über-Ich] appears independent of the treatment of it (*unabhängig von ihr*), a child brought up very leniently (*sehr milder Erziehung*) can acquire a very strict conscience. But it would also be incorrect to exaggerate this independence (*diese Unabhängigkeit übertrieben*), it is not difficult to convince oneself (*sich zu überzeugen*) that the strictness of upbringing also exerts a strong influence (*einen starken Einfluß übt*) on the formation of the child's Über-Ich. What it amounts to (*Es kommt darauf hinaus*) is that in the formation of the Über-Ich and emergence of a conscience, inborn constitutional factors (*mitgebrachte konstitutionken Faktoren*), and influences from the real environment act in combination (*Einflüsse des Milieus der realen Umgebung zusammenwirken*); and that is in no way surprising, rather it is a universal aetiological condition (*allgemeine ätiologische Bedingung*)⁴⁴⁵ for all such processes.⁴⁴⁶ One can also say that when a child reacts to his first great frustration of desire with very strong aggression and a corresponding strictness of the Über-Ich he is following a phylogenetic model

---

⁴⁴⁴ Bk. 7, 413. Freud's footnote 1 cites Melanie Klein and English writers who have 'rightly emphasized' this point. There was another controversy between Klein and Anna Freud. Freud in private supported Anna's side. The Klein - Anna Freud dispute revolved in part over who was the more authentic Freudian (a parallel to the Marxists arguing over who was closer to the Master's thought). b) There is a minor sub-text in *DUK* in which Freud engages with opponents, but generally he avoids polemical comments on current psychoanalytical issues.

⁴⁴⁵ Idem. a) We learned about 'nature and nurture' in first-year sociology. The basic point is how they interact. b) '*ätiologische*' is from the Greek αιτιολογικ-ός (without some diacritics): 'an inquiry into causes and reasons.' This claim of universality, one of the strongest philosophical claims in *DUK*, lacks adequate elaboration and support. However, some evidence is presented in Freud's footnote on Fr. Alexander. See fn. below.

⁴⁴⁶ Bk. 7, 413. a) The sentence has a redundant quality. JS (p. 131) splits it in two. b) Freud's second footnote: "Fr. Alexander has assessed in his *The Psycho-analysis of the Total Personality* (1927) both types of pathogenic methods of rearing, i.e. over-strictness and spoiling, in connection with Aichorn's study of delinquency (*Studie über die Verwahrlosung* [1925]). The "too-lenient and indulgent father" is the cause of an over-severe *Über-Ich* because under the impact of the love they receive, they have no outlet for their aggression except to turn it inwards (*nach innen*). With delinquent children, brought up without love, [and] lacking the tension between the 'I' and the *Über-Ich,* their whole aggression can be directed outwards. Thus one sees, apart from a constitutional factor which may be present, that the severe conscience arises (*entstehe*) from the joint operation of the two influences of life, the frustration of drives, which unleases aggression and the experience of being loved, which turns this aggression inward and hands it over (*überträgt*) to the *Über-Ich.*" [This is a concise and insightful footnote, especially on the theme of aggression, but 'being loved' escapes the simplicity of a handing over to an *Über-Ich.*]

ud

(*phylogenetischen Vorbild*) and is going beyond the response currently justified, because the prehistoric father (*der Vater der Vorzeit*) was certainly frightful (*fürchterlich*), and the highest degree of aggression may be attributed to him.[447] If one shifts from the individual to the phylogenetic development [model] the differences between the two theories of the genesis of conscience become reduced further. Instead of it, an important new difference between these two events appears. We cannot get away from the assumption that the guilt feeling of humans derives from the Oedipus complex[448] and was acquired with the death of the father through the joining together of the brothers (*der Tötung des Vaters durch die Brüdervereinigung erworben wurde*).[449] At that time an act of aggression was not suppressed but was carried out, the same act whose suppression in the child was supposed to be the source of his sense of guilt (*die Quelle des Schuldgefühls sein soll*). Now I would not be surprised if a reader cried out angrily (*wenn ein Leser ärgerlich ausriefe*): "So it makes no difference if one kills one's father or not, a guilt feeling will come in either case! We are

---

[447] No doubt there were *Vater der Vorzeit* or prehistoric fathers (is this a reference to the 'Neanderthal'—mentioned by Darwin in 1871?) who were very fearful and frightening; but Freud here, as elsewhere, mixes a mythic construct with observation of children. Moreover, while observation of children is valuable, it should not ignore context. That is, neglect mothers and mother figures and hence implicitly endorse a gendered image of development, and/or shift attention away from the violence of the father and authority figures.

[448] a) This is strange. In the Oedipus drama it was the father who sought to kill the son. It is disconcerting that Freud, now advanced in years, repeats the abstract construct of the 'Oedipus complex' within a theory of malaise and *Kultur*. The concept has value if used in the specific context of young people in ambivalent relationships to father or father-like authority figures, or in relation to certain types of obsessional neurosis. In a letter to Jung (14 April 1907) he said that "(the original Oedipus was himself a case of obsessional neurosis—the riddle of the Sphinz)" *F. J. Letters*, p. 33. b) Ambivalance, the central feature of obsessional neurosis, was explored in *Totem und Tabu*. In that work, Freud argued, unconvincingly, that the oedipal complex had prehistoric status and was the core of the neuroses. He also failed to establish that totemism and the Oedipus complex were universal phenomena. c) The term 'oedipal', slaying of the father and marriage with the mother, is not identical with 'family romance' or 'father complex.' On the Oedipus complex, see Bennett Simon and Rachel B. Blass in chapter 6 of *The Cambridge Companion to Freud*, edited by Jerome Neu (Cambridge University Press, 1991), pp. 161-174.

[449] A primal murder of a/the father by a band of brothers is historical fiction. There is no evidence to confirm or falsify it. And given the reality of ambivalence, it is just as likely that the *Vater* wanted to destroy the sons. b) Freud's footnote is to *Totem und Tabu* (1912-13), oben s. 314). This page number corresponds to the one in this volume, *Freud ZB*.

ud

permited here to raise a few doubts. Either it is false that the feeling of guilt comes from suppressed aggression or the whole story of the killing of the father is a fiction (*Roman*) and the children of the primal man did not kill their fathers anymore than they do today. Besides, if it is not a fiction but a plausible narrative (*Historie*),[450] it would be an instance of something happening which all the world expected to happen, namely of a person feeling guilty because he really was, had done something that could not be justified (*nicht zu rechtfertigen ist, getan tun*).[451] And of this event (*Fall*) which afterall happens all the time, psychoanalysis has failed to give any explanation (*die Erklärung schuldig geblieben*)." [452]

That is true and we must attend to the omission (*soll nachgeholt werden*). There is also no special mystery about it. When one has a sense of guilt after and because of an offense the feeling should more correctly be called *remorse* (*eher Reue nennen*). It relates only to an action (*Tat*) already done and presupposes a *conscience* (*Gewissen*) ready to feel guilty before the deed was done (*bereits vor der Tat bestand*). [453] Remorse of this kind can, therefore, never help us discover the origin of conscience and the feeling of guilt in general (*des Schuldgefühls überhaupt zu finden*). What happens in the course of these everyday events is usually this: an instinctual need (*Triebbedürfnis*) acquires the strength for satisfaction in spite of the conscience, which is, after all, limited in carrying through with

---

[450] Freud was sometimes a captive of his own insights. He lacks credibility on the 'fiction' and 'history' distinction, or on the two families and two images of Moses, one invented, one real, posited in *Der Mann Moses*. In essay II of that work, he followed E. Sellin's 'discovery' that there was a tradition, found implicitly in *Hosea*, of 'the people' who were angry with Moses and put him to death. But Freud was not pleased with the 'historical' part of his late study of Moses and he told Max Eitingon that he was not good at historical romances and they should be left to Thomas Mann (cited in our paraphrase from E. Jones, volume 3, p. 194). Freud blurred the distinction between 'fiction' and 'history' because he thought a primal killing of the father, even if not factual, was basic to the formation of culture and the emergence of the *Über-Ich*.

[451] Any speculative approach to history must interact with fiction, hence SF wavered between the primal murder as fact or useful fiction. There are fascinating parallels and interactions between fiction and purported historical fact, but the enlargement of the role of narrative should not be at the price of epistemological scepticism.

[452] Bk. 7, 414. a) Note Freud's inventive style in using a fictional reader (*Leser*) to explore the fiction versus fact question in the topos of the killing of the father. Also, lest we fret too much over the history-fiction contrast, we should recall that in Freud's thinking, image has priority over thing. b) JS generally has 'psychoanalysis' for '*Psychoanalyse*', e.g. Bk 2, (his p. 62). However, twice in this passage in Bk. 7, JS has 'psycho-analysis' (p. 133).

[453] Bk. 8, 414. '*Reue*' and '*Gewissen*' are in italics in the original.

ud

its strength; and with the natural weakening of the [instinctual] need because of its satisfaction, the earlier balance of power is restored (*durch seine Befriedigung das frühere Kräfteverhältnis wiederhergestellt wird*). Psychoanalysis is therefore justified in excluding the case of a feeling of guilt derived from remorse from this discussion (*von diesen Erörterungen auszuschließen*) no matter how frequent they occur and how great their practical importance. [454]

But if the human feeling of guilt goes back to the killing of the primal father (*Urvaters zurückgeht*) that was a case of "remorse" ("*Reue*"), and yet are we to assume that conscience and a feeling of guilt did not exist before that act (*vor der Tat nicht bestanden haben*)? [455] In that instance, where did the remorse come from? Certainly, this case must explain the mystery of guilt feeling and put an end to our difficulties

---

[454] **Idem. Freud's refusal to consider guilt that emerges from remorse is based on the assumption that remorse relates only to a deed already done. Hence, as we stated before, remorse does not help us discover the origin of conscience and guilt feelings. But if this is true, what is remorse related to? In later sentences, Freud answers that it relates to the primordial ambivalence of the sons toward the father, i.e. after slaying him, their love for him arises and this ambivalence creates remorse. The dimension of love creates identification with the father and through that identification the *Über-Ich* is constructed and endowed with the power of the father, as if it were a punishment (*wie zur Bestrafung*) for the aggression carried out against him. The *Über-Ich* created restrictions intended to prevent a repetition of the deed. This analysis and conclusion, a mix of mythical appreciations about a primal patricide, functions to reinforce the reality of ambivalence and the mechanist 'balance of power' thinking that Freud had explored, without the postulate of the slaying of a primal father, in his 1895 'Project.' (His friend L. Binswanger had called this type of thinking too close to "the current materialist rationalism"). If remorse is to have any value in an image of moral responsibility it must be connected with guilt feeling. But this requires that we bracket or exclude psychic or organic brain factors, and interpret the slaying of an *Ur*-father not as a fact of pre-history, but as a symbolical truth about autonomy and authority and the complementary functions of the good and the bad father figure (e.g. the archetype of Saturn). Social conditioning and willed egoism on individual and collective levels can dim or negate authentic moral obligations, but otherwise their violation invariably brings remorse.**

[455] **Bk. 8, 414. a) The attempt to explicate the difference between guilt and remorse through a hypothetical construct of a primal father parricide is rather curious (*ganz sonderbare*). b) JS (p. 133) breaks the sentence into two, and has 'before the deed'. The 'before that act' clause seems to accept 'the killing of the primal father' as a fact. However, Freud wavers on the point. This is shown in his use of "*aber wenn*" (but if), and is also attested in the statement on p. 415 that regardless of having done it or not ("*oder sich der Tat enthalten hat*") guilt arises because of the eternal struggle between Eros and the destruction or death-drive. c) This raises another point: in giving credence to Eros and the death-drive as interacting archetypal structures, Freud has moved closer to C. G. Jung, his one-time 'crown prince', friend, rival.**

ud

(*Verlegenheiten ein Ende machen*). And I think it does (*Und ich meine, er leistet es auch*).[456] This remorse was the result (*Ergebnis*) of the primordial ambivance of feeling towards the father: his sons hated him, but they also loved him; after their hatred had been satisfied through the [act of] aggression, their love appeared (*Vorschein*) in their remorse over the action; through identification with the father [remorse] set up the *Über-Ich*, it [remorse] gave it the power of the father, as though as a punishment (*gab ihm die Macht des Vaters wie zur wie zur Bestrafung*) for the aggression carried out against him, and it created the restrictions intended to prevent a repetition of the deed (*schuf die Einschränkungen, die eine Wiederholung der Tat verhüten sollten*).[457] And since the aggressive tendency against the father repeats itself in succeeding generations, the feeling of guilt remains in existence (*Schuldgefühl bestehen*) and becomes stronger through every case of aggression that was oppressed and carried over to the *Über-Ich*. Now, I think, we can grasp two things with full clarity; the part love plays in the origin of conscience, and the fateful inevitability of the feeling of guilt (*den Anteil der Liebe an der Enstehung des Gewissens und die verhängnisvolle Unvermeidlichkeit des Schuldgefühls*). Whether one has killed the father or has not (*oder sich der Tat enthalten hat*), one must feel guilty in both cases because the feeling of guilt is an expression of the ambivalence-conflict (*Ambivalenzkonflikts*), the eternal struggle (*ewige Kampfes*) between Eros and the destruction or death-drive (*Todestrieb*). This conflict is stimulated as soon as men are faced with the task of living together (*Zusammenlebens gestelt wird*); so long as the community knows no other form of the family, the conflict must express itself in the Oedipus complex (*Ödipuskomplex*) to establish (*einsetzen*) the conscience and create the feeling of guilt. When an attempt to widen the community is made, the same conflict is carried on in forms dependent upon the past; stronger, and results in an increased (*Steigerung*) feeling of guilt. Because culture obeys an inner erotic drive (*inneren erotischen Antribe gehorcht*), which commands (*heißt*) human beings to unite in a closely connected multitude (*innig verbundenen Masse vereinigen*) this goal can only be

---

[456] JS (idem) connects this sentence with the previous one by using 'at that time' in brackets.

[457] JS (p. 134) divides this long sentence into four sentences. The influence of Lamarck is shown in the sentence following: "...the aggressive tendency against the father repeats itself in succeeding generations..."

ud

reached through an ever increasing reinforcement of the feeling of guilt (*immer wachsenden Verstärkung des Schuldgefühls erreichen*). What began with the father is completed in the masses (*Was am Vater begonnen wurde, vollendet sich an der Masse*). If civilization (*Kultur*) is a necessary tendency of development (*Entwicklungsgang*) from the family to humanity, then as a result of the innate ambivalence conflict (*mitgeborenen Ambivalenzkonflikts*) arising from the eternal strife (*ewigen Haders*) between love and the death-drive there is inextricably bound up with it an increase of guilt feelings perhaps to the point that an individual finds difficult to bear.[458] One thinks of the moving charge (*ergreifenden Anklage*) of the great poet against the 'heavenly Powers':

> To earth, this weary earth, ye bring us
> To guilt ye let us heedless go,
> Then leave repentance fierce to wring us:
> A moment's guilt, an age of woe![459]

And one may heave a sigh of relief at the recognition (*aufseufzen bei der Erkenntnis*) that it is given to individual human beings, from the whirlpool of their individual feelings, to recover without difficulty (*mühelos heraufzuholen*) the deepest insights; toward which the rest of us have to make our way through tormenting uncertainty and with restless

---

[458] **Bk. 7, 415. a) Freud used *mitgeborenen* (innate) several times but never clarified the meaning. If 'innate' is taken as a biological or genetic given it differs radically from 'innate' as the 'eternal strife' between Eros and the death-drive. b) The sentence 'what began with the father is completed in the masses', one of the best lines in *DUK*, is contradicted by Freud's earlier statements in Bk. 4 on women's love as the foundation of civilization. c) On the *Ödipuskomplex*: this interpretative construct was based largely on his tendentious interpretation of the Oedipus saga in Sophocles, his own self-analysis of the late 1890's, and clinical data from others. The evidence is slim and the concept should not be generalized across cultures and epochs that have different forms of family and sociality. But the concept could be reformulated so that its meaning-use related to the renunciation necessary for the emergence of culture, the historicity of desire, and the conflict between the pleasure priniciple and the reality principle. d) The historical determinism in this section reflects a reification of *Kultur* which conflicts with Freud's critique of progress and images of an ideal world. However, the determinist motif is not even comprehensive because 'the masses' are not aware of the inner erotic drive of *Kultur*. [This resembles the ancient notion of 'double-truth'.] This lack of awareness by the masses of their own misery is analogous to the lack of awareness of 'class conflict' as the driving force of history in Leninist theory.**

[459] **Thomas Caryle's translation of Goethe's "*Lieder des Harfners*" in *Wilhelm Meister*.**

ud

groping (*durch qualvolle Unsicherheit und rastloses Tasten den Weg zu bahnen haben*). [460]

VIII

Having reached the end of his path (*Weges angelangt*), the author must beg forgiveness from the readers (*Leser*) for not having been a more able guide (*geschickter Führer gewesen*), and for not having spared them the experience of empty deserts and inconvenient detours (*ihnen das Erlebnis öder Strecken und beschwerlicher Umwege nicht erspart hat*). There is no doubt that one could have done it better. I will attempt, belatedly, to make some amends (*nachträglich etwas gutzumachen*). [461]

First, I expect that the reader has the impression that our discussions about the sense of guilt disrupt (*sprengen*) the framework of this essay, in that they take up too much space; and other content, not always closely connected with it, gets pushed to the side (*an den Rand drängen*). This may have destroyed the structure of our essay, but it fully corresponds to my intention to represent the feeling of guilt as the most important problem in the development of culture, and that the price we pay for the progress of culture is a loss of happiness (*Glückseinbuße*) through an increase of the sense of guilt.[462] What still sounds strange in this proposition (*Satz*), the

---

[460] **This sentence of grace and beauty assumes a cultural division between 'individual human beings' who can recover the 'deepest insights', and the masses or 'the rest of us' who can only grop tentatively toward them.**

[461] **Bk. 8, 415-6. '*Leser*' (singular) does not match '*ihnen*' (dat. plural); JS (p. 137) has 'readers' with aposthrophe, and '*détours*' for '*Umwege*'. b) Freud's modesty should probably not be taken literally, e.g. "*Aufbau der Abhandlung gestört haben*" ('have destroyed the structure of our essay'). This may suggest that his 'the reader' is a projection of his own dissatisfaction with *DUK*.**

[462] **The assertion that progress in culture is at the price of diminished happiness because of guilt is a basic conceptual proposition of *DUK*. b) In his footnote, Freud cites in German the line in Hamlet: "Thus conscience does make cowards of us all..." III, 1. This is followed by a long moralistic discourse, which should be in the text itself, on the inauthentic education of young people. Concern for the young was basic to Freud and to his daughter Anna. The issue of adult hypocrisy, a theme integral to his critique of 'religion', is also raised. There is sarcasm and irony in his use of the 'sin' vocabulary which he had earlier identified with the 'pious.' c) The footnote reads: "That the present day education of young people conceals from them the role which sexuality will pay in their lives is not the only reproach (*Vorwurf*), that one can bring against it. Its other sin is that it does not prepare them for the aggression that they will become the objects of (*deren Objekt er zu werden bestimmt ist*). In that the young are send out into life with such**

ud

final conclusion of our inquiry (*Endergebnis unserer Untersuchen*), can probably be traced back to the quite curious (*ganz sonderbare*), as yet not fully understood, connection of the feeling of guilt with our consciousness. In the common cases of remorse, which we think normal, this feeling makes itself clearly perceptible enough to consciousness; thus we are accustomed (*gewöhnt*) to say 'consciousness of Guilt' ('*Schuldbewußtsein*') instead of a feeling of guilt (*Schuldgefühl*). Out of our study of the neuroses, to which we owe valuable clues (*wertvollsten Winke*) to an understanding of normal [people], yields a condition which is full of contradictions (*ergeben sich widerspruchsvolle Verhältnisse*). In one of those emotional disturbances (*Affektionen*), obsessional neurosis (*der Zwangsneurose*), the feeling of guilt makes itself noisily heard in consciousness, it dominates the clinical picture (*Krankheitsbild*) as well as the patient's life, and allows almost nothing else to arise beside it (*läßt kaum anderes neben sich aufkommen*). But in most other cases and forms (*Fällen und Formen*)[463] of neurosis it remains fully unconscious, without as a result producing any less significant effects. Our patients do not believe us when we expect (*zumuten*) an 'unconscious guilt feeling' of them, and when we tell them, in order to be half understood, of an unconscious need for punishment in which guilt feeling is expressed.[464] But its connection with a specific form of neurosis must not be over-rated (*überschatz werden*); there is even within the obsessional neurosis type patients who are not aware of their sense of guilt or experience it as a tormenting malaise (*quälendes Unbehagen*) or form of anxiety, and then not until they are blocked from doing certain acts (*gewisser Handlungen verhindert werden*). We should eventually be able to understand these things, but as yet we do not (*man kann es noch nicht*). Here perhaps the comment is welcome (*Bemerkung*

---

incorrect psychological orientation is like equipping people on a Polar expedition with summer clothes and maps of the lakes of Italy. In this a certain misuse of ethical demands (*ethischen Forderungen*) is apparent. The strictness of these [ethical demands] would not be so shameful if the education said: 'This is how one ought to be if one wants to be happy and have others happy but you have to reckon (*rechnen*) that they are not like that.' Instead the young are made to believe that eveyone else fufills those ethical demands, that they are virtuous (*tugenhaft sind*). On this, the demand is grounded that the young, too, should become virtuous."

[463] **Bk. 8, 416. Synonymous lexical parallelism.**

[464] **Idem. JS (p. 139) divides the sentence; renders '*zumuten*' (*beimessen, zuschreiben*) as 'attribute,' and has 'In order to make outselves at all intelligible' for "*nur halbwegs von ihnen verstanden zu werden*".**

ud

willkommen) that guilt feeling at bottom is nothing else than a topical variety of anxiety (*topische Abart der Angst*), in its later phases it fully merges with the *anxiety of the Über-Ich* (*Angst vor dem Über-Ich*). [465] And the relation of anxiety to consciousness exhibits the same extraordinary variations. [466] Anxiety is present somewhere behind every symptom, but at one time its clamor (*larmend*) takes over the whole of consciousness, while at another it completely conceals (*verbirgt*) itself so fully that we are forced (*genötigt*) to speak of unconscious anxiety (*unbewußter Angst*) or —if we want to have a purer psychological conscience, since indeed anxiety in the first instance is simply a feeling—to speak (*zu reden*) of possibilities of anxiety. [467] And therefore it is very conceivable (*denkbar*) that the consciousness of guilt produced (*erzeugte*) by culture is not recognized as such, to a large part it remains unconscious or comes to expression as a kind of malaise (*Unbehagen*), or appears as a dissatisfaction (*Unzufriedenheit*) for which people seek other motivations. The religions have at least never overlooked (*nie verkannt*) the role of guilt feeling in culture (*die Rolle des Schuldgefühls in der Kultur*). [468] Indeed, they assume (*Sei treten ja*), [a point] which I had not appreciated elsewhere (*an anderer Stelle nicht gewürdigt hatte*), [469] to redeem humanity from this feeling of guilt, which they call sin (*Sünde heißen*). [470] From the way in which this salvation was achieved in Christianity (*wie im Christendom diese Erlösung gewonnen wird*), through the sacrificial death of an individual who in this

---

[465] Bk. 8, 416-7. The German text has italics, hence the English italics. JS (idem) has *'fear of the super-ego'* in italics.

[466] As mentioned before, Heidegger in his *Sein und Zeit* explored the problem of anxiety and consciousness on an onthological dimension. While he ignored Freud, he used the Freudian terminology of 'urge' and 'repress (*Drang and verdrängen*) in *Prolegomena zur Geschichte des Zeitbegriffs* (GA 20, 1970). Of course the usage was not psychoanalytical but 'existential' in an ontological sense.

[467] Bk. 8, 417. The sentence makes no sense unless one literally follows Freud's use of the dash marks. b) This link between language and the possibilities of anxiety relates to the role of speaking as a 'cure' for deep, hidden anxiety. The connection has deep potentialities that move beyond *DUK*.

[468] Idem. a) Note the use of the key term '*Unbehagen*.' b) In this passage, Christianity is the context for Freud's 'the religions.' As mentioned before, he was too undifferentiated and unspecific about 'religion' and the 'religions'; he ignored Islam and only glanced at the Eastern noetic traditions. There is a brief mention of the Japanese *Mikado* in the context of taboo and ambivalence in Part II: B of *Totem and Taboo*.

[469] Freud's footnote here is to his *Die Zukunft einer Illusion* (1927c; *The Future of an Illusion*, 1927c).

[470] But Freud used the the German terms for 'sin' and 'sinful' in Bk. 7.

ud

way takes upon himself a guilt common to everyone, we have been able to infer (*gezogen*) what the first ocassion may have been on which this primal guilt (*Urschuld*), which was also the beginning of culture, was acquired. [471]

Although it cannot be very important, it may not be superfluous (*überflüssig*), to clarify the importance (*Bedeutung*) of some words like *Über-Ich, Gewissen* (conscience), *Schuldgefühl* (guilt feeling), *Strafbedürfnis* (need for punishment), *Reue* (remorse), which we perhaps have used too loosely and interchangeabily. [472] They all relate to the same condition but indicate different aspects of it. The '*Über-Ich*' is a court (*Instanz*) [473] inferred by us (*erschlossene*), and conscience is a function that, along with other functions, we ascribe to it; this function consists of keeping watch over and judging the actions and intentions of the 'I' (*des Ichs*), [i.e.] in exerting a censorious activity (*die die Handlungen und Absichten des Ichs zu überwachen und zu beurteilen hat, eine zensorische Tätigkeit ausübt*). [474] The sense of guilt, the harshness of the *Über-Ich* (*des Über-Ichs*) is thus the same as the severity of the conscience, it is the perception that the 'I' has of being watched-over in this way, the evaluation (*Abschatzung*)[475] of the tension between its own striving and the demands of the *Über-Ich* (*den Forderungen des Über-Ichs*) and that the whole relationship at bottom is anxiety toward this critical court (*Angst vor dieser*

---

[471] *DUK*, Bk. 8, 417. Note the leaps of logic from a hypothetical primal guilt acquired at the beginning of culture to a peculiar use of the image of salvation in Christianity within an atheistic framework. On the atheistic issue: Ludwig Feuerbach (1804-1872), whom the young Freud revered, was a major influence. Evidence for this is in Freud's letters to Eduard Silberstein (Harvard, 1990). Freud has two footnotes to this sentence, the first is to *Die Zukunft einer Illusion* (1927c, *The Future of an Illusion*) and the other is to *Totem und Tabu* (1912[-13],*Totem and Taboo*).

[472] *DUK*, Bk. 8, 417. The paragraph begins on an ironic note, and then adopts a nominalist and historicist perspective. We think there is more need for clarification of these and other keywords.

[473] Idem. Or 'authority.' JS (p. 140) has 'agency.' *The New Cassel's German Dictionary* has "court (of justice); stage (of proceedings)…" p. 246.

[474] Note the complementary parallelism of 'actions and intentions'. b) JS (p.140) has "in exercising a censorship' for "*eine zensorische Tätigketi ausübt*." c) On the construct of the *Über-Ich* and the 'I', one must ask how the conscience can attain autonomy; and how the 'I', under the watchfulness and judgment of the 'super-ego' relates to itself and how an 'I' to 'I' relationship possible? Without that relationality the human Dasein has no reflexive interiority.

[475] The important term '*Abschatzung*' was used in the first sentence of *DUK* in the form of '*unterschätzen*' ('undervalue').

ud

kritischen Instanz): the need for punishment is a drive manifestation (*Triebäuberung*) of the 'I', which has become masochistic under the influence of the sadistic *Über-Ich*; that is, it is a part of the drive towards internal destruction present in the 'I', [and] used for forming an erotic attachment to the *Über-Ich*.[476] We should not speak of a conscience before the existence of an *Über-Ich* is authenticated (*nachweisbar ist*), one must admit that a consciousness of guilt exists before the *Über-Ich* and, therefore, before conscience, too.[477] It [consciousness of guilt] is then the immediate expression of anxiety toward the external authority, the recognition of the tension between the 'I' and the latter [external authority], [and] the direct descendant (*Abkömmling*) of the conflict between the need for love and the drive for the satisfaction of desire, whose inhibition) creates the inclination to aggression (*Hemmung die Neigung zur Aggression erzeugt*). The superimposition (*Übereinanderlagerung*) of these two strata of the sense of guilt—one coming from anxiety of the outside authority, the other from anxiety of the inner authority—has in respect to conscience impeded (*erschwert*) our insight in many ways. Remorse is a general term (*Gesamtbezeichnung*) for the reaction of the 'I' in a case of guilt feeling. It contains, in little (*wenig*) altered form, the sensory material working behind the anxiety (*Empfindungsmaterial der dahinter wirksamen Angst*);[478] it is itself a punishment and can include the need for punishment, hence it [remorse] can also be older than conscience.

It can also not do any harm if we once more review the contradictions (*Widersprüche*) that for a time has confused our inquiry (*Untersuchen verwirrt haben*). At one point the sense of guilt was the result of uncommitted acts of aggression (*unterlassener Aggressionen*); but at another point and exactly at its historical beginning, [i.e.] the killing of the father, [it was] the result of an aggessive act that was carried out

---

[476] *DUK*, Bk. 8, 417. This is a very long sentence with unclear phrasal references. JS (p. 141) inserts parenthetical marks, breaks the sentence up, however it is incorrect to render *Angst* as 'fear.'

[477] Idem. In a major lexical error, JS (idem) translates '*Schuldbewußtsein*' ('consciousness of guilt') as 'sense of guilt.' On the existence of guilt before conscience, see M. Heidegger in *Sein und Zeit* (1927).

[478] Bk. 8, 417. a) That the inhibition of desire for satisfaction creates the inclination to aggression contradicts statements elsewhere on aggression as an innate given. See our Index, 'aggression'). b) Bk. 8, 418. JS (p. 141) has 'the sensory material of the anxiety…' and divides the sentence.

ud

(*ausgeführten*). But we found a way out of this difficulty. The installation (*Einsetzung*) of the inner authority, the *Über-Ich*, radically changed the situation. Before this, the feeling of guilt belonged together with remorse; besides we note that the term 'remorse' should be reserved for the reaction after an aggression has been carried out.[479] After this, because of the all-knowingness (*Allwissenheit*) of the *Über-Ich* the difference between intended and carried out (*beabsichtigter und erfüllter*) aggression lost its power;[480] from now a sense of guilt could be produced (*erzeugen*) by an an act of violence (*Gewalttat*) actually carried out—as all the world knows—and also by a simple intention—as psychoanalysis has recognized (*erkannt hat*). Regardless of this change of the psychological situation, the ambivalent conflict between the two primal drives (*Ambivalenzkonflikt der beiden Urtriebe*) leaves the same result behind. We are tempted to look here for the solution to the enigma of the changeable relation of the sense of guilt to consciousness (*hier die Lösung des Rätsel von der wechselvollen Beziehung des Schuldgefülts zum Bewußtsein zu suchen*). The sense of guilt from remorse over an evil deed must always remain conscious, whereas [sense of guilt] from the perception of evil impulses may remain unconscious (*das aus Wahrnehmung des bösen Impulses könnte unbewußt bleiben*).[481] That alone is not so simple, obsessional neurosis speaks strongly against it (*die Zwangsneurose widerspricht dem energisch*).[482]

The second contradiction was [concerned with] the aggressive energy with which one thinks the *Über-Ich* was endowed (*ausgestattet denkt*): according to one view, that energy simply carries on the punitive energy of the external authority and preserves it in the life of the mind (*seelenleben erhält*); while, according to another view, it consists, on the contrary, of one's own aggression which has not been used (*die nicht zur Verwendung gelangte*), and which one now directs against that inhibiting authority (*die man gegen diese hemmende Autorität aufbringt*). The first

---

[479] **Idem. The analysis of language usage and psychic dimensions is impressive. Oddly, JS (p. 142) puts the final clause within brackets.**

[480] **Note how the complementary lexical parallelism supports the argument. At this point, JS (idem) breaks up the sentence.**

[481] **Bk. 8, 418. JS (p. 142) introduces the sentence with 'It might be thought...' puts 'deed' and 'impulse' in italics, and has the singular case for "*bösen Impulses*".**

[482] **If this sentence modifies the second clause of the previous sentence, it is not clear why 'obsessional neurosis' would count against a perception of evil impulses remaining unconscious.**

ud

theory (*Lehre*) fits in with the history (*der Geschichte*), the second fits better with the theory of the sense of guilt (*die zweite der Theorie des Schuldgefühls besser anzupassen*). More detailed reflection has obliterated (*verwischt*) this apparent unresolvable contradiction, almost too much so; what remained as the essential and common (*wesentlich und gemeinsam*)[483] factor was that in both cases we are dealing with an aggression displaced inwardly (*innen verschobene Aggression handeln*). Moreover, clinical observation (*klinische Beobachtung*) has allowed us to distinguish two sources for the aggression which we attribute to the *Über-Ich*; one or the other of them exerts the stronger effect in specific cases, but in general they work together *(Zusammenwirken)*.

Here is the place, I think, at which to seriously defend a view which I had recommended awhile ago for provisional acceptance (*zur vorläufigen Annahme empfohlen hatte*). In the newest analytical literature there is a predilection for the theory (*Vorliebe für die Lehr*) that any kind of frustration, any blocked satisfaction of desire; results, or may result, in an intensification of the sense of guilt (*Steigerung des Schuldgefühls*).[484] I believe one creates a great theoretical simplification if one regards this as applying only to the *aggressive* (*aggressiven*)[485] drives, and little will be found to contradict this view. For how are we to give a dynamic and economic explanation of an increase in the sense of guilt appearing in a place of unfulfilled erotic demands (*nicht erfüllten erotischen Anspruchs eine Steigerung des Schuldgefühls auftritt*)? This seems possible only in a round-about way (*Umwege möglich*): that the prevention of an erotic satisfaction causes a portion of aggression to be directed against the person who had interfered with the satisfaction (*welche die Befriedigung stört*), and that this aggression itself must in turn be suppressed. But then, after all, it is only the aggression which is transformed into a sense of guilt by becoming suppressed and pushed over (*zugeschoben wird*) to the *Über-Ich*.[486] I am convinced that many processes will allow a simpler and clearer

---

483 '*verwischt*' (v.a.) literally, 'wiped away'. JS (p. 143) has 'resolved.' Note the complementary parallelism of "*wesentlich und gemeinsam*."

484 Bk 8, 418-19. Freud's footnote (his reference is to the 'newest analytical literature'): 'In particular by E. Jones, Susan Isaacs, Melanie Klein; and I understand, also by Reik and Alexander.' A subtext here was the ongoing controversy with Ernest Jones on the death-drive, and the disagreements between Anna Freud and Melanie Klein.

485 '*aggressiven*' is in italics in the text, p. 419.

486 Bk. 8, 419. Aggression is changed into guilt by being suppressed and turned over to the

ud

description (*einfacher und durchsichtiger Darstellung*) if the discovery (*Fund*) [487] of psychoanalysis on the derivation of the sense of guilt is restricted to the aggressive drives. The examination (*Befragung*) of the clinical material gives us here no unequivocal answer (*keine eindeutige Antwort*) because in conformity with our preassumption (*weil unserer Voraussetzung gemäß*) both forms of desire seldom appear in pure form, isolated from each other; but the assessment of extreme cases would probably point in the direction I expect. [488]

I am tempted to extract a first advantage (*ersten Nutzen zu ziehen*) from this more restricted view by applying it to the process of repression (*Verdrängungsvorgang anwende*). The symptoms of neurosis are, as we have learned, essentially substitute satisfactions (*Ersatzbefriedigungen*) for unfulfilled sexual wishes. In the course of our analytical work we have to our surprise discovered that perhaps each neurosis conceals an amount (*Betrag*) of unconscious guilt feeling, which in return fortifies the symptoms through using them as punishment (*ihre Verwendung zur Strafe befestigt*). It now seems credible (*nun liegt es nahe*) to formulate the proposition (*Satz*): when an instinctual tendency (*Triebstrebung*) undergoes repression, its libidinal components turn into symptoms, its aggressive components into a sense of guilt. Even if this proposition is only an average approximation (*durchschnittlicher Annäherung*) to the truth, it serves our interest (*verdient er unser Interesse*).

Some readers of this treatise may further stand under an impression that the formula of the struggle between Eros and the death drive (*Todestrieb*) is heard too often.[489] It was alleged to designate the process of

---

Über-Ich. However, the sentence is unclear, i.e. what stands in contrast to 'it is only the aggression which is transformed into a sense of guilt'? Is it aggression because of unfilled erotic demands or the person who had interfered with their satisfaction?

[487] Bk. 8, 419. Note the synonymous lexical parallelism. JS (p. 144) has 'exposition' for '*Darstellung*' and 'findings' for '*Fund.*'

[488] This cautious method of suveying the evidence and where it might point is impressive. *DUK,*, in some respects a Wisdom tradition type reflection, needed more critical scrutiny of keywords, e.g. *Libido, Eros, Liebe, Tod, Destruktion,* and their conceptual fields. SF admitted the same, although with an ironic tone, on p. 417.

[489] a) Perhaps, although for different reasons, the critics ('readers of this treatise') were right, e.g. the struggle between Eros and the death drive has poetic power but violates Ockham's principle: "*entia non sunt multiplicanda praeter necessitatem*" (entities are not to be multiplied beyond necessity). b) Also, Freud in the late 1920's was in a debate with other analysts about the 'death drive.' That polemic, however, is not relevant to our suggestion that the Eros-Death duality gives mythopoetic force to the treatise and

ud

civilization (*Kulturprozeß*) that humans undergo, but it was also connected with the development of the individual (*die Entwicklung des einzelnen bezogen*) and, moreover, [it was said] revealed the mystery of organic life in general. Investigation of the relations of these three processes to one another appears unavoidable (*Es scheint unabweisbar*). Hence, the repetition (*Nun ist die Wiederkehr*) of the same formula is justified by the consideration (*Erwägung gerechfertigt*) that both the process of human culture (*Kulturprozeß der Menschheit*) and the development of the individual are life processes (*Lebensvorgänge sind*), also that they must share in the most general characteristic of life. On the other hand, evidence of this general feature fails, because its general nature [leads to a] lack of differentiation [of the general processes], so long as this is not narrowed down through specific qualifications (*Anderseits trägt gerade darum der Nachweis dieses allgemeinen Zuges nichts zur Unterscheidung bei, solange dieser nicht durch besondere Bedingungen eingeengt wird*).[490] We can only be calmed by the assertion (*Aussage beruhigen*) that the process of culture is only a modification of the life processes, which is under the influence of a task set by Eros and of *Ananke*, the realm of Necessity (*der realen Not*) and that this task is uniting separate individuals into a community bounded by libidinal ties (*Vereinigung vereinzelter Menschen zu einer unter sich libidinös verbundenen Gemeinschaft*).[491] When, however, we view the relation between the process of human culture and the developmental or educative process (*Entwicklungs oder Erziehungsprozeß*) [492] of the individual person we shall conclude without much hesitation that they are very similar in nature, if not everywhere the same process [applied] to different kinds of objects. The process of human civilization

---

consequently supports our suggestion that *DUK*, in some respects, is a 'wisdom' treatise. c) The death-drive issue was not the only debate that Freud was involved with in his later years. There was the debate about lay analysis, and debates with early female analysts, e.g. Melanie Klein. H. Westerink (cited above, p. 229 ff.) points out the importance in *DUK* of debate with other analysts and asserts that "most of them [were] women". Many were but the statement is exaggerated.

[490] Bk. 8, 419-20. The requirement that the general be subject to differentiation and restricted by specificity is sound, but it is contradicted in the next sentence by the abstract, ontic claim about the 'task set by Eros and of *Ananke.*'

[491] Bk. 8, 420. Freud's spelling is '*Ananke*' but the Greek 'e' is long. The mythical Eros and *Ananke* breaks in here like a revelatory and bewildering experience, especially so after the careful stress in the previous two sentences on concrete differentiation.

[492] Bk. 8, 420. Close conceptual parallelism.

ud

(*Kulturprozeß*) is, of course, an abstraction (*eine Abstraktion*) of a higher order than the development of the individual, therefore more difficult to grasp in concrete terms (*anschaulich zu erfassen*), nor should we trace out analogies (*Aufspürung von Analogien*) to a compulsive extreme; but given the similiarity of the goals of the two processes—here (*hier*) the integration of an individual into a human group (*Masse*), there (*dort*) the creation of a unified group out of many individuals—we cannot be surprised at the closeness of the means used and the phenomena that result.

We must not long postpone mention (*nicht lange unerwähnt bleiben*) of one feature, of exceptional importance, which distinguishes between the two processes. In the developmental process of the individual person, the programme of the pleasure principle, the satisfaction of happiness, is retained as the principal goal (*Hauptziel festgehalten*), alignment in or adjustment to (*Einreihung in oder Anpassung an*) a human community, appears as a scarcely avoidable condition which must be reached (*Erreichung*) before this goal of happiness can be fulfilled. If it could succeed without that condition (*ohne diese Bedingung*), it would perhaps be better. Expressed otherwise (*Anders ausgedrückt*), the development of the individual appears to us as a product of the interaction between two strivings, the striving after happiness, which we generally call 'egoistic' ("*egoistisch*") and the urge toward union with others in a community which we generally call 'altruistic' ("*altruistisch*").[493] Both of these descriptions fail to go much beneath the surface (*Überflache hinaus*). As we have said, in the case of individual development the principal accent falls on the egoistical or the striving for happiness, the other which may be called a 'cultural' ("*kulturell*")[494] one is usually content with the role of imposing restrictive rules. Things differ with the process of culture (*Kulturprozeß*); here the most important thing by far is the goal of

---

[493] **Idem. As stated before, JS and the *S.E.* translators rendered '*Ich*' with 'ego' and '*Über-Ich*' with 'super-ego'. Freud only used 'ego', in the form of '*egoistisch*', in this passage in *DUK*. The context is the striving toward happiness versus the urge toward union. Freud thought that neither of these positions went deep enough. But the arguments against the former differ from those against the latter. It also depends on how the issue is formulated, e.g. a Buddhist view of co-dependent arising includes the interests of self and other, not one at the expense of the other.**
[494] **Idem. This use of '*kulturell*' cuts against the practice of the translators of the *S. E.* of assuming that when Freud wrote "*Kultur*" he meant 'civilization.' [Although it is likely that sometimes he did.]**

ud

producing a unity (*Herstellung einer Einheit*) out of the individual human beings, the goal of happiness still exists (*besteht zwar noch*), but it is pushed into the background, it almost seems (*fast scheint es*) as if the creation of a great human community would be most successful if no concern for the happiness of the individual had been required (*nicht zu kümmern brauchte*).[495] Hence, it can be expected that the developmental process of the individual has special characteristics (*besonderen Züge haben*), which one does not find repeated (*nicht wiederfinden*) in the cultural process of humanity; only in so far (*nur insofern*) as the first of these processes has union (*Vorgang den Anschluß*) with the goal of humanity as its aim does it have to coincide with the second process (*letzteren zusammenfallen*).[496]

Like a planet circles (*kreist*) around a central body, as well as rotates on its own axis, so the human individual (*einzelne Mensch*) takes part in the development of humanity at the same time as he goes on his own life path (*eigenen Lebensweg geht*). But to our dull eyes, the play of forces in the heavens (*Kräftespiel am Himmel*) seem solidified in an ever-lasting order (*ewig gleicher Ordnung erstarrt*), but in the field of organic life we can still see how the forces contest one another, and how the results of conflicts (*Ergebnisse des Konflikts*) are continually changing.[497] Hence, also, the two urges, one toward individual happiness and the other toward union with other human beings must struggle with one another in each individual; and, hence, the two processes of individual and of cultural development must encounter one another in hostile opposition (*einander feindlich begegnen*) and mutually dispute the ground (*gegenseitig den Boden*

---

[495] Idem. The sentence is long (JS breaks it into four) and difficult, but it is the important premise for the sentence that follows.

[496] Bk. 8, 420. If I understand this, the two processes are not the 'egoistic' and the 'altruistic', but the process of culture and the process of individual development. In *DUK*, however, the image of 'love' as a specific and limited quantity and the dualism of Eros and *Ananke* make it difficult to theorize human community. The dualism is like a poetical overlay which reinforces a point, but the point can be made without it. That is, the struggle between the individual and society is literally speaking 'a derivative of the probably irreconcilable opposition (*unversöhnlichen Gegensatzes*) of the primal drives of Eros and death', Bk. 8, 421.

[497] The revolve/rotate analogy is central to *DUK*, but it is partially spoiled by the literalism of 'play of forces in the heavens' contrasted to 'the field of organic life'. JS (p. 148) renders '*geht*' as 'pursues.'

ud

bestreiten).[498] But this struggle between the individual and society is not a derivative of the probably irreconcilable opposition (*unversöhnlichen Gegensatzes*) of the primal drives of Eros and death; it means a dispute within the economy (*Haushalt*) of the libido, comparable to the strife over the distribution (*Augteilung*) of the libido between 'the I' and objects; and it does admit of an eventual adjustment (*Ausgleich*) for the individual, as one also hopes for in the future of civilization (*Kultur*), however much that civilization now oppresses the individual.[499]

The analogy between the process of civilization (*Kulturprozeß*) and the path of individual development (*Entwicklungsweg des Individuums*) allows an extension in an important respect.[500] It can be asserted that society also develops (*ausbildet*) an *Über-Ich,* under whose influence cultural development proceeds. It would be a tempting task (*verlockende Aufgabe*) for a specialist (*Kenner*) on human cultures to follow out this comparison (*Gleichstellung*) in detail.[501] I will confine myself to bringing forward a few striking points. The *Über-Ich* of an epoch of culture (*Kulturepoche*) has an origin similar to that of an individual person, it is based on the impression left behind by the personalities of great leaders (*große Führerpersönlichkeiten hinterlassen haben*), men of over-powering force of mind or men in whom one of the human aspirations (*Strebungen*) has its strongest and purest (*stärkste und reinste*), and also often one-sided

---

[498] **Bk. 8, 421. The dualist conflict posited here contrasts with Heraclitus who saw the opposites as a unity. Freud denies that the struggle between the individual and society is a derivative of the primal opposition of Eros and death, but it is vigorously implied elsewhere.**

[499] **Idem. a) Note the antithetical parallelism of "*Individuum und Gesellschaft*", "*Eros and Tod*", and the complementary parallelism of "*Ich und den Objekten*". b) The context here requires that '*Kultur*' be translated as 'civilization.' Freud was more positive on the integration of the individual than of the larger human construct (cf. Camus' *La Peste* (1947). He tried to avoid the options of optimism and pessimism toward civilization, but on the whole, and especially after the First World War, he had little faith in human beings.**

[500] **Idem. Freud's image of the primal family, elaborated in *Totem und Tabu* (1911-1913), was the basis for this analogy. The central analogy of religion and neurosis was also developed in *Totem und Tabu* (1912-1913, III, 4, 84-5). As we mentioned before, the neuroses had a significant correspondence (*Übeinstimmungen*) to the great social productions of art, religion, and philosophy (*der Kunst, der Religion und der Philosophie*), but they were also a distortion and caricature of them, e.g. religion was a caricature (*Zerrbild*) of a compulsion neurosis.**

[501] **Bk. 8, 421. JS (p. 148) renders '*Kenner*' as 'knowledge of' and '*Gleichstellung*' as 'analogy.'**

ud

development, expression.[502] The analogy in many cases goes further in that these persons—frequently enough, even if not always—during their lifetimes were mocked, mistreated by others or eliminated (*beseitigt*) in a cruel way, as, indeed, the primal father did not become a divinity (*Gottlichkeit*) until long after his violent death. The most affecting example of this fateful conjunction (*Schicksalsverknüpfung*) is the person of *Jesu Christi*, if that is not something belonging to mythology which called it into life from obscure memory of that primal event (*Urvorgan ins Leben rief*).[503] One other point of accord (*Übereinstimmung*) between the cultural *Über-Ich* and the individual *Über-Ich* is that the cultural *Über-Ich*, entirely like the individual [*Über-Ich*], has strict ideal demands *(strenge Idealforderungen)*, [and] not following them brings anxiety of conscience ("*Gewissensangst*"). Here, indeed, there is set up a remarkable circumstance that the mental processes are more familiar to us, and accessible (*zugänglicher sind*) to consciousness when seen in the group than in the individual person.[504] In the latter, when tension arises it is only the aggressiveness of the *Über-Ich* in the form of noisily heard reproaches (*Vorwürfe*), while the actual demands often remain unconscious in the

---

[502] The loose and free-floating notion of an *Über-Ich* of an epoch, which resembles Herder's 'folk-soul', is countered to some extent by Freud's theme of 'renunication.' We note the lexical parallelism of "*stärkste und reinste.*" The stress on 'great leaders', a motif probably based in part on Nietzsche's 'highter types', was expounded in somewhat incoherent ways in the images of Moses and Paul in *Der Mann Moses und die monotheistische Religion* (1937-39), translated as *Moses and Monotheism* (1939, *S.E.*, 23). On Freud's attitude toward the apostle Paul, see H. Westerink, *A Dark Trace*, cited above, pp. 290-292; and Jacob Taubes, *Die Politische Theologie des Paulus* (Wilhelm Fink Verlag, 1993).

[503] Bk. 8, 421. a) Obscure memory "of that primal event" may suggest the influence of Plato's view of reminiscence. In 1933 he acknowledged that he had been impressed by that notion. He also stated that his knowledge of Plato was "very fragmentary", but that "he wove some suggestions of Plato's into his book, *Beyond the Pleasure Principle.*" (cited in E. Jones, *Life and Work*, one vol. edition, p. 37). b) We leave 'Jesu Christi' as written in the text. JS (p. 149) has 'Jesus Christ.' c) The dissonance of this move from characterizations of strong personalities to a violent death of a primal father reminds one of how, like the ancient Greeks, Freud liked to use mythical stories and narratives, interweaving the given with the imaginary. The Eros and Death duality reinforced his insight on ambivalence. But Freud went way beyond this in asserting that there were memories of a primal father, the prototype of images of God (*Urbild Gottes*), and this *Urvater* was slain by the band of brothers. Hence, in part, the Biblical commandment against killing is a disguised reflection of an historical truth (*historische Wahrheit*).

[504] "*Gewissensangst*" has double quotation marks in the text. On group and individual, compare Plato's methodology in *Republic*.

ud

background. If one brings them to conscious knowledge (*bewußten Erkenntnis*) we find that they coincide with the precepts (*Vorschriften*) of the prevailing cultural *Über-Ich* (*Kultur-Über-Ichs zusammenfallen*). At this point, so to speak, both processes, the cultural development process of the group and that of the individual are normally stuck together (*regelmäßig miteinander verklebt*).[505] For that reason, some of the manifestations and properties (*Äußerungen und Eigenschaften*) of the *Über-Ich* can be easier to detect in its behavior in the community of culture (*Kulturgemeinschaft*) than in the separate individual.[506]

The cultural *Über-Ich* has developed its ideals and set up its demands. Among the latter, those that concern (*betreffen*) the connections of human beings with one another are grouped together under the name of ethics (*als Ethik zusammengefaßt*). At all times, the greatest value has been set on ethics as if one expected that it would produce especially important results. And ethics is really a turning point toward what can easily be recognized as the sorest point (*wundeste Stelle*) in every civilization. Ethics is thus to be grasped (*aufzufassen*) as a therapeutic attempt: an effort to achieve through a command (*Gebot*) of the *Über-Ich* what before could not be attained through any other cultural work (*Kulturarbeit*). We already know that the question before us here is how to remove (*wegzuräumen*) the greatest hindrance to culture, the constitutional inclination of human beings to aggression against one another; and exactly for that reason we are very interested in what is probably the most recent (*wahrscheinlich jüngste*) of the command of the cultural *Über-Ich* (*Kultur-Über-Ichs*): love your neighbor as yourself. In our research into neurosis and the therapy of neurosis we came to two reproaches (*Vorwürfe*) against the *Über-Ich* of the individual: in the severity of its commands and prohibitions (*Gebote und Verbote*)[507] it troubles (*kümmert*) itself too little about the happiness of the

---

[505] Bk. 8, 421. *Kultur*, as 'culture' or 'civilization', is complex and historically mutable. This one reason why the move to a cultural *Über-Ich'* which borders on a notion of collective or group mind is questionable. b) JS (p. 150) has 'always interlocked' for "*regelmäßig miteinander verklebt*".

[506] Note the complementary parallelism and how the method resembles Plato in *Republic*, i.e. features of the ideal state are a map and key to understanding our own souls.

[507] Bk. 8, 422. Freud's perspective on 'ethics' recognizes the force of aggression, the drive of the '*Es*' or 'It', and 'the difficulty of the real environment.' But he deals with this recognition in simplistic and polemical ways. He repeats his earlier attack on "love your neighbor as yourself"; and while sensibly asking about the possibility of fulfilling that

ud

'I', in that it takes insufficient account (*Rechnung*) of the resistance (*Widerstände*) against obeying them, [i.e.] the strength of the drive (*Triebestärte*) of the 'It' (*Es*), and [second] the difficulty of the real environment (*Umwelt*). Therefore we are often obliged for therapeutic purposes to oppose the *Über-Ich,* and we strive to lower its demands. Exactly the same objections (*Einwendungen*) can be raised against the ethical demands of the cultural *Über-Ich.* It also does not trouble itself enough with the facts of the mental constitution of human beings (*seelischen Konstitution des Menschen*), it proclaims a command and does not ask if it is possible to comply with it. It assumes rather that all is psychologically possible to the 'I' of a person (*daß dem Ich des Menschen*): what is mandated of one (*was man ihm aufträgt*), [and] that the 'I' has unrestricted domination over his 'It' (*über sein Es zusteht*). This is a mistake, and even in what are called normal people the 'It' [id] cannot be dominated beyond fixed limits (*des Es nicht über bestimmte Grenzen steigern*). If more is demanded of them, one produces a revolt or neurosis (*Auflehnung oder Neurose*),[508] or makes them unhappy (*macht ihn unglücklich*). The commandment "Love your neighbor as yourself" is the strongest defense against human aggression and an excellent example of the unpsychological procedure of the cultural *Über-Ich* (*unpsychologische Vorgehen des Kultur-Über-Ichs*). It is impossible to fulfill the commandment; such a huge inflation of love can only degrade its value (*deren Wert herabsetzen*) and not eliminate the difficulty.[509] Civilization disregards all this, it merely admonishes (*mahnt*) us that the more difficult it is to obey the precept (*Vorscrift*), the more meritorious doing so is (*desto verdienstvoller ist sie*).[510] Anyone in present-day civilization who follows

---

commandment is important, Freud only considers the question within the topography of *Über-Ich* and cultural *Über-Ich.* Had he ingested Kant's Categorial Imperative he would have seen the mutual entailment of rights and obligations and that regarding self and other as ends, never simply as means, upholds the unique autonomy of human beings. b) Note the synonymous parallelism of 'commands and prohibitions.'

[508] Bk. 8, 422. Note the use of antithetical parallelism in this summary type passage.

[509] The insight rests upon a quantitative view of 'love'.

[510] Idem. On 'meritorious' ("*Verdienstvoller*"): the conceptual problems include the reification of *Kultur,* as if it were an active entity. There is also the lack of evidentiary sources for the assertion of a correlation of difficulty and merit, e.g. Christian ascetic practice and the concept of merit in (non-ascetic) Talmudic literature. In the sentence following, the transition from *Gebot* (commandment) to *Vorscrift* (precept, rule) is as if they were the same.

ud

such a precept puts himself at a disadvantage (*Nachteil*) in relation to those who put off following it. Aggression must be a powerful obstacle to civilization if the defence against it can cause as much unhappiness as aggression itself! The so-called natural ethics (*natürliche Ethik*) has nothing here to offer except the narcissistic satisfaction of deeming oneself better than others.[511] Ethics modelled on religion (*an die Religion anlehnt*)

---

[511] Bk. 8, 422. JS (p. 151) has "'Natural' ethics". a) I don't know what Freud meant by "*natürliche Ethik*". Natural in contrast to what and in what context? 'Natural' suggests a reductive meaning, but ethics involves normative claims. The underlying issue is how the Right, justice as fairness and Kant's moral law, relates to the Good as the most rational and harmonious, given the conditions, satisfaction of interests and desires. The sentence following makes it clear, as elsewhere in *DUK*, that Freud rejects an ethics based on religion which he attacked for imposing its vision of the Good ('doctrines and promises'). [And by implication critiques it for giving priority to the Good over the Right.] Consequently, the contrast between 'natural ethics' and an ethics based on 'religion' suggests that 'natural ethics' refers to good/bad distinctions based on facts determined by scientific study of the natural world. This is acceptable except that the 'natural world' is unstable flux and hence an inadequate basis for determining the Right. Second, the larger textual context does not support a view of 'natural ethics' as a view of the Good in the sense ascribed to the 'religions'. By textual context, I mean that Freud is still talking here about how *Kultur* insists on humans following the precept of 'love' and how that precept ignores the power of aggression and disadvantages those who follow it. Moreover, the demand of *Kultur* to fulfill the commandment of 'love' only inflates love and hence devalues it. There is a valuable insight here: a commandment that cannot be fulfilled may become a form of aggression. However, the 'love' your enemy commandment is a non-quantitative vision of the Good, and Freud's critique of the commandment reflects his belief in the priority of the Right as justice over the Good as a specific view of how one should live. There are hints in *DUK* on what constitutes a good life, e.g. the reduction of suffering, but there is no comprehensive vision of it. b) The other objection or premise for a rejection of 'natural ethics' is that the defense against aggression causes as much unhappiness as aggression itself. But if this is true, why would it lead to 'the narcissistic satisfaction of thinking oneself better than others'? This might imply that by 'natural ethics' Freud is thinking of a psychological form of social Darwinism. I doubt this. Darwin was a major influence on Freud, but Freud rejected his optimistic vision of human progress (cf. the sentence on the last page of *The Origin of the Species*). c) Freud thought his method was a rigorous science opposed to religion, an attitude shared by Engels and the Russian Bolsheviks. However, Freud's belief that progress increases unhappiness through an increase of guilt-feeling combined with his view of the innate tendency toward aggression distanced him from classic Marxism and the varied forms of socialism. I don't know if Freud was aware of anarcho-communism, especially the views of Kropotkin that humans were essentially cooperative and the state was an instrument of oppression. However, his comments on a 'change in relation to possessions' and the need for 'virtue' to be rewarded on earth rather than in an illusionary afterlife suggests that 'ethics' should include a socialist-like component. But that component was in tension with his realism about human aggression. This realism could lead to a resigned form of passivity rather than opposition to injustice. For a chilling example, see our fn. 347 on the *Letter* to Georg Fuchs (1931[f]. *S.E.* 22, 251). d) Freud once called himself "a liberal of the old school." I am not sure what this means. It might refer to Mill's "government by discussion"; but

ud

intervenes here with its promises of a better afterlife (*ihre Versprechungen eines besseren Jenseits eingreifen*). I think that as long as virtue (*Tugend*) is not rewarded on earth, ethics will preach in vain (*wird die Ethik vergeblich predigen*).[512] I also think it quite certain that a real change in the relationship of humans to their possessions would be more helpful in this direction than any ethical commandment (*als jedes ethische Gebot*), but the recognition of this insight (*Einsicht*) among the socialists has been clouded and rendered useless by a new idealistic misconception of human nature.[513]

It appears to me that the line of thought which seeks to pursue in the phenomena of cultural development the role played by an *Über-Ich* has the promise of further disclosures (*andere Aufschülsse zu versprechen*). I hurry to close. But one question is by all means difficult for me to avoid. If the development of culture has such a wide-reaching similarity to the development of the individual and works with the same means, would not the diagnosis be correct that, under the influence of cultural strivings

---

according to P. Roazen, it refers to someone unsympathetic to the communist left and the fascist right (*Freud and His Followers*, p. 533). But that type of liberalism, grounded in mid-19th century thought, died in the trenches of the Great War. The older Freud of *DUK* showed sympathy for what he called *Sozialisten* (Bk. 8, 423) and *Kommunisten* (Bk. 5, 401, 403). [Freud (like individuals on the European left at that time) used the terms interchangeably, although Marx was heatedly explicit on these distinctions.] Freud distained the "*kommunistische Kultur in Rußland*" (Bk. 5, 403), and his sympathy for socialism did not include proletarian revolution but a top-down managerial system. To repeat: in his view socialists or communists were naïve in their optimism about human nature and failed to recognize innate aggressive tendencies. In some ways he was a Viennese middle-class Victorian with a touch of superiority toward the "psychological poverty of the masses ("*das psychologische Elend der Masse*") contrasted to respect for 'leaders with individuality' (*Führerindividualitäten*), Bk. 5, 403.

[512] Freud refuses the consolations of a belief in an 'afterlife'. This applies not only to the Western monotheisms, but presumably to the great karmic-cosmic structures of ancient India and Asia. b) In *DUK*, Freud uses the German for 'ethics' nine times, 'ethical' six times. No definitions or historical delineations are given. The context suggests that 'Christian' and 'Christianity' was the central context, and the fundamental point is his rejection of an 'ethics' based on 'religion'. It is an implicit theme of the treatise that the search for 'happiness' as the reduction of misery is an ethical pursuit. But in this passage he implies that 'ethics' is a Christian type preaching and commandment which is less helpful than a real change in the relationship to 'possessions', although as we just noted those who advocate this ('socialists') have a naïve conception of 'human nature.' We suggest that he inverted the relationship of 'morality' and 'religion'. That is, the direction, counsel, judgment of the 'I' and *Über-Ich* vis à vis the *Es* fulfills the role of commandments and precepts in the Western religions.

[513] Bk. 8, 422-3. Freud loved philosophy as a youth but later turned away from it. He is not using '*idealistisches*' in the sense of Schelling and Hegel ('*Idealismus*,' 1786, < Latin '*idea*' < Greek '*eidos*') but in the sense of 'visionary,' 'impractical,' 'impracticabe.'

ud

(*Kulturstrebungen*), human culture—or epochs of culture, possibly the whole of humanity, have become 'neurotic' ("*neurotisch*")? [514] An analytical dissection (*Zergliederung*) of these neuroses might lead to therapeutic proposals (*Vorschläge*) which could claim great practical interest. I would not say that such an investigation of the transference (*Übertragung*) of psychoanalyis to the cultural community was meaningless or doomed to be unfruitful (*unsinnig oder zur Unfruchtbarkeit verurteil wäre*). But one should be very careful (*sehr vorsichtig sein*) and not forget that we are dealing only with analogies and that it is dangerous, not only with humans but also with concepts to tear them from their region of origination and development (*sie aus der Sphäre zu reißen entstanden und entwickelt*). [515] Also, the diagnosis of communal neurosis (*Gemeinschaftsneurosen*) is confronted (*stößt*) with a special difficulty. With individual neurosis we use as our starting-point the contrast that distinguishes the ill-person from his assumed 'normal' ("*normal*") environment. No such background could exist for a group (*Masse*) whose members were all affected by the same disorder; it would have to be found elsewhere (*anderswoher geholt werden*). And concerning the therapeutic application of our understanding (*Einsicht*), what would be the use of the most correct analysis (*zutreffendste Analyse*) of social neuroses, since no one has the authority to impose such a therapy upon the group? However in spite of all these difficulties, one can expect that one day someone will boldly venture (*Wagnis*) to undertake such a pathology of cultural communities (*Pathologie der kulturen Gemeinschaften unternehmen wird*). [516]

---

[514] Bk. 8, 423. Freud's footnote refers to "eine Passage in *Die Zukunft einer Illusion* (1927c), oben, s. 357." b)The socialist humanism of Erich Fromm's *The Sane Society* (1955), along with the Marx of the 1844 mss., reflects the thought in this sentence and the one following and the concluding phrase of the paragraph on 'a pathology of cultural communities' ("*kulturellen Gemeinschaften*"). Marxist perspective was broadened and deepened by Freud's focus on the family, but he lacked Freud's sense of tragic conflict and focus on aggresstion. According to Robert R. Holt, Fromm said that Freud and Marx were indispensable for students in many disciplines but practically everything they said "was wrong." But Fromm was probably exaggerating and/or the comment reflects his last works, e.g. the overly simplistic *To Have or to Be* (1976).

[515] Idem. Complementary lexical parallelism. b) Freud sometimes forgot his own methodological caution, i.e. his over-confidence in *Kultur-Über-Ichs* as a reality of nature when in part it is a social construction which mixes observation with in-reading.

[516] Idem. But this project, from different starting points and with different conclusions, was already in motion, e.g. by W. Reich, C. Jung, and later by E. Fromm and H. Marcuse.

ud

From diverse motives, I am very far from giving an evaluation (*Wertung*) of human culture. I have tried hard (*bemuht*) to guard myself against an enthusiastic partiality (*Vorurteil*) which holds that our culture is the most valuable that that we possess or could obtain and that its path will lead necessarily to heights of unimagined perfection (*ungeahnter Vollkommenheit führen*). I can at least listen without anger to the critic who is of the opinion that if one surveys the goals of cultural striving and the means used one must conclude that the entire exertion (*Anstrengung*) is not worth the trouble (*sei nicht der Mühe wert*) and the result can only be a condition that the individual must find unbearable. My impartiality (*Unparteilichkeit*) is made easier for me because I know very little about all these things,[517] I know only one thing with certainty and that is that human value judgments accompany his wishes for happiness (*Glückswünschen geleitet werden*); accordingly, they are an attempt to prop up his illusions with arguments (*also ein Versuch sind, ihre Illusionen mit Argumenen zu stützen*).[518] I can understand very well if someone were to point out the obligatory character (*zwangsläufigen Charakter*) of the course of human culture and were to say, for instance, that the tendencies (*Neigung*) toward restriction of sexual life or to the carrying through (*Durchsetzung*) of a humanitarian ideal at the expense of natural selection (*natürlichen Auslese*) were developmental trends which cannot be averted or diverted (*nicht abwenden und nicht ablenken*) [519] and to which it is best for us to yield as if they were necessities of nature. I also know the objection against this, that such unsurmountable strivings (*Strebungen*) have often in the course of

On '*Einsicht*' (one sentence above) JS (p. 153) has 'knowledge', as he did throughout the translation, with the single exception of one use of 'perception.' '*Einsicht*' translates as 'insight,' 'understanding,' 'reason,' 'look' (in, at).'

[517] I suspect this is a Socratic-type tactical modesty. At this point, JS (p. 154) divides the sentence in two.

[518] Bk. 8, 423. Determinism, a thesis with a long history and many interpretations, is the key problem in this passage. b) The phrase '*geleitet werden*' has the sense of 'accompany' or 'escort', meanings which don't support a strong version of causality. JS's (p. 154) 'follow directly' does support a strong form. However, a tight causal connection between value judgments and the wish for happiness conflicts with Freud's opening remarks on the false standards of value measurement (*falschen Maßstäben messen*). That assertion implied that value-choice is not determined by wish or preference, some standards are better than others, and value judgments cannot be reduced to the deployment of argument to support illusions or desires. However, that anti-determinist statement was immediately qualified by recognition of the variety of the human world (*Buntheit der Menschenwelt*).

[519] Bk. 8, 424. Vivid assonance and complementary lexical parallelism.

ud

human history been thrown aside (*beiseite geworfen*) and replaced by others. So my courage to rise up as a prophet before my fellow-humans falls (*der Mut, vor meinen Mitmenschen als Prophet aufzustehen*),[520] and I bow (*beuge*) before their reproach that I can offer no consolation (*Trost*), for at the foundation that is what they all crave (*verlangen*), the wildest revolutionaries no less passionately than the most upright, pious believers (*die wildesten Revolutionäre nicht weniger leidenschaftlich als die bravsten Frommgläubigen*). [521]

The fateful question for the human species appears to me to be if and to what extent their cultural development will succeed in the mastery of the disturbance of communal life (*Störung des zusammenslebens*) by the human drives of aggression and self-destruction. In this connection the present time perhaps deserves a special interest. Human beings have gained control over the forces of nature to such an extent that with their help they would have no trouble exterminating one another down to the last man (*einander bis auf den letzten Mann auszurotten*). They know this and from that comes a large portion of their current disquiet, their unhappiness and their mood of anxiety (*Angststimmung*). And now it is to be expected that the other of the two 'heavenly powers' ("*himmlischen Machte*"), eternal Eros, will strain to assert himself in the struggle with his equally immortal opponent (*ebenso unsterblichen Gegner*). But who can foresee his success and the final result? (*Aber wer kann den Erfolg und Ausgang voraussehen?*) [522]

---

[520] **Idem. Freud rejects the role of prophet ("the best quesser", Hobbes) out of respect for the arguments for and the arguments against a deterministic view of culture. One appreciates the modesty.**

[521] **This wonderful clause reminds one of Erasmus' satirical criticisms in his *In Praise of Folly* of the Roman Church, the Protestant reformers, and current social values. Unlike Erasmus (1466-1536), Freud recognized that resistance was ambiguous or a compromise formation. Hence, while rejecting consolation at the cost of critical thought Freud did not advocate political disengagement or pietism either Jewish or Christian.**

[522] **JS has a final footnote: "[The final sentence was added in 1931—when the menace of Hitler was already beginning to be apparent.]" b) The image of exterminating one another rebuts a view of Freud as a progressivist. He accepted sociobiological evolution ("new erect gait against his earlier animal existence") but his scheme of cultural development from the early and barbaric, even cannibalistic, to later civilized forms was subjected to innate human aggression. c) '*Erfolg*', 'success, result, issue, outcome, and effect' was in the first and last sentence. According to the German editor, Freud added it to the treatise in 1931 ("*Diesen Schußabsatz fügte Freud 1931 hinzu*"). According to E. Jones, Freud had ended his treatise "with the hopeful words": 'And now it may be expected…'. However, four**

ud

Bibliography, also see footnotes.

Freud, *Werkausgabe in Zwei Bänden,* (S. Fischer Verlag, 1978, 2006), cited as *Freud ZB*). Anna Freud and Ilse Grubrich-Simitis did the selection and editing of the texts. It contains indexes, bibliographical and didactic notes, and links to psychoanalytical literature. This is the best German critical edition now available but it is far from complete.

_____*Das Unbehagen in der Kultur,* in vol. 2 of *Freud ZB,* 367-424 (cited as *DUK*).

_____*Gesammelte Werke* (18 vols.), London, from 1940, (cited as *G. W.*) Not the needed historical-critical edition, see comments on it by Ilse Grubrich-Simitis (1996, 1993).

_____*The Standard Edition of the Complete Psychological Works of Sigmund Freud* (24 vols.) Translated under the general editorship of James Strachey, in collaboration with Anna Freud, assisted by Alix Strachey, Alan Tyson and Angela Richards (London and New York, 1953-1974.) Cited as *S.E.*

_____*Collected Papers* (5 volumes, London, 1924-50). Citation in fn. from volume 4.

_____*Civilization and its Discontents* (London, 1930, New York, 1962; *S.E.*, 21, 59-145.) The citations in our text are from the W. W. Norton edition of 2005 with Introduction by Louis Menand. It incorporates two sentences added after the 1930 translation by Joan Riviere. Because of the introduction, the text begins on page 5. James Strachey, the translator, is cited as JS. The first translator is cited as JR.

---

years later, after Hitler was on the verge of total power, he added the final sentence "But who can predict his [Eros] success and the final outcome?" (E. Jones, *Life and Works*, vol. 3, p. 348). d) After a coma of two days, Freud died on the morning of September 23, 1939. He anticipated the atomic age, and the emerging evil in Europe, but died before the mass murder of the *sho'ah* or *hurban* ('catastrophe, devastation'.)

ud

_____*The Freud/Jung Letters*, edited by William McGuire, translated by Ralph Manheim and R. F. C. Hull (Princeton, Bollingen series, 1974) cited as *F J Letters*.

_____*The Origin of Psycho-Analysis. Letters to Wilhelm Fliess, Drafts and Notes: 1887-1902*, edited by Marie Bonaparte, Anna Freud, Ernst Kris, authorized translation by Eric Mosbacher and James Strachey, Introduction by Ernst Kris (Basic Books, 1954). The introduction is valuable, but this work was subject to some censorship and is superseded by *The Complete Letters of Sigmund Freud to Wilhelm Fliess*, edited and translated by Jeffrey M. Masson (Cambridge, 1985).

_____*The Letters to Eduard Silberstein 1871-1881*, edited by Walter Boehlich, translated by Arnold J. Pomerans (Harvard University Press, 1990).

_____*The Sigmund Freud---Ludwig Binswanger Correspondence 1908-1938*, edited by Gerhard Fighter, translated by Arnold J. Operands, Introduction, editorial notes and additional letters, translated by Thomas Roberts (New York and London: Other Press).

_____*Sigmund Freud and Lou Andreas-Salomé LETTERS*. Edited by Ernst Pfeiffer, translated by William and Elaine Robson-Scott (New York: Harcourt Brace Jovanovich, Inc., 1972, 1966).

_____*Totem und Tabu* (Vienna, 1913, *Freud ZB*, 201-328), translated as *Totem and Taboo* (London, 1950); *Totem und Tabu* (London: Imago, 1940; Frankfurt am Main und Hamburg, Fischer-Bücherei, 1956).

_____*Das Ich and das Es* (Vienna, 1923, *G. W.*, 13), translated as *The Ego and the Id* (New York, 1961, *S.E.*, 19). Fuller information in notes.

_____*Die Zukunft einer Illusion* (Vienna, 1927, *G. W.*, 14), translated as *The Future of an Illusion* (London, 1928, *S.E.*, 21).

_____*Jenseits des Lustprinzips* (Vienna, 1920, G. W., 13), translated as *Beyond the Pleasure Principle* (London, 1961, *S.E.*, 18).

ud

_____ *Obsessive Actions and Religious Practices* (*S.E.,* 9, 117-204).

_____ *Dostoevsky and Parricide* (*S.E.,* 21, 175-196). See fn. 440.

_____ *Three Essays on the Theory of Sexuality* (*S.E.,* 7, 125-243).

_____ *The Question of Lay Analysis* (1926e), *S.E.,* 20, 236ff, *Die Frage der Laienanalyse* in *Freud ZB,* vol. 1, 17- 69.

_____ *Charakter und Analerotik* (*Character and Anal Erotism*) (*S.E.,* 9, 167-175).

_____ *Zeitgemässes über Krieg und Tod* (*Thoughts for the Times on War and Death*), (*S.E.,* 14, 274-300).

_____ *Massenpsychologie und Ich-Analyse,* Vienna, 1921, in *Freud ZB,* vol. 2. Translated as *Group Psychology and Analysis of the Ego* (London, 1959, *S.E.,* 18, 67-143).

_____ *An Autobiographical Study* (1925), translated by James Strachey with Freud's 1935 Postscript (W.W. Norton, 1963, in *S. E.,* vol., 20, 3-7. Original title: "*Selbsdarstellung*" (1925), complete edition with introduction by Ilse Grubich-Simitis (Frankfurt am Main: Fischer Taschenbuch Verlag, 1971. Freud's 1935 copyright title was *Autobiographie.*

Adorno, Theodor W., *History and Freedom: Lectures 1964-1965,* edited by Rolf Tiedemann, translated by Rodney Livingstone (Polity Press, 2006).

Adorno, Theodor W., and Max Horkheimer, *Dialectic of Enlightenment* (1944; translation, 1972, Verso Edition, 1979).

Alexander, Franz, *Die Psychoanalyse der Gesamtpersönlichkeit,* (Vienna, 1927); cited by Freud in fn. to *DUK,* Bk. 7, 414 (Trans.: *The Psychoanalysis of the Total Personality,* New York, 1930). Alexander's paper on Amenhotep IV anticipated Freud's *Der Mann Moses,* but Freud did not openly acknowledge the influence (see Carol Delaney (1998), 208-10).

Anselm, Saint (c. 1033-1109) of Canterbury. Mentioned in fn. 3, in relation

ud

to the ontological argument (in the *Proslogion*), and in fn. 326 in relation to *credo ut intelligam*.

Aristotle (384-322 BCE.). *Nicomachean Ethics.* Translated with an Introuduction and Notes by Martin Ostwald (Library of Liberal Arts, 1999). *see also* Annotated Index.

Babylonian Talmud, *Shabbat*, cited in fn. 473.

Bakan, David, *Freud and the Jewish Mystical Tradition* (Princeton, 1958). The focus on the 'uncanny' and the insight on Moses as representative of the *Über-Ich* is valuable. While there are some positive comments on mystical traditions in *DUK*, Freud was basically indifferent to negative (Bk. 1-2), and I have seen no evidence of a Kabbalist influence. In Lecture 29 of *New Introductory Lectures*, he referred to psychoanalysis as a "new found land which has been reclaimed from the regions of Folklore and Mysticism".

Barnes, Julian, *Nothing to Be Frightened Of* (N.Y., Knopf, 2008).

Benjamin, Walter, *One-Way Street and Other Writings*, Introduction by Susan Sontag (Verso, 1979).

Beauvoir, Simone de, *The Second Sex* (Knopf, 1952, Vintage Books, 1989; Translated and edited by H. M. Parshley, Introduction to the Vintage edition by Deirdre Bair; published by Gallimard in two volumes; *Le Deuxieme Sexe*: I. *Les Faits et Les Mythes*, II. *L'Expérience Vécue*). See, especially, chapter 5 of Bk. I; quoted phrases on p. 197 from Introduction, p. IX.

Michael Billig**,** *Freudian Repression*: *Conversation Creating the Unconscious* (Cambridge, 1999**).**

Binswanger, Ludwig. This Swiss psychiatrist (1881-1966) developed *Daseinanalyse* (existence analysis), which sought to unite psychoanalysis with phenomenology. His close friendship with Freud is evident in his *Erinnerungen an Sigmund Freud* (Berne, 1956), English translation by Norbert Guterman: *Sigmund Freud: Reminiscences of a Friendship* (London and New York, 1956). Their correspondence shows that the

ud

intellectual differences between them did not diminish their friendship. This contrasts with the Freud-Jung relationship and other cases of dissenters.

Bleuler, Eugen, '*Der Sexualwiderstand*', *Jahrbuch fur psychoanalyt. und psychopathol. Forschungen,* Bd. V, 1913. Cited in a fn. by Freud at the beginning of Bk. 5.

Bloom, Harold, *Where Shall Wisdom Be Found*? (Riverhead Books, 2004). Bloom's enormous erudition and enthusiasm sometimes becomes vatic and dogmatic. His marking out 'strongest' poets and writers within a model of 'anxiety of influence' reflects the literary impact of Freudian themes.

Bonaparte, Marie, *The Life and Works of Edgar Allan Poe: A Psychoanalytic Interpretation* (1933). Freud wrote the Preface to (*S.E.,* XXII, 254) to this work.

Bowie, Malcom. *Proust Among the Stars* (Columbia Univ. Press, 1988), cited in fn. 46.

Brandes, Georg, Danish critic and scholar whom Freud admired and read in German translation. Freud cites his *William Shakespeare* (1896) in fn. to *DUK*, 387.

Burkhardt, Jakob, Kultur der Renaissance in Italien. Swiss-German Romantic, nationalist visionary, art-critic, journalist, historian. As famous titles go, this and Freud's *Unbehagen in der Kultur* had '*Kultur*' translated by 'civilization.'

Daly, C. D. "Hindumythologie und Kastrationskomplex," *Imago* XIII, 1927; cited by Freud in footnote to Bk. 4, 392.

Dammapada, edited by O. van Hinüber and K. R. Norman (Oxford: The Pali Text Society, 1995).

Decker, Hannah S., *Freud, Dora, and Vienna 1900* (The Free Press, 1900) and *see also* P. J. Mahoney, *Freud's Dora. A Psychoanalytic, Historial, and*

ud

Textual Study (Yale University Press, 1996).

Delaney, Carol, *Abraham on Trial: The Social Legacy of Biblical Myth* (Princeton University Press, 1998). See, especially, Part Four, "The Testimony of Psychoanalysis."

Dollimore, Jonathan, *Sexual Dissidence: Augustine to Wilde, Freud to Foucault* (Oxford, Clarenton, 1991).

Dostoevsky, Fyodor. See Freud's study "Dostoevsky and Parricide" (1928, *S.E.*, 21, 175-196.) Freud wrote: "As a creative writer he has his place not far behind Shakespeare. *The Brothers Karamasov* is the greatest novel that has ever been written…" See our fn. to Bk. 7, 412.

Dworkin, Ronald, *Justice for Hedgehogs* (Harvard University Press, 2011).

Ecclesiastes (*Kohelet*). As a type of wisdom text, see our study *An Inquiry Concerning Qohelet…*(2016). Some Stoic-like themes found in *Kohelet* are: the flux of things, a division of wise and foolish, the futility of effort. There is also the motif of grasping joy now, see chap. 3, verses 12-13, 22.

Ellenberger, Henri F., *The Discovery of the Unconscious: the History and Evolution of Dynamic Psychiatry* (New York: Basic Books, 1970).

Ellmann, Richard, *James Joyce* (1959, Galaxy Book, 1965), cited in fn. 285,401..

Emerson, Ralph W. *Essays: First and second series*, with an introduction by Douglas Crase (Vintage Books: The Library of America, 1990). His essay *Nature* was published anonymously in 1836; and "The American Scholar", an oration given at Harvard, was published in 1837. H. Bloom has called 'Emersonianism' the "American religion". That characterization would have made Freud very uneasy. However, there are themes that he shared with Emerson, most importantly, although on a highly abstract level, the transfer of power/s from god to man.

Fisch, Jörg, *'Zivilisation, Kultur'*, in *Geschichtlich Grundbegriffe:*

ud

Historisches Lexikon zur politisch-sozialen Sprache in Deutschland, edited by O. Brunner, W. Conze, and R. Koselleck (Stuttgart, Klett-Cotta, 1992), vol. 7, 679-774.

Fox, Robin. *The Search for Society: Quest for a Biosocial Science and Morality* (Rutgers University Press, 1989).

Freud, Anna (1895-1982). A pioneer in the psychoanalysis of children, especially in respect to the problem of aggression, and research on the mother-child dyad. *The Ego and the Mechanisms of Defense* (1936) is Vol. II of the VII volume collection of writings.

Firestone, Shulamith. *The Dialectics of Sex: The Case for Feminist Revolution* (Farrar, Straus, and Giroux, 1970).

Fromm, Erich (1900-1980), *The Sane Society* (1955). Fromm is cited in our fn. 290, 303, 514, 515t,see *DUK*, Bk. 4, 396; Bk. 8, 423. Fromm develops an idea found in Bk. 8 of *DUK*.

Gay, Peter, *Freud: A Life for Our Time* (Norton, 1988).

German Loanwords in English (Cambridge, 1994), ed. by Pfeffer and Cannon (Cambridge, 1994).

Geuss, Raymond, *Morality, Culture, and History: Essays on German Philosophy* (Cambridge University Press, 1999).

Glymour, Clyde, "Freud's Androids" in *The Cambridge Companion to Freud*, edited by Jerome Neu (Cambridge University Press, 1991), pp. 44-85.

Goethe, Johann Wolfgang. Freud's citation of Mephistopheles in *Faust* I, Scene 3 with introductory statement: "The identification of the principle of evil with the destruction-drive in Goethe's Mephistopheles is exceptionally convincing." Freud quotes: "*Denn alles, was entsteht, / Ist wert, daß es zugrunde geht.... So ist denn alles, was Ihr Sünde,/ Zerstörung, kurz das*

ud

Böse nennt, / Mein eigentliches Element." [deadly destruction or briefly stated: Evil, that is my proper element]. Five more lines are cited. *see also* our fn. 2,16, 63, 64, 69, 71, 98, 226 (Brandes on), 291, 326, 372, 384, 387, 459.

Gilman, Sander L., *The Jew's Body* (Routledge, 1991). See esp., chapter 3 on 'Dora.'

——————————, *The Case of Sigmund Freud* (John Hopkins Press, 1993).

——————————, edited by and with introduction. *Sigmund Freud. Psychological Writings and Letters.* (The German Library 59; Continuum, 1995.) The introduction is important, but this volume, as others in the series, lacks adequate bibliographical information for the entries.

Grabbe, D. Chr. *Hannibal* (1835). Grabbe (1801-36) was a German journalist and dramatist. Cited in Freud's fn. 2, Bk. 1, 368.

Greenblatt, Stephen. *The Swerve. How the World Became Modern* (Norton, 2011). On the great poem by Lucretius, see review by Anthony Grafton in *The New York Review of Books* (Decenber 8-21, 2011).

Griffiths, David B., *The Keywords of Martin Heidegger: A Philosophical-Lexical Analysis of 'Sein und Zeit'* (The Edwin Mellen Press, 2006); cited in fn. 2 to *DUK*, Bk. 1, fn.205, 206; 406 to Bk. 7; 466, 467 to Bk.8.
——————————, *Buddhist Discoursive Formations: Keywords, Emotions, Ethics* (The Edwin Mellen Press, 2004); cited in fn. to *DUK*, Bk. 3, 389-390; fn. to Bk. 5, 399.
——————————, *'Transport of the Aim,' and Voice of Reason. Dialogues on Kant's moral theory, social and intellectual environments* (Createspace, 2016).
——————————, *An Inquiry concerning Qohelet: context, text, keywords, themes* (Createspace, 2016).

Groddeck, Georg, author of *Das Buch vom Es. Psychoanalytische Briefe an*

ud

eine Freundin (Zurich, 1926); not mentioned in *DUK* but cited in *Das Ich and das Es* (*Das Ich and das Es* (1923), p. 377, and in Freud's fn. 1 and 2: "Groddeck himself no doubt followed the example of Nietzsche, who habitually used this grammatical term (*Es,* our insertion) for whatever in our nature is impersonal, and so to speak, subject to natural law."

Grubrich-Simitis, Ilse, *Back to Freud's Texts: making silent documents speak*. Trans.: Philip Slotkin (Yale University Press, 1996.) German: *Züruck zu Freuds Texten* (S. Fischer Verlag, 1993). This is a major achievement toward a complete, historical-critical edition of Freud's works. See page 65 for her comment on the German edition we have used. Her critique of the *Gesammelte Werke* reminds one of the deficiencies of Heidegger's *Gesamtaugabe* (GA., Frankfurt am Main: Klossterman, 1975-). Now about 100 volumes, it has been subject to censorship and lacks critical editorial scrutiny.

Grünbaum, Adolf, *The Foundations of Psychoanalyis: A Philosophical Critique* (Berkeley: University of California Press, 1984). In this influential critique, Grünbaum argued that Freud's clinical data do not support his central concepts. See the evaluation by David Sachs "In fairness to Freud" in *The Cambridge Companion to Freud*, pp. 309-338.

Harris, Johanna and Elizabeth Scott-Baumann, editors, *The Intellectual Culture of Puritan Women, 1558-1680* (Palgrave Macmillan, 2011). This collection of 15 essays contains evidence that piety for women was a form of power.

Havelock, Eric A. *The Muse Learns to Write: Reflections on Orality and Literacy from Antiquity to the Present* (Yale University Press, 1986).

Hebrew Bible, *Biblia Hebraica*, edited by Rud. Kittel; 7th edition with Alt. Eissfeldt. Kahle (Leipzig, 1951).

Heidegger, Martin, see fn. 2, 3, 10, 68, 145, 188, 203, 205, 206, 224, 406, 418, 466, 477.

ud

Heine, Heinrich, *Gedanken und Einfälle.* Freud cites a passage in a fn. to Bk. 5, 399.

Hitchens, Christopher, *god is not Great. How Religion Poisons Everything* (Hachette Book Group, 2007). Cited in our fn. to "*Priesterreligion*", Bk. 7, 411; fn. 185, 431.

Hobbes, Thomas, *Leviathan or the Matter, Form, and Power of a COMMONWEALTH Ecclesiastical and Civil* (1651, Latin version 1668, Pelican Books, 1968, Penguin Classics, 1985), see our fn. to Bk. 5, 401.

Hrdy, Sarah Blaer Hrdy, *The Woman That Never Evolved* (Harvard, 1981); *Mothers and Others: The Evolutionary Origins of Mutual Understanding* (Cambridge, Harvard, 2011). Mentioned in fn. 299. See also A. Zihlman "Women the gatherer: the role of women in early hominid evolution" (1989).

Hunt, Tristram*, Marx's General. The Revolutionary Life of Friedrich Engels* (Holt, 2009).

Huston, Nancy. Author of *Les Variations Goldberg* (1981), translated by her into English as *Goldberg Variations* (2008).

Isbister, J. N. *Freud. An Introduction to his Life & Work* (Polity Press, 1985).

James, William (*Principles of Psychology*, 1890), See fn. 2 to Bk. 1, fn.326 to Bk.5, 400; fn.359 to Bk. 6, 367.
———————, *The Varieties of Religious Experience* (The Gifford Lectures on 'Natural Religion', 1901-2; published June, 1902; The Library of America, 1990).
See p. 260: "Psychologically and in principle, the precept 'Love your enemies" is not self-contradictory. It is merely the extreme limit of a kind of magnanimity…Yet if radically followed, it would involve such a breach with our instinctive springs of action as a whole, and with the present world's arrangements, that a critical point would practically be passed, and we should be born into another kingdom of being."
I don't know if Freud knew this book. As a tribute to complexity over dogmatism, it checks and enlarges his critique of 'love your enemies', and it could have given him a more balanced view of 'religion'.

ud

Jameson, Fredric, *Marxism and Form*: *Twentieth-Century Dialectical Theories of Literature* (Princeton, Princeton University Press, 1974).

——————, *Late Marxism: Adorno, or, The Persistence of the Dialectic* (Verso, 1990).

Jaspers, Karl, "Philosophical Autobiography" in *The Philosophy of Karl Jaspers*, The Library of Living Philosopers, edited by Paul Arthur Schilpp (Open Court Press, 1957).

Jones, Ernest, *The Life and Work of Sigmund Freud* by Ernest Jones, 3 volumes (N.Y.: Basic Books, 1953-1957). One volume edition, edited and abridged by Lionel Trilling & Steven Marcus (Basic Books, 1961). On Jones, See Brenda Maddox, *Freud's Wizard: Ernest Jones and the Transformation of Psycho-analysis* (De Capo Press, 2006), and discussion in Peter Gay's *Freud. A Life for Our Time, see* Index, p. 708.

Jonte-Pace, Diane, *Speaking the Unspeakable: Religion, Misogyny, and the Uncanny Mother in Freud's Cutlural Texts* (University of California Press, 2001).

Josepheus, *Flavius* (c. 37-c. 100) *Jewish Antiquities* (Loeb Classical Library, Harvard Univ. Press, 1965). Mentioned in fn. 354.

Jung, Carl G., see fn. 15, 56, 124, 145, 179, 206, 270, 291, 292, 359, 370, 448, 455, 516.

Kafka, Franz, *Letters to Felice,* edited by Erich Heller and Jürgen Born. Trans.: James Stern and Elizabeth Duckworth (Schocken Books, 1973.) H. Arendt worked on this project. Kafka and Freud, central European intellectuals and assimilated Jews, assumed that nothing is as it appears. It is important to study them within the range of Western thought and not only within biographical and ethnic-national-religious contexts.

Klett's Modern German and English Dictionary, third Edition (NTC Publishing Group, 1998).

Kant, Immanuel, *Kritik der praktischen Vernunft* (Hamburg, Felix Meiner

ud

Verlag, 2003; 1788). Cited in fn. 2, 10, 164, 171, 252, 304,316, 320, 323, 327, 396, 408, 410, 411, 507, 511

——————, *Groundwork of the Metaphysics of Morals* (1797; translated by Thomas Kingsmill Abbot). Cited in fn. 442; p. 47 in the Abbot translation (Wilder Pubs., 2008), superseded by the translations by H. Paton, and M. Gregory.

Lacan, Jacques, *The Four Fundamental Concepts of Psycho-Analysis* (1977, French, 1973.) See on *'Trieb'* as related to the 'psychical *pulsion.'* Lacan retains influence among a few intellectuals and a few analysts, but his 'return to Freud' was an obscure and radical alteration. See review by R. Wollheim in *The New York Review of Books* (January 25, 1979, 36-45) and see Wollheim's Supplementary Preface (1990) to *Freud* (2nd ed., Fontana, 1991), xxxviii-xl.

Lash, Christopher. *The True and Only Heaven. Progress and Its Critics* (Norton, 1991).

Laqueur, Thomas, *Making Sex. Body and Gender from the Greeks to Freud* (Harvard University Press, 1990).

Mack, Michael, *German Idealism and the Jew. The Inner Anti-Semitism of Philosophy and German Jewish Responses* (University of Chicago Press, 2003).

Marcuse, Herbert, *Eros and Civilization. A philosophical Inquiry into Freud,* with a new preface by the author (Beacon Press, 1966). Marcuse attempts to synthesize Freud and Marx (much earlier he had unsuccessfully tried to synthesize themes in Heidegger and Marx). Contains a critique of "neo-Freudians", notably E. Fromm. Marcuse distinguishes biological repression from surplus societal repression, and asserts that sexuality under non-repressive conditions develops into Eros as meaningful relationships with self and others.

May, Rollo. May developed 'existential analysis' in America and was the author of *Love and Will* (1969) and other works. He was one of the editors

ud

of *Existence: A New Dimension in Psychiatry and Psychology* (Simon and Schuster, 1958). In that volume, see his "The Origins and Significance of the Existential Movement in Psychology" and "Contributions of Existential Psychotherapy." See L. Binswanger.

Mill, John Stuart (1806-73). *On Liberty* (1859), *Utilitarianism* (1861), *The Subjection of Women* (1869). *On Liberty and The Subjection of Women.* Ed. Alan Ryan (Penguin Group, 2007). *The Subjection* was written eleven years after the death of Harriet Taylor Mill in 1851. It incorporated her ideas on sexual equality. She wrote "Enfranchisement of Women" (1851). According to Mill in his *Autobiography*, Harriet was the joint-author of most of his books and articles.

Monk, Ray, *Ludwig Wittgenstein: the duty of genius* (London: Jonathan Cape, 1990).

Neu, Jerome, ed. *The Cambridge Companion to Freud* (Cambridge University Press, 1991).

Okin, Susan Moller, *Justice, Gender, and the Family* (Basic Books, 1989).

Oxford English Edition of the English language (2004), cited as *OED*.

Plato. See fn.2, 256, 257, 307, 320, 338, 404, 503, 504, 506.

Phillips, Adam. *On Kissing, Tickling and Being Bored: Psychoanalytic Essays on the Unexamined Life* (Harvard Univ. Press, 1993).

Rawls, John. *A Theory of Justice* (Original Edition, Harvard University Press, 1971).

Ricouer, Paul, *Freud and Philosophy. An Essay on Interpretation.* Trans.: from the French by Denis Savage (New Haven and London: Yale University Press, 1970).

Rieff, Philip, *Freud: The Mind of the Moralist, with a new Epilogue*

ud

(University of Chicago Press, 1979, 1959).

_____, *The Triumph of the Therapeutic. Uses of Faith after Freud*. With a new Preface (University of Chicago Press, 1987, 1966).

Roazen, Paul, *Freud and His Followers* (New York University Press, 1984, 1974). Based mainly on interview data from 128 people.
Supplements the less critical works by E. Jones and P. Gay. For critical appraisal, see R. Wollheim, *Times Literary Supplement*, March 26, 1976, p. 341.

Robert, Marthe, *From Oedipus to Moses: Freud's Jewish Identity*. Trans.: from the French, *d'Oedipe à Möise: Freud et la conscience juive* (1974), by Ralph Manheim (Anchor Books Edition, 1976).

Rosenzweig, Franz, *The Star of Redemption*. Trans.: from the German 2nd edition of 1930 by W. W. Hallo (Holt, Reinhart and Winston, 1970). On Rosenzweig, see Nahum N. Glatzer, *Franz Rosenzweig: His Life and Thought* (Schocken, 2nd. revised edition, 1967).

Rothgeb, Carrie Lee, editor, *Abstracts of the Standard Edition of the Complete Psychological Works of Sigmund Freud, with an Introduction ON READING FREUD by Robert R. Holt* (Jason Aronson, 1973, softcover edition, 1993).

Saramago, José, *Death with Interruptions* (*Intermitências da morte*), Trans.: from the Portuguese by Margaret Jull Costa (Lisbon, 2005, First Mariner Books edition, 2009).

Sartre, Jean-Paul, *L'Etre et le néant* (Paris, 1947).

Sellen, Ernst. Biblical and Arabic scholar and author of *Mose und Seine Bedeutung für die israelitisch-jüdische Religionsgeschichte* (Leipzig and Erlangen, 1922). Sellin's argument was based on comments in the prophetic literature. He was the source for Freud's assumption that Moses was killed by his own people.

Scanon, T. M. *What We Owe to Each Other* (Harvard University Press, 1998).

ud

Sen, Amartya, *The Idea of Justice* (Penquin Books, 2010; Allen Lane, 2009).

Sheldrake, Rupert, *A New Science of Life: The Hypothesis of Morphic Resonance* (1981).

Tadié, Jean-Yves, *Marcel Proust: A Life.* Trans.: from the French by Euan Cameron (Viking, 2000; Edition Gallimard, 1996).

The New Cassell's German Dictionary (New York: Funk & Wagnalls, 1958).

The Oxford Companion to The Mind, edited by Richard L. Gregory with the assistance of O. L. Zangwill (Oxford University Press, 1987).

Thomas Aquinas, St. (c. 1225-74). Dominican philosopher and theologian. Cited in fn. to Bk. 1, 367 in connection with the Five Ways (*Quinque Viae*) or proofs of God (*Summa Theol.* 1, q 2, art. 3) and mentioned in fn. 3 to Bk. 1.

Thomashow, Mitchell, *Ecological Identity. Becoming a Reflective Environmentalist* (MIT, 1996).

Trotsky, Leon, *Literature and Revolution*, cited in our footnotes to *DUK*, fn. 259, 343, 355.

Young-Bruehl, Elizabeth, *Anna Freud: A biography* (Yale University Press, second edition, 2008, 1988).

_____, *Freud on Women: A Reader*, edited by Young-Bruehl and with her Introduction (W. W. Norton, 1990).

Lowith, Robert, *Lectures on the Sacred Poetry of the Hebrews.* Trans.: from the Latin by G. Gregory (Boston: Croker and Brewster, 1829).

MacCannell, Juliet Flower, "Sigmund Freud," in *The Continuum Encyclopedia of Modern Criticism and Theory*, general editor, Julian Wolfreys (N.Y.: Continuum, 2002), 50-70.

ud

MacNeice, Louis, *Autumn Journal* (The Faber Library 7, 1939).

Maddox, Brenda, *Freud's Wizard: Ernest Jones and the Transformation of Psycho-analysis* (De Capo Press, 2006).

Nancy, Jean-Luc, *The Experience of Freedom*, translated by Bridget McDonald (Stanford Univ. Press, 1993; French *L'Experience de la liberté* (Editions Galilée, 1988).

New Testament: KJV and Greek text.

Parfit, Derek, *On What Matters*, 2 volumes (Oxford University Press, 2011). Mentioned in fn. 323.

Rank, Otto, *The Trauma of Birth* (1925, Eng. translation, 1929). Dedicated to Freud.

Schorske, Carl, *Postcards from the End of the World: An Investigation into the Mind of fin-de siècle Vienna* (London: Collins, 1988). Cited in fn. 33, and based on M. Billig, cited above, pp. 117, 119.

Storr, Anthony, *Freud & Jung* (Barnes & Noble, 1989).

Sulloway, Frank J. *Freud, Biologist of the Mind: Behind the Psychoanalytic Legend* (Harvard University Press, 1992). For a critical appraisal, see R. Wollheim in *The New York Review of Books*, November 8, 1979, pp. 25-28.

Taubes, Jacob, *Die Politische Theologie des Paulus* (Wilhelm Fink Verlag, 1993). Available now in translation: *The Political Theology of Paul* (Stanford Univ. Press, 2004). Trans.: by Dana Hollander.

Turner, Victor, *Dramas, Fields, and Metaphors. Symbolic Action in Human Society* (Cornel University Press, 1974).

Zihman, Adrienne and Frances Dahlberg, *Woman the Gatherer*, see Melvin Konner "It Does Take a Village" *New York Review of Books* (Decenber 8-21, 2011), p. 37.

ud

Westerink, Herman, *A Dark Trace: Sigmund Freud on the Sense of Guilt*, Trans.: from the Dutch (Leuven University Press, 2009; Dutch, 2005).

Wharton, Edith (1862-1937), author of *The Age of Innocence* (1920).

Wilson, Edmond O., *Biophila.* (Harvard University Press, 1984).

Wittgenstein, Ludwig (1889-1951), *Culture and Value*, ed. by G. H. von Wright in collaboration with Heikki Nyman, translated by Peter Winch (Blackwell, 1980; Univ. of Chicago Press, paperback edition, 1984). German title: *Vermischte Bemerkungen* (1977).

Wollheim, Richard. *Freud*, 2nd edition (Fontana, 1991, 1971).

Woolf, Leonard, review of *The Psychopathology of Everyday Life*, see fn. 3.
Woolf, Virgina, *To The Lighthouse*, see our fn.3.

Yerushalmi, Yosef Hayim, *Freud's Moses*: *Judaism Terminable and Interminable* (Yale University Press, 1991).

ud

www.ingramcontent.com/pod-product-compliance
Lightning Source LLC
Chambersburg PA
CBHW081827280526
45789CB00007B/2371